D0944646

152.4
H2364   Handbook of humor
vol.2   research.

$51.00

DATE		
DEC 21 1992		
MAY 21 1993		
ILL 11/06		
8/1/12		

WITHDRAWN

© THE BAKER & TAYLOR CO.

HANDBOOK OF HUMOR RESEARCH

Volume II

Volume II
Applied Studies

HANDBOOK OF HUMOR RESEARCH

Edited by

PAUL E. MCGHEE *and*
JEFFREY H. GOLDSTEIN

Springer-Verlag
New York Berlin Heidelberg Tokyo

Paul E. McGhee
Department of Home and Family Life
Texas Tech University
Lubbock, Texas 79409, U.S.A.

Jeffrey H. Goldstein
Division of Social Psychology
Temple University
Philadelphia, Pennsylvania 19122, U.S.A.

With 4 Figures

Library of Congress Cataloging in Publication Data
Main entry under title:
Handbook of humor research.
  Includes bibliographies and indexes.
  Contents: v. 1. Basic issues—v. 2. Applied studies.
  1. Wit and humor—Psychological aspects—Addresses,
essays, lectures. 2. Wit and humor—Social aspects—
Addresses, essays, lectures. 3. Wit and humor—Research
—Addresses, essays, lectures. I. McGhee. Paul E.
II. Goldstein, Jeffrey H.
BF575.L3H36 1983   152.4   83-6675

© 1983 Springer-Verlag New York Inc. except Chapter 1
© 1983 Joel Goodman

All rights reserved. No part of this book may be translated or reproduced in any form without written permission from Springer-Verlag, 175 Fifth Avenue, New York, New York 10010, U.S.A.
The use of general descriptive names, trade names, trademarks, etc., in this publication, even if the former are not especially identified, is not to be taken as a sign that such names, as understood by the Trade Marks and Merchandise Marks Act, may accordingly be used freely by anyone.

Jacket illustration by Stuart Leeds.
Typeset by Ampersand Inc., Rutland, Vermont.
Printed and bound by R.R. Donnelley & Sons, Harrisonburg, Virginia.
Printed in the United States of America.

9 8 7 6 5 4 3 2 1

ISBN 0-387-90853-6 Springer-Verlag New York Berlin Heidelberg Tokyo
ISBN 3-540-90853-6 Springer-Verlag Berlin Heidelberg New York Tokyo

Preface

Progress in understanding humor and developing a comprehensive, testable theory of humor has been slow in coming. Fortunately, we do not need to have at our command a thorough understanding of a phenomenon in order to make use of it. In Volume II, *Applied Studies,* of the *Handbook of Humor Research,* there is a movement away from theoretical issues that lay beneath humor and laughter as biological, psychological, and social acts. Rather than attempting to deal with the dynamics of humor—with why a particular situation or object elicits laughter—the chapters in Volume II explore humor and laughter as behaviors that are correlated with and have effects upon a great many other realms of social and psychological life. In this volume we explore the uses and consequences of humor.

Joel Goodman is one of only a handful of individuals who teaches the development of humor, not for purposes of entertainment, but for the enhancement of human relationships. He has taught humor techniques to business executives and rank and file workers, teachers, medical and mental health practitioners, and government employees. In recognizing that humor is an important form of social communication, Goodman focuses on making conscious the often unthinking use of humor.

What does a card-carrying comedian think of humor? More than you may have supposed. In Chapter 2, Stanley Myron Handelman likens humor to religion, a set of beliefs and a foundation for interpreting the cosmos. The comic perspective and comic creation also emerge as central topics in Chapter 3 by Maurice Charney, and Chapter 4 by Seymour Fisher and Rhoda Fisher. Charney examines characteristics of various comic personae in drama, festival, and joking. The Fishers report on their study of professional and amateur comics in which a variety of methods are brought to bear on the themes and conflicts of comedic performance. The use of humor in psychotherapy is explored briefly by Fisher and Fisher, and in great depth by Waleed Salameh in Chapter 5. In recent years there has been increasing emphasis on the therapist's openness and self-revelation, features that include humor and laughter. Salameh reviews the literature on humor and therapy and provides a much-needed structure for examining the uses and effects of humor in the therapeutic relationship.

The uses of humor in medicine have been hotly debated, both in the popular and professional literature, especially since the publication (in both the popular and professional literature) of Norman Cousin's *Anatomy of an Illness*.* Michael Duchowny, a pediatric neurologist, reviews the literature on laughter from a neurological perspective. His focus in Chapter 6 is on pathology, particularly gelastic epilepsy, and he speculates on the types and neurological structures likely to be involved in pathological laughter. Furthermore, he, like Robinson in Chapter 7, distinguishes healthy from pathological laughter and humor. Vera Robinson discusses the uses of humor in medicine, nursing, and in medical education. She also presents an overview of the literature on the relation between humor and health.

Comedy is a ubiquitous feature of popular culture and mass media. Lawrence Mintz in Chapter 8 presents a summary of the forms that humor takes in American popular culture, focusing on the prevalence and history of the changing forms of humor. In Chapter 9, Dan Brown and Jennings Bryant summarize the research on the practices and effects of using humor in mass media. The focus is primarily on the medium of television and includes studies on the effects of children's educational programming.

Humor in education is discussed by Dolf Zillmann and Jennings Bryant in Chapter 10. They present considerable research of their own on the relationship between humor and learning, retention, and interest among students. For the past decade, textbooks from the elementary through the college level have attempted to increase attention and retention by relying on humorous drawings and illustrations (e.g., Adams, 1982†; Ziv, 1983‡). Such efforts do not have uniformly positive effects, but depend instead on the relevance of the humor, the difficulty of the material to be learned, and the manner of presentation.

Both volumes in the *Handbook of Humor Research* are intended for students, researchers, and practitioners in psychology, sociology, anthropology, linguistics, mass communications, medicine and nursing, education and human development interested in (a) and handy source of information about humor, laughter, and comedy, (b) a rich source of fresh theoretical and research insights

---

*Cousins, N. *Anatomy of an illness*. New York: Norton, 1979.

†Adams, D., Ed. *Using humor in teaching sociology: A handbook*. Washington, D. C.: American Sociological Association Teaching Resources Center, 1982.

‡Ziv, A. The influence of humorous   atmosphere on divergent thinking. *Contemporary Educational Psychology*, 1983, *8*, 68–75.

into the nature and functioning of humor, and (c) a guide for the enhancement, use, and application of humor. With regard to information, the *Handbook* summarizes current and classical literature on humor and laughter. Literature reviews focus on theories of the nature of humor, on the relationship of humor to language, cognition, and social functioning, on biological and physiological features, and on the presence, use, and effects of humor in a wide variety of settings. Included also are theoretical integrations, philosophical speculations, methodological suggestions, and thoughtful analyses of humor and all its attendant phenomena. Indeed, we hope the *Handbook* will serve as a fertile ground for research ideas. Finally, the *Handbook of Humor Research* contains chapters that instruct on the development and enhancement of humor, both in oneself and in others. As a whole, then, these chapters should help the reader to further develop his or her own sense of humor as well as to understand the nature, development, and functions of humor.

Paul E. McGhee
Jeffrey H. Goldstein

Contents

Contributors

Dan Brown, Department of Communication, University of Evansville, Evansville, Indiana 47702, U.S.A.

Jennings Bryant, Department of Communication, University of Evansville, Evansville, Indiana 47702, U.S.A.

Maurice Charney, Department of English, Rutgers University, New Brunswick, New Jersey 10024, U.S.A.

Michael S. Duchowny, Seizure Unit and Division of Neurology, Miami Children's Hospital and Departments of Neurology and Pediatrics, University of Miami School of Medicine, Miami, Florida 33155, U.S.A.

Seymour Fisher, Department of Psychiatry, Upstate Medical Center, State University of New York College of Medicine, Syracuse, New York 13210, U.S.A.

Rhoda L. Fisher, Department of Psychiatry, Upstate Medical Center, State University of New York College of Medicine, Syracuse, New York 13210, U.S.A.

Joel Goodman, The Humor Project, Sagamore Institute, Saratoga Springs, New York 12866, U.S.A.

Stanley Myron Handelman, Valencia, California 91355, U.S.A.

Lawrence E. Mintz, American Studies Program, University of Maryland, College Park, Maryland 20742, U.S.A.

Vera M. Robinson, Department of Nursing, California State University, Fullerton, California 92634, U.S.A.

Waleed Anthony Salameh, Patton State Hospital, Patton, California 92369, Psychotherapy Institute of San Diego, San Diego, California, 92126, U.S.A.

Dolf Zillmann, Department of Communications, Indiana University, Bloomington, Indiana 47401, U.S.A.

Chapter 1

How to Get More Smileage Out of Your Life: Making Sense of Humor, Then Serving It

JOEL GOODMAN

We are all here for a spell. Get all the good laughs you can. (Will Rogers)

There are three things which are real: God, human folly, and laughter. The first two are beyond our comprehension. So we must do what we can with the third. (John F. Kennedy)

Humor is essential to any smoothly functioning system of interaction, to any healthy person, and to any viable group. Humor is, in the last analysis, no joke. (Dr. Gary Alan Fine quoted in HUMOR RESEARCH NEWSLETTER)

IN THE BEGINNING ...

I first became aware of the positive power of humor during one of the most stressful times of my life—when my father faced major surgery. Our family is very close, and the anxiety and tension were high before, during, and after the operation. This is when humor came to the rescue.

In 1977, my father discovered that he had an aneurysm in his aorta, a life-threatening situation. My parents flew from their home in Maryland to Houston, Texas, where Michael DeBakey was to perform the necessary surgery. Even though a well-known surgeon was involved, the outcome was in no way certain. The few days prior to the operation were incredibly stressful for all of us (I had flown from Saratoga Springs to join my parents and lend support).

Then, a funny thing happened on the way to the hospital. My mother and I were staying in a nearby hotel, and each morning we were shuttled to the hospital by a hotel van. The driver of the van had been selected as Bellman of the Year, and it soon became evident that this was well-deserved. The driver had the wonderful ability to joke with, tease, and invite laughter from people wrapped in fear and tension (as they went to visit relatives and friends who were hospitalized). His sense of humor helped others to come to their senses . . . of humor. It didn't take long for the laughter to melt through the people frozen with fear and tension. People facing (in some cases) grave situations were discovering humor as a beautiful giver of hope and reliever of tension. It created a powerful contagion—my mother and I, for instance, found ourselves following Robin Williams's notion that "comedy is acting out optimism." After leaving the hotel van (which we dubbed "The Good Humor Truck"), we were in a much better position to help my father laugh off the tension of the upcoming operation. In looking back at that situation, I am convinced that our ability to keep ourselves "in stitches" played a vital part in Dad's successful recovery from surgery.

As a result of this powerful personal experience, I became intrigued with the positive power of humor. Always one to appreciate the serendipity and spontaneity of humor, I began to wonder if it might be possible to invite and apply humor intentionally—without killing it in the process. Why should such a beautiful gift be left to chance? Couldn't we be more intentional about calling on humor in our lives and the lives of others? I began to explore how we could make sense of humor and then serve it; or more accurately, explore how it could serve us. My purpose was not to "analyze humor to death" but rather to discover practical ways of "bringing it to life."

THE HUMOR PROJECT

In 1977, I founded the HUMOR Project, which is sponsored by Sagamore Institute, a nonprofit educational resource and training organization. The goals of this new project were twofold: (1) to explore the nature and nurture of humor by helping people to learn, practice, and apply *skills* for tapping their own sense of humor; (2) to develop and disseminate *practical uses* of humor that managers, teachers, parents, helping professionals, business people, and young people could integrate into their own work and life-style.

The HUMOR Project addresses these goals by providing workshops, speeches, graduate courses, training seminars, and consulting services for individuals, schools and organizations interested in the constructive applications of humor in everyday life and work. The Project also publishes a quarterly journal, *Laughing Matters*, which has subscribers from throughout the United States and ten foreign countries, and a syndicated column, *The Grinning of America.*

To date, over 30,000 people have participated in programs sponsored by the

Project. There has been a great deal of media attention focusing on the work of the Project—including national and local television, radio, newspaper, and magazine features. This has been a reflection of the enormous—and growing—interest nationwide in the positive power of humor. More and more people are realizing that laughing matters . . . it really does!

WHY SHOULD WE BE SERIOUS ABOUT HUMOR?

When I first started the HUMOR Project, I asked myself the question "Why should we be serious about humor?" Now, on a regular basis, I continue to ask it of myself—just to keep me honest and focused. I have generated three basic responses to the question; these three answers are the ones I give myself and the participants in workshops, courses, and speeches (Goodman, 1982).

Humor for the Health of it

The old adage, "Laughter is the best medicine," may not be far from the truth. Norman Cousins's (1979) book, *Anatomy of an Illness as Perceived by the Patient*, on the best-seller list for many months, certainly has opened up many people's eyes to the notion that "he who laughs lasts." Cousins describes how he intentionally tapped various sources of humor (books, films, etc.) in order to tap his own sense of humor, hope, and optimism in recovering from a painful and debilitating illness. Raymond Moody, M.D. (1978), also has a provocative book, *Laugh after Laugh: The Healing Power of Humor*, in which he describes research, case studies, and anecdotes related to the positive health benefits of humor. William Fry, Jr., another medical doctor who has done research on the physiological impact of humor for more than 30 years, also lends support to Cousins' notion that laughter is like "internal jogging." Laughter may have a positive effect on blood pressure, oxygenating the blood, massaging vital organs, facilitating digestion, and causing the release of endorphins in the brain (the body's natural pain killer, without the side effects of external drugs). As Cousins suggests, humor provides "that apothecary inside you."

In these times, when "stress" and "burn out" have become household words, humor can certainly play a significant role. My perspective is given by a sign that appeared on a plumber's truck: "A flush beats a full house." If we can flush ourselves and our lives of the stress that can accumulate, then our lives will be fuller of joy, laughter, hope, optimism, and good relationships. Humor can be instrumental in helping people to recover from illness—and in preventing it in the first place. Humor can serve as an effective "mental floss" and "fortified ironic supplement"—a way of promoting mental and physical health.

From Haha! To Aha!: Humor and Learning

The second reason I am serious about humor is that it has important implications for people involved in teaching and learning, whether that teaching/learning takes place in a classroom, in an office, in the home, or elsewhere. My perspective is that laughter (haha!) and learning (aha!) can go hand-in-hand, and that in many cases, laughter can liberate learning.

Avner Ziv (Note 1) of Tel Aviv University has done powerful research showing how humor can enhance learning and creativity. When used appropriately, humor maximizes memory. I am convinced that this is how it works: Humor serves first to capture students' attention ("tickling" their curiosity about the subject at hand), to free up their attention (by allowing for the release of stressors that might otherwise have preoccupied them), and to hold their attention (thus providing motivation and momentum for learning). Once you capture, free, and hold attention, then retention has a better chance of happening.

In the past, many schools discouraged humor. Phrases like "Don't smile until Christmas" (told to new teachers) reinforced the myth that education and enjoyment are mutually exclusive. However, in recent years, the positive power is being recognized. For instance, each year, The Council of Chief State School Officers, *Encyclopaedia Britannica*, and *Good Housekeeping* magazine sponsor a contest for the Teacher-of-the-Year. Here is a brief excerpt describing the 1980 winner:

> Perhaps one quality more than any other enables Beverly Bimes to serve as an inspiration and as a role model in her school and community: That quality is her sense of humor.
>
> She uses her sense of humor, quipping with students, laughing at herself, and easing tensions of overwork at home with her husband, Jim. On her 18th wedding anniversary she sent herself a single red rose with an enclosed card that read, "I love you," signed "Jim". Jim's puzzlement over who really sent the rose lasted until he received the florist's bill on his credit-card account. (*Good Housekeeping*, May 1980, pp. 48, 50)

Whether used in one's own personal life to lighten the load or as a teacher to enlighten, humor can be a powerful tool if used well.

Humor as Aikido

What is aikido? It is one of the only forms of Eastern martial arts that does not involve an offensive posture. It simultaneously prohibits aggression and invites graceful responses to "attacks." The essence of aikido is "going with the flow (of the attack)." This approach emphasizes harmony and blending with your "partner" rather than discord and defeating your "opponent."

By way of example, if you were being physically attacked, in addition to running away you would have three basic options: (1) you could fight back—this would be good in that you would be standing up for yourself, but it runs the risk of escalating the conflict; (2) you could be passive and allow yourself to be "pushed up against the wall"—this might help avoid a big blowup, but it is no fun for you to have footprints all over your face; or (3) you could go with the flow of the attack by standing your own ground, pivoting as your attacker reaches you, and ushering him on his way—this use of aikido enables you to maintain your integrity while simultaneously honoring the direction in which the attacker was going. As described by Eric Zorn, in aikido an attack is not to be prevented, but guided so the attacker is subdued by the force of his own motion. The key is not strength, but position, timing, and focusing of energies.

Aikido is a metaphor for how we can use humor to defuse confrontations, disarm attackers, and turn situations from abusing to amusing. What does this look like in "real life"? Here are six examples of "attacks" and how humor as aikido was used in response.

(1) The first attack came from Mother Nature. In June 1981, I flew to Minneapolis to teach a graduate course on humor. I arrived on the day that a series of tornadoes had devastated the Minneapolis metropolitan area. It was an awful and awe-inspiring demonstration of the power of Nature. Trees were uprooted and tossed about, smashing everything in their path.

Now what could you do in the face of this "attack" by the tornadoes? You couldn't fight back (clearly the tornadoes are stronger than you). You also would not want to roll over and "play dead" (and have the situation devastate you emotionally and financially). So, what you could do is call on humor as aikido in order to roll with the punches. After all, stress is not an event—it is a perception of an event. And we can control our perceptions and attitudes by having an aikido orientation.

This was exemplified by one Minneapolis man whose car was crushed by a huge tree trunk. He responded by standing next to his car and waving to all the passers-by. On his car was a hand-lettered sign reading, "Compact Car."

(2) The second attack came in the form of a practical joke. It involved Eve Arden, who was on stage during a play. The phone on stage began to ring when there was no ringing called for in the script. She could see by the look on her leading man's face that he was in on the gag. Rather than confront him directly in front of the audience (this clearly would have been inappropriate), and rather than let him "get away with it," she had the presence of mind to play along with him in using aikido. She picked up the phone, said "Hello," turned to him and said, "It's for you."

(3) The third true aikido story involved a man, Lieutenant Paul Tomb, who pronounced his last name, "TOM." Lieutenant Tomb went in to be interviewed by an admiral for a particular job. "Sit down, Toom," said the admiral. The

lieutenant replied with, "Excuse me, sir, my name is pronounced 'TOM'." To this, the admiral shouted, "I didn't ask you to speak. You'll only speak in response to my questions! Now, TOOM, when did you first become interested in nuclear power?" After thinking a moment, the lieutenant came up with this aikido response, "Well, sir, I guess I first became interested in nuclear power on the day the United States dropped the first atomic boom."

In this case, the lieutenant did not have the position power to confront the admiral head-on. He also did not want to be passive while his name was being mispronounced. So, he turned to aikido, essentially saying to the admiral, "I can *name* the game you are playing . . . by using aikido I can *tame* it . . . and thus *claim* my own integrity."

(4) The fourth example is drawn from *Let the Buyer be Aware* (Goodman & Huggins, 1981): Once there were five tailors who lived on the same block. They were quite competitive and began to advertise as a way of attracting customers. The first tailor hung a sign outside his shop. It said "best tailor in the city." Upon seeing this sign, the second tailor did a little bit of one-upmanship and produced a sign that said "best tailor in the state." Not to be outdone, the third tailor put up a shingle announcing "best tailor in the country." Of course, it wasn't long before the fourth tailor had a plaque publicizing "best tailor in the world." After all of this, the fifth tailor went into his shop and came out with an aikido sign that read simply, "best tailor on this block."

(5) In September 1982, I had an opportunity to do an in-house humor training program for managers and engineers in a California utility company. One of the participants shared this personal aikido anecdote with me. Earlier in his career, he had been a policeman and was being considered for promotion to captain. During the course of one of his interviews, he was tossed a curve ball, a trick question, that went like this: "Suppose you were involved in a high-speed chase. The car you were chasing sped through the intersection ahead, and then all of a sudden a big battleship moved across the intersection, blocking your way. What would you do?" The man responded with "Of course, I'd sink it." The interviewers were taken aback and asked, "How would you sink it?" The interviewee quickly replied, "With my submarine." Astonished, the interviewers pushed further, "And just where did you get the submarine?" At this point, the interviewee pulled out his final aikido ace and said, "The same place you got your battleship." They all enjoyed a good laugh—and he got the job.

(6) The final attack came in the form of a conspiracy hatched by a group of students. Unbeknownst to the teacher (a friend of mine), the class had all arranged that each student would knock a book off his/her desk at precisely 10:18 in the morning. Sure enough, the students got their act together at exactly the same time. The teacher, who was working at the board, was completely surprised. As she turned around to face the class, she had three options. She could have "counterattacked" by punishing the students (e.g., having them stay after school, marking them down on grades)—but this would have run the risk of alienating them and escalating the confrontation. She could have ignored the situation and hoped that by not acknowledging the situation it might "go

away"—but this would have just led the students the next day to try knocking off two books per person. What she actually did was to call upon humor as aikido by blending with the students. She proceeded over to her desk, and with a wry smile, knocked one of her books off her desk while saying. "Sorry, I'm a little bit late." The class broke up with laughter—but they didn't break stride with the lesson at hand. As a fringe benefit, the students realized, "Hey, teacher is a human being; teacher has a sense of humor!" This is a wonderful example of how we can use humor as a simple yet powerful way to share our humanity.

MAKING SENSE OF HUMOR: FOUR KEY INGREDIENTS

The previous section examined the "So What?" of humor—so what's the big deal? Why should we be serious about humor? After people become aware of the potential power of humor, they often ask, "Now what? . . . Now what can I do to develop my own sense of humor?" The following four ingredients will provide you with some food for thought on this:

1. The Eye of the Behohoholder
2. Discover the ELF in YoursELF
3. Get With It
4. Follow the Rule of the 5 Ps.

The Eye of the Behohoholder

Humor is a matter of perspective and perception. A very simple paradigm seems to work: If you look for humor, humor will find you. It could be as simple as putting on your "Candid Camera glasses" for 5 minutes each day. The human condition is inherently humorous—if you use your sense of sight, then you are bound to get some "in-sights" vis-a-vis humor. For example, take a look at the following stimulus consisting of a row of letters:

OPPORTUNITYISNOWHERE

How do you read the line above? Some may see it as "opportunity is no where." I would like to suggest, however, that the "opportunity is now here." The opportunity is now here for you to see the humor that surrounds you and lives within you.

How can you put this ingredient into action? It could be as simple as keeping a log of funny perceptions. For instance, one teacher has collected such classroom boners as the following:

An active verb shows action; a passive verb shows passion.
A census taker is a man who goes from house to house increasing the population.

Water is composed of two gins. Oxygin and Hydrogin. Oxygin is pure gin. Hydrogin
is gin and water.
A triangle which has an angle of 135 degrees is called an obscene triangle.

Other people might look to other arenas in their life for their humor. For
example, the following quotes are taken from church bulletins—exactly as they
appeared:

This afternoon there will be meetings in the north and south ends of the church.
Children will be baptized on both ends.
Wednesday the Ladies Literary Society will meet. Mrs. Johnson will sing "Put Me in
My Little Bed" accompanied by the Reverend.
Thursday at 8 P.M. there will be a meeting of the Little Mother's Club. All those
wishing to become Little Mothers will please meet the minister in his study.
On Sunday a special collection will be taken to defray the expense of the new carpet.
All those wishing to do something on the carpet, please come forward and get a
piece of paper.

The ability to develop a comic vision of life can be nurtured intentionally. For
instance, Hanoch McCarty passed along to me one ritual that he has developed
with his 6-year-old son, Ethan. After dinner each night, father and son sit down
together and review the day for any situations that were "ridiculous." This
provides a good excuse to focus on the humor around them and within
themselves. After deciding on the daily event that receives the "That's
Ridiculous!" award, they proceed to write several paragraphs describing it in a
notebook. They then take a Polaroid picture that captures the essence of the
event, and place the photo above the paragraphs. Coauthoring a humor book of
this kind is a delightful way to operationalize Victor Borge's notion that
"laughter is the shortest distance between two people." Keeping an ongoing
"That's Ridiculous!" book in the home, office, or classroom could be an
enjoyable way of keeping things in perspective while strengthening your comic
vision muscles.

Discover the Elf in YoursELF

In order to develop your sense of humor, one of the first places you might look is
to your*self* as a source of humor. This is what many professional comics have
done. Bill Cosby, for instance, notes that you can turn painful situations around
through laughter. If you can find humor in something (even poverty) you can
survive it. It's just a matter of having the elf inside you come out to play.
One way of inviting the elf is to play with new ways of doing things. For
instance, many previous workshop participants now take a 1-minute "humor
break" each day. During this time, they draw two pictures. In the first 30
seconds, they draw a picture in as much detail as they can of anything in the

Table 1-1. Performance rating guide

Performance Factors	Excellent	Good	Fair	Poor	Awful
Communications	Talks with God	Talks with the Angels	Talks to himself	Argues with himself	Loses these arguments
Adaptability	Walks on water consistently	Walks on water in emergencies	Washes with water	Drinks water	Passes water in emergencies
Initiative	Is stronger than a locomotive	Is stronger than a bull elephant	Is stronger than a bull	Shoots the bull	Smells like a bull
Timeliness	Is faster than a speeding bullet	Is as fast as a speeding bullet	Not quite as fast as a speeding bullet	Would you believe a slow bullet	Wounds self with bullet when attempting to shoot
Quality	Leaps tall buildings with a single bound	Must take running start to leap over tall buildings	Can leap over short buildings only	Crashes into buildings when attempting to jump over them	Cannot recognize buildings at all

room—the only catch is that they do it with the hand not normally used for writing or drawing. The second 30 seconds offers a new challenge—to draw a detailed picture of someone's face (e.g., self-portrait, colleague, friend, family member). This picture is drawn by their regular writing hand—the only catch is that the people do it with their eyes closed. The inevitable outcome of this 1-minute humor meditation is uproarious laughter coupled with the ability to take themselves with a grain of salt, since it is almost impossible for the pictures to be "perfect." Humor is a wonderful gift for living with our imperfection; it is the synapse between the perfection we seek and the imperfection we have. Giving yourself permission to be imperfect is one of the keys to discovering the elf in yourself. Taking your job or role seriously, but not taking yourself too seriously, is essential. The Performance Rating Guide (see Table 1-1), authored by Dr. Anonymous, is an excellent way to help you to laugh at yourself.

Many people have springboarded off the Performance Rating Guide by keeping their own humor notebook consisting of a running list of their own foibles, times they could laugh at themselves, and humorous ways of defining their own reality. For instance, one teacher who was under much stress one day, looked at her own adaptability with tongue in cheek by saying, "A teacher is someone who can drink three cups of coffee before 8 A.M. and hold 'em until 3

P.M." Another teacher, who was ready to pass water in emergencies, included in her humor diary the following incident: As a high-school English teacher, one day she was helping her students to rehearse a play. She began by asking, "Would all the boys with small male parts please stand up. . . . " She almost fell over—with laughter—when she and the rest of the class realized the double entendre.

Another way of playing around with the elf in yourself is to play with your reality—by creating your own personalized Murphy's Laws. For instance, one group of managers with whom I worked generated the following perspective-givers/sanity-savers:

1. The importance of reports is in inverse proportion to their size.
2. The more you need it, the more likely the computer will be down.
3. The harder you work, the harder the work.
4. The sooner someone is needed, the longer Personnel will take.
5. Taking the time to manage your time doesn't leave you any time to do your work.
6. Anyone who can sue, will.
7. You always meet the boss when you are arriving late.
8. If a mistake is made, it will be at the beginning, so the error will be included throughout.

A group of college dorm counselors came up with a list of Murphy's Laws just for their particular role as a way of laughing at themselves and some of the situations in which they found themselves:

1. When you're in the mood for a good time, you're always on duty.
2. The importance of any floor meeting is inversely proportional to the number of people present.
3. The guy with the loudest stereo on the floor lives next door.
4. You'll always be the last one to hear about a problem for which you are responsible.
5. The number of people who are locked out of their rooms increases exponentially after midnight.
6. The number of people who need you is inversely proportional to the amount of time you have.
7. The phone always rings right after you fall asleep.
8. You're always needed when you're not in.

Holding up a mirror to ourselves and our reality is one of the best ways of taking ourselves less seriously and of playing with situations rather than getting stuck in them. As Steve Allen notes, "Nothing is quite as funny as the unintended humor of reality."

Get with It

Humor is a powerful tool. It can be used for constructive purposes or it can be used in destructive ways. How can you tell which is which? The key question, I believe, looks like this: "Is the humor that is being used a form of 'laughing with' as opposed to 'laughing at'?" The more you can get *with* it, the more effective humor will be for you. The checklist below will give you a taste for how to distinguish between "laughing with others" and "laughing at others."

Laughing with	*Laughing at*
1. going for the jocular vein	1. going for the jugular vein
2. based on caring and empathy	2. based on contempt and insensitivity
3. builds confidence	3. destroys confidence through put-downs
4. involves people in the fun	4. excludes some people
5. a person makes a choice to be the butt of a joke (as in "laughing at yourself")	5. a person does not have a choice in being made the butt of a joke
6. amusing—invites people to laugh	6. abusing—offends people
7. supportive	7. sarcastic
8. brings people closer	8. divides people
9. leads to positive repartee	9. leads to one-downmanship cycle
10. pokes fun at universal human foibles	10. reinforces stereotypes by singling out a particular group as the "butt"

Sometimes it is difficult to distinguish between "laughing with" and "laughing at." There are a number of grey areas to be sure. At the same time, it is clear that humor at the expense of others can be very harmful, it can destroy positive working and learning environments and can diminish self-esteem. As one 16-year-old Chicago student put it, "The exploitation of people for the entertainment of others has to be one of the worst things you can do to a person."

The key here is that in order to develop an effective sense of humor, it makes sense to develop simultaneously a sensitivity to humor. For me, it all boils down to a matter of choice—am I choosing to be the butt of a joke? In most cases, I have observed that people who are the butt of a joke (either against themselves personally or against their race, religion, sex, or ethnic background) have not chosen to be in that position. This is contrasted to people who express their ability to laugh at themselves: "At least my neurosis is creative. It could have been writer's block" (Woody Allen). . . . "I do not care to belong to a club that accepts people like me as members" (Groucho Marx). . . . "Humor is just another defense against the universe" (Mel Brooks).

The more we can help ourselves and others to move to the "laughing with" side of the humor fence, the more we can minimize the use of put-down humor, then the likelihood increases of following Robin Williams's notion that humor is "acting out optimism." How can we do this? Here are some sample humor action projects that workshop participants have pursued in the past; feel free to use or adapt them.

(1) In order to develop your sensitivity to humor, simply ask people such questions as: "what is your least favorite kind of humor, and what is it that you don't like about it?" "Have you ever observed/been a part of another person having a painful or negative experience with humor? What made it painful or negative?" "Can you remember a painful experience you've had that involved humor? Describe it."

(2) Listen to situation comedies on television for an evening. Count the number of put-down statements that evoke laughter. Take one of the put-downs and see if you can turn it into a "put-up" that evokes laughter.

(3) Take some time to brainstorm a list of ways that a person could interrupt an ethnic or put-down joke. Pick one of the ways that feels comfortable or potentially effective for you. The next time you hear an ethnic/put-down joke, try out this behavior and make note of the reactions (both in yourself and in the other person). The key here is to move from awareness into action. Here are some sample responses generated by previous workshop participants:

In response to a sexist or racist joke: "I like you but I don't appreciate your 'isms.' "

In response to a joke about people with handicaps: Hand out a little card with the following words printed on it—"THANK YOU FOR NOT JOKING ... about ethnic groups, people with handicaps, etc. You don't have to blow out their candle to make yours glow brighter."

In response to a put-down of you: Say with tongue-in-cheek, "I resemble that statement!"

In response to a derogatory ethnic joke: "That's unethnical!"

Humor is laughter made from pain—not pain inflicted by laughter. If we can interrupt and help others become aware of destructive humor patterns, and if we can replace these with positive, nourishing humor models, then sensitivity to humor will lead to more effective and appropriate sense of humor—or you + more (an approach to life to help *you* feel *more* connected with others, to help *you* feel *more* self-esteem, etc.).

Follow the Rule of the 5 Ps

Contrary to popular belief, it *is* possible to make sense of humor. There are specific ingredients and recipes that we can follow intentionally to invite laughter in ourselves and others. I see humor as a set of skills, attitudes, and guidelines that we can consciously access, and like any set of skills, humor can be nurtured through practice. How do you get to Carnegie Hall? How do you get to tickle funnybones? The same way—practice ... practice ... practice ... practice ... practice. This is the Rule of the 5 Ps.

I see the development of humor as comparable to the development of listening skills. For many years, people thought that some people are "born listeners" while others just "missed the boat" when the quality was being handed out. Then, Carl Rogers, Thomas Gordon, and others came along with a different perception; they were able to identify people who were effective listeners, and in turn, identified the characteristics, qualities, and skills that these people seemed to possess. This enabled them to develop paradigms and training models to help people to practice these skills to become better listeners. I believe we can walk (or skip) down a similar path to help people develop their own humor muscles and skills.

In addition to perceptual skills (the eye of the behohoholder), the ability to laugh at yourself, and sensitivity to humor (laughing with others), what other qualities can we work on (or play with—depending on how you look at it) in order to increase our Humor Quotients? One suggestion I make in my workshops is for people to observe professional comics and comedy writers to see what kinds of skills and techniques they use. They often observe such mirth-girth skills as exaggeration, understatement, mirroring reality, juxtaposition, reversals, playing (with words, with situations), creating new ideas, and so forth. Let's take a look at a number of these skills, ways of developing them, and examples of how people have applied them in different personal and professional settings.

Exaggeration. If I've told you once, I've told you a million times in this chapter that exaggeration is *the* most important humor skill. In fact, this is the most important sentence you will ever read in your life. Would you believe . . . .

Exaggeration is *one* of the most important and versatile humor skills you can have in your repertoire. If you want to s-t-r-e-t-c-h your exaggeration muscles, you might try filling in the blanks on the following format:

I'd rather (exaggerated undesirable behavior) than (real behavior).

Here is what it looks like in action:

I'd rather have chewed 50 feet of barbed wire than to lose this election. (Jody Powell after 1980 election)
I'd rather wear a gasoline suit through hell than face the boss when I'm late.

You'll notice that in each of the examples above one of the keys to exaggeration is to ask yourself "*What else* could I do to make this even more un-real?" For instance, the thought of chewing barbed wire alone is enough to get you on the soap opera "As the Stomach Turns", adding "50 feet" to the sentence heightens the exaggeration even more. In the second example, going through hell is a lot in itself, to wear a gasoline suit through hell, however, makes a quantum leap in the power of the exaggeration. So, keep asking yourself "What else could I do to stretch and exaggerate the idea even further?"

Now you're up to bat! Think of some of the things that cause you stress. Then see if any of them would fit the blanks below:

I'd rather sit on a bed of nails than _____.
I'd rather be locked in a room with a flatulent hippo than _____.
I'd rather go to the dentist once every day than _____.
I'd rather sit on a cold toilet seat at the North Pole than _____.
I'd rather pull a Band-Aid off one hair at a time than _____.
I'd rather listen to a cassette tape of a mime than _____.

For practice, see if you can stretch any of the above exaggerations even further—for example, "I'd rather sit on a bed of nails with an elephant on top of me than _____." Keep asking yourself "what else?" Next, see if you can create some of your own exaggerations. Start with a common experience or behavior (e.g., going to the dentist, listening to a cassette tape, taking off a Band-Aid, etc.) and then continually blow it up by asking "what else?"

Many people have found billions of practical applications for exaggeration (would you believe . . . 346,792 practical applications?). Previous workshop participants report that exaggeration is often a helpful way to blow up a particular problem out of proportion, so that they can get perspective on how big (or small) the problem really is. For example, counselors and therapists have used the "Dear Blabby" technique: Clients pick a problem from their own life and then play with it by writing a letter to "Dear Blabby." This letter exaggerates the problem to unbelievable proportions—blowing up the causes, the consequences, and the clients' own reactions. Here are some samples to wit (sic) your appetite:

Dear Blabby, My husband always wears socks to bed—4 pair on each foot! If I've toe'd him once, I've toe'd him a thousand times that I think this particular habit really stinks (it really does—the neighbors have had exterminators come to our house three times in the last week alone!). If he doesn't stop, I'm going to sock him right in the kisser. Signed, The Wife of a Socks Maniac

Dear Blabby, I have been teaching for ten years and my salary is so bad that I can't pay my bills (not to mention the bills of my spouse and children). I love teaching, but I'm so poor I can't even pay attention. What should I do? (And speaking of dues, I am going to get kicked out of the teacher's union for not paying my dues. . . . I can't even pay my don'ts.). Signed, Pay-Me-No-Mind

Basically, people are like tea bags. You see how strong they are when they're in hot water. Writing exaggerated letters to "Dear Blabby" is one way to keep us from boiling over, as noted by people who have used this strategy:

Exaggeration of a problem helps us to laugh at it, minimize it, defuse it.

Stretch it out once a day . . . more than likely it will go away.

Exaggeration helps to put issues into perspective. The bigger you make a problem, the smaller it becomes.

You can call upon Dear Blabby in many ways; for example, having a daily 5-minute "humor meditation" that involves writing Dear Blabby about the day's events, or collecting your Dear Blabby letters in a personal notebook or journal and periodically reviewing and relaughing. In our workshops and courses, we have also had fun by having people write exaggerated responses *from* Blabby to help solve some of the exaggerated problems.

Mirroring Reality.   Art Buchwald recently won the Pulitzer Prize. His comic vision of the world basically involves simply holding up a mirror to reality (and sometimes giving it a slight twist). Erma Bombeck often holds up a mirror to the commonplace everyday events as a way of inviting people to laugh. The Candid Camera television show was based on the premise that the human condition is inherently funny—we just need to hold up a mirror (or a camera) to capture the humor that is staring us in the face. Where can you hang up your mirror for maximum results? Right in front of yourself (your own foibles), habits, routines, office memos, mundane events, and jargon. Here are four examples of how people have held up a mirror to portray their humorous realities:

(1) Amity Hallmark, a professional printer, is a fun organization with which to do business. One reason is that with each order, they send out a humorous or tongue-in-cheek view of some piece of reality. Here is one story they sent to customers that portrays and pokes fun at (funny) business:

The story that follows is about four people named Everybody, Somebody, Anybody, and Nobody. There was an important job to be done and Everybody was asked to do it. Everybody was sure that Somebody would do it. Anybody could have done it, but Nobody did it. Somebody got angry about that because it was Everybody's job. Everybody thought that Anybody could do it, but Nobody realized that Everybody blamed Somebody when Nobody accused Anybody.

There are probably 8 million stories in your naked city—holding up a mirror to them is one way of taking reality as a tourist—with a grain of salt.

(2) In order to deal with the stress of the job, many professionals look into their humor mirrors. In some cases, you can combine mirroring reality and exaggerating it in order to liberate laughter. This is reflected in the following sign that was posted in an office:

The objective of all dedicated insurance company supervisors should be to thoroughly analyze all situations, anticipate all problems prior to their occurrence and help solve these problems when we are called upon. . . . However, when you are up to your ass in alligators, it is difficult to remind yourself that your initial objective was to drain the swamp.

(3) A number of people have found it helpful to use a particular "formula" as a running gag in their lives—a way to hold the humor mirror up to reality in an ongoing fashion. You can do this by simply drawing upon things that have actually happened to you, or things that you have brought on yourself. For example, one group laughs about their reality by creating every week a series of "You know it's going to be a bad day when...." sentences. Here's a taste:

You know it's going to be a bad day when...
 you wake up face down on the pavement.
 you see a 60 Minutes *news team waiting for you in your office.*
 your twin sister forgets your birthday.
 you hit a hole-in-one in golf, and you're playing alone.

Another group regularly creates spoof memos that mirror (and at times, slightly corrupt) the usual memos that fill their mailboxes. For instance, they recently circulated a memo on the new sick-leave policy (e.g., you must report all illnesses a week in advance; death is no longer an excuse for absence—if you are well enough to go to your own funeral, you are well enough to report to work).

The staff of one organization chose a different arena in which to hold up the mirror. They saw a great deal of humor in their own language—specifically, in their use/misuse/overuse of jargon words. This led them to create their own Jargon Dictionary. Here are several of the entries:

"where are you at" means "you look like I feel"
"negotiate" is a substitute word for "argue"
"I'm comfortable with that" means "I trust you to do the work"
"brainstorm" means "no one knows the answer, but if we all talk at once...."
"under consideration" means "the issue is dead"

(4) Another way to mirror the humor in reality is simply to use your perceptual skills, your Candid Camera within you to capture the humor around you. You might challenge yourself to come up with a quota of humor for each day or week by viewing bumper stickers, T-shirts, buttons, signs, and so forth. Here are some bumper stickers, for example, which have been spotted through our front-view mirror:

Teachers have a lot of class.
Librarians make novel lovers.
Have an electrician check your shorts.
Tobacco chewer: Pass with care!
The Moral Majority is neither.
Be kind to animals—kiss a rugby player.
Priests do it with Amazing Grace.
Give peas a chance.... Be a human bean!

And then there are numerous examples of how business people have held up a humor mirror so that their customers could chuckle at themselves. One restaurant that found it difficult to tell patrons that substitutions were not allowed finally turned to humor—on the menu were the words, *"No substitutions. Survivors will be prosecuted!"* An auto repair shop faced the problem of customers being in the work area. Humor served to open the door to help the customers to stay out. The manager posted a sign: *"Labor Rates: Regular, $24; If you wait, $30; If you watch, $35; If you help, $50; If you laugh, $75."*

If you laugh, it will probably help. And one way of helping yourself to laugh is to hold up a mirror to your reality—to the world around you and the world within. You'll be in for some mirroraculous laughter.

Reversals.   When things seem to be going from "bad to worse," I encourage people to go from "bard to reverse." There can be real poetry in the ability to view the world from a 180 degree reverse perspective. Reversing reality carries with it much liberated laughter as people get distance on their immediate stressors.

For instance, many teachers have combined laughter and learning by freeing students of the fear of taking risks and fear of "looking stupid." A simple yet powerful way to accomplish this is to exaggerate how *not* to do a new skill. For example, if you were leading a session on "motivation," you might start it by role playing in an exaggerated way the most unmotivating, boring speaker you could possibly imagine. This would enable people to learn many "how to's" by seeing so clearly the "how not to's." Or, if you are teaching a lesson on listening skills, it might be instructive to have people engage in "non-sense" before trying to make sense of this topic. This could be accomplished by having pairs take turns for 30 seconds each to do their best *not* to listen to their parenters (the speaker in his/her 30 seconds would address such topics as "your favorite ice cream flavor," "your favorite tv show," etc.). The exaggeration of the nonlistening behaviors brings into perspective the importance of and ingredients of effective listening and affords participants a chance to laugh while they learn. A third example comes from a colleague, Elliott Masie, who led a workshop on "Public Relations Skills for Non-Profit Agencies." During the workshop, he taught participants how to identify an effective press release by first having them create some awful press releases; teaching through reversal proved to be very effective. The beauty of it is that you can apply this skill to any content area. Just teach the subject first from a "how-not-to" perspective, and people will have perspective on the flip side of the flop side.

Another way to spread the contagion of laughter throughout the land is by creating what Jack Canfield calls "inverse paranoids"—people who think the world is out to do them good. By creating some positive self-fulfilling prophecies (thus reversing the "negative tapes" many people carry around in their heads), we simultaneously can aid people in building self-esteem and spreading smiles.

Here are some positive seed-planting activities for you to help people reverse negative mind-sets and to get more smileage out of life:

- Clip out a cartoon from the newspaper that you think will make someone laugh—give it or send it to that person.
- Send a humorous greeting card to someone who might not expect it from you—be sure to do this on a day other than a holiday or the person's birthday.
- Say hello and smile at ten strangers in one day.
- On the turnpike, pay for the car in back of you at the tollbooth.
- In leaving a tip at a restaurant, be sure to include a funny note, joke, or cartoon for the waiter or waitress.
- Throw a surprise "unbirthday" party for a friend, colleague, or family member.
- Be a "secret pal"—send someone an anonymous positive note or joke on a regular basis.
- During a conversation, say "To be perfectly honest with you . . . "—then finish the sentence with something positive rather than negative.
- Send the author of this chapter examples of successful ways in which you have used or adapted successfully ideas from this chapter.

Reversal is a funderful way to move from a "grim and bear it" mentality to a "grin and share it" orientation. You might want to use the creativity skills described in the next section to help you create dozens of other ways to spread inverse paranoia across the land.

Creating New Ideas.   Humor and creativity are at least kissing cousins. The gut response to humor is one of the best four letter words in the language: HAHA. The gut response to creativity is AHA (as in "Aha! Why didn't I think of that before?!" or "Aha! I've got it!"). In terms of gut response and the word-play level (from HAHA to AHA), humor and creativity are certainly linked. One often leads into the other, for example, funny ideas leading to break-throughs in perspective or solution to a particular problem; creative ideas having the tendency to liberate laughter. They can often be described in similar ways, too. For instance, here is a series of descriptors for "humor" or "creativity"; I challenge you to see if you can figure out which of these two concepts the author is clarifying:

a familiar surprise . . . an unexpected certainty . . . a vital triviality . . . a disciplined freedom . . . an intoxicating steadiness . . . a repeated initiation . . . a difficult delight . . . a predictable gamble . . . a unifying difference. . . .

In his book *The Practice of Creativity*, George Prince (1970) used the above compressed conflicts to describe "creativity." However, I think you can see that these phrases could just as easily be used to describe "humor." The implication of all this is that one way of developing your humor muscles is to strengthen your creativity muscles.

How do you make the light bulb go on when you need it? How can you overcome the times when you feel "uncreative" or stuck? How can you move from a "yes, but . . . " mentality to a yes, and . . . " orientation? How can you create humorous ideas? With LOVE:

Let 'em fly!
Off-beat ideas are encouraged!
Vast number and variety of ideas encouraged!
Expand and piggyback on others' thinking!

Let 'em fly: Let your ideas out; defer judgment, debate, discussion, and "yes, buts"—the basic notion here is that when you are in an idea-generating mode, it doesn't make sense to drive with one foot on the accelerator and one foot on the brake (yes, but) at the same time. Let your exaggeration muscles flex by going for

Off-beat ideas: Weird ideas and impossible dreams often help to break us out of our perceptual ruts. They can also add a great deal of energy and laughter to your creativity. The basic notion here is that it's a lot easier to tame down an idea than it is to think one up in the first place. You can come up with more off-beat ideas by going for a

Vast number and variety of ideas: Aim for quantity, knowing that the quality check will come later. The basic notion here (which is backed up by research) is that the more ideas you have, the more good ideas you have. You can generate many more ideas by trying to

Expand on others' thinking: Piggybacking and hitchhiking on other people's ideas is one of the most direct ways of moving from "yes, but" to "yes, and." The basic notion here is that it makes more sense to build rather than destroy ideas. And expanding is really at the heart of the humor skill of exaggeration.

It might be fun for you to try using (either by yourself or with a group) the LOVE guidelines. You might start with problems that are not "close-to-home" (so that you can focus first on the skill before needing to apply it to real-life situations). Just as athletes warm-up first before engaging in physical exercise, it makes perfect sense of humor for us to limber up our creativity muscles at the beginning. The following sample problems could serve as humorous brainstorming warm-ups:

- What would happen if the human body was rearranged so that our mouths were relocated to the tops of our heads?
- What would happen if our eyes were relocated to the tips of our thumbs?
- What would happen if a popcorn popper didn't stop popping?
- What would happen if orchestras played colors, not sounds?
- What are all the ways you can think of to send love long distance?

- What are all the different uses you can think of for a rubber band . . . for an "Exit" sign . . . for old tennis balls . . . for unmatched socks?
- What other examples can you think of for humorous brainstorming warm-up questions?

If you engage in this kind of warm-up activity before tackling real problems, you may very well find that you can easily go from being the "Wizard of Aha's" to the "Wizard of Haha's." As many teachers, counselors, business people, and others have found, problem solving does not have to be painful—there can be a great deal of play, laughter, and creativity involved as we take on personal and professional challenges. All you need to do is LOVE your ideas.

SUMMARY

For the past 6 years, I have been working (and playing) through The HUMOR Project to help in "The Grinning of America." The Project—and this chapter—have tried to help people to get more smileage out of their lives by making sense of humor, then serving it in personal and professional contexts.

The approach taken has involved exploring the "why?" and "how to?" of humor: (1) Why should we be serious about humor? and (2) How can we develop and apply our sense of humor in constructive ways in our lives? Once people realize that (1) laughing matters . . . it really does, then they become quite interested in learning (2) practical guidelines, activities, and skills (how to's) for nurturing their own and others' senses of humor.

I agree with James Thurber's notion that "Humor is a serious thing. I like to think of it as one of our greatest and earliest national resources which must be preserved at all costs." One of the best ways to preserve humor is to use it: Jest in case you find yourself starting at 9 sharp and ending at 5 dull!

REFERENCE NOTE

1. Ziv, A. *Creative ways to encourage humor and humorous ways to encourage creativity*. Paper presented at the 3rd International Conference on Humor, Washington, D.C., 1982.

REFERENCES

Cousins, N. *Anatomy of an illness as perceived by the patient*. New York: Norton, 1979.

Goodman, J. *Laughing matters* (Vol. 1). Saratoga Springs, N.Y.: The HUMOR Project at Sagamore Institute, 1982.

Goodman, J., & Huggins, K. *Let the buyer be aware.* La Mesa, Cal.: Wright, 1981.

Moody, R. *Laugh after laugh: The healing power of humor.* Jacksonville, Fla.: Headwaters Press, 1978.

Prince, G. *The Practice of Creativity.* New York: Collier Books, 1970.

Chapter 2

From the Sublime to the Ridiculous— the Religion of Humor

STANLEY MYRON HANDELMAN

Religion, to be religion, must free us from the restraints we impose upon ourselves, as well as those imposed upon us by the particular societies to which we belong. It must sanctify all life, and undermine (with love) any force opposed to life, such as inertia or gravity. It must help us to distinguish between sense and nonsense and to accept both as an integral part of life. It must enable us to find heaven here on earth—now—the way it is. All of this is possible through the sense of humor. Comedy is my religion, and I would like to see it become everyone else's . . . soon.

Christ said, "Love thine enemy." Chaos is the enemy, and for most people, a difficult one to love. By chaos, I mean meaninglessness, emptiness, or the void. It seems to go against our nature to live in peaceful coexistence with it. This idea is very well expressed in a children's nursery rhyme: "Humpty Dumpty sat on a wall. Humpty Dumpty had a great fall. All the king's horses and all the king's men couldn't put Humpty together again."

The same idea is expressed in the Book of Genesis, although not exactly in these words. In the beginning, there was nothing. Nothing doesn't make any sense, so we could say that, in the beginning, there was nonsense, and it was good. Then God, who was, and remains, nonsensical Himself, created man in His image, and that was good. After that, He looked around and was tickled and amazed at what He had made out of nonsense. He loved it just the way it was. He cautioned man not to try to make any sense of it or he would lose it—maybe even go crazy. Man could enjoy everything just the way it was as long as he didn't look for meaning. Not a bad deal considering the fact that, in the beginning, nothing had any meaning anyway.

Everything was hunky dory, until one day a miserable snake in the grass crawled over to God's first creatures and asked them how they would like to double their pleasure. They were all ears. Although they were already living in ignorant bliss, there was always room for improvement. "What must we do?" they queried. "All you have to do is to make sense out of it," the snake replied. "What's sense?" they wanted to know. "It is what God is keeping from you so that you won't be like Him." This, of course, was a pack of lies. God kept nothing back. But man, in his ignorance, took the bait, and to this day, has alienated himself from himself and from the nonsense that surrounds him and gave rise to him. Most of us can no longer enjoy anything unless it makes sense. Chuang Tzu, a Chinese Taoist, put it this way:

> The ruler of the Southern Ocean was Shu the Heedless. The ruler of the Northern Ocean was Hu the Sudden. And the ruler of the Center was Chaos. Shu and Hu were continually meeting in the land of Chaos, who treated them very well. They consulted together as to how they might repay his kindness and said, "All men have been given orifices for the purpose of seeing, hearing, eating, and breathing, while this poor ruler, alone, has not one. Let us try to make them for him." Accordingly, they dug one orifice in him every day. At the end of seven days, Chaos died. (1971, p. 110)

Many religious leaders, philosophers, scientists, artists, and poets realize that there is a limit to knowledge, and that ultimate knowledge is impossible. The ultimate truth is that there is no ultimate truth. Everything comes from nothing. Sense comes from nonsense. Not understanding is true understanding.

Bodhidharma, the man who brought Buddhism from India to China, was sitting in meditation, when he was approached by a seeker of the truth who cried,

> "My mind has no peace as yet! I beg you, master, please pacify my mind!"
> "Bring your mind here, and I will pacify it for you," replied Bodhidharma.
> "I have searched for my mind, and I cannot take hold of it," and the man.
> "Now your mind is pacified," said Bodhidharma. (Reps, 1957, p. 52)

According to Paul Steinhart (1982), a physicist at the University of Pennsylvania, "All of the matter and energy that exists in the universe originally came from a near vacuum state that contained essentially no atoms or any particle of matter. What we call the universe, the stars, the galaxies, all the matter that composes us, was really produced out of a vacuum. The universe, as we know it, came from virtually nothing."

Lao Tzu (1963, p. 57) a Chinese Taoist, said, "The way that can be spoken of is not the constant way. The name that can be named is not the constant name. The nameless was the beginning of heaven and earth . . . thus something and nothing produce each other."

From the *Theologia Germanica* (Kepler, 1952) " . . . And man cannot find all satisfaction in God unless all things are one to him, and one is all, and something and nothing are alike."

A rabbi of a wealthy synagogue, in the course of one of his sermons, said, "Although I happen to be the rabbi of one of the most renowned synagogues in America, I am, in reality, really nothing. Nothing is my true nature and all else is delusion and pretension." Upon hearing this, one of the congregation lept to his feet and testified, "Even though I have a very successful law practice, a beautiful wife, and two wonderful sons, both in medical school, I, too, am nothing." Then another member, catching the spirit, arose and exclaimed, "In this world I am a banker, and I have enough money to retire for ten lifetimes, but in the real world, I am nothing, just like you, rabbi." During all this, the janitor, who happened to be doing a little mopping in the back of the synagogue, got caught up in the fever, dropped his mop, and shouted, "Me too. I'm nothing also." Upon hearing this, the banker turned to the lawyer and said, "Look who thinks he's nothing."

The world can never be completely figured out, and humor points to the futility of trying. Humor deflates the pride we take in our reasoning ability. It loves and thrives on chaos.

From *The Search for Solutions* by Horace Freeland Judson (1980, p. 22), in an interview with Murray Gell Mann, the physicist and discoverer of "Quarks":

> Mann: Everything we do is explained mathematically. But there's apparently some beautifully subtle way in which perfectly symmetrical equations produce asymmetrical physics, in certain cases.
>
> Judson: The super system, in order to be perfectly not quite perfect, would have to have the imperfection of being perfectly symmetrical in some places?
>
> Mann: That's exactly, apparently, what happens. Yes, and we don't understand it perfectly.

Werner Heisenberg, a founder of the quantum theory, established the uncertainty or indeterminacy principle that states that it is impossible to determine both the position and momentum of a subatomic particle like an electron. The effect of this principle is to convert the laws of physics into statements about relative probability instead of absolute certainty. Reason has its limits.

A traveling salesman stopped at a farm house and asked the farmer if he could put him up for the night. The farmer told the salesman that he could share the barn with a college professor of logic who was currently staying there. The farmer then told the salesman that at 10 o'clock he locked the barn doors, and that if, for any reason, the salesman had to go outside, he had better do it before then. The salesman thanked the farmer. He went into the barn and met the professor, with whom he struck up a friendly conversation. He liked the professor, and he found him to be very reasonable and friendly, and they talked until 11 o'clock. Then both went to sleep. In the middle of the night, the salesman woke up with a sudden urge to defecate. Finding the barn doors locked, he had no choice but to relieve himself where he was. Ashamed and not wanting to be found guilty of such a heinous deed, he gathered it up and went to the sleeping professor, and stealthily put it inside the professor's trousers. The salesman left early the next morning, while the professor was still asleep. Several years later, the salesman returned to this territory, and again asked the same farmer to put him up for the night. The farmer agreed, and told him that this time he could have the barn all to himself. The salesman asked what had happened to the professor. The farmer told him that the last time, when the two of them were sharing the barn, the professor had had an accident and had defecated in his pants while he was asleep, and three days later, ended up in a mental institution trying to figure out how he could do a thing like that without getting it through his underwear.

Religion's job is to "re-legare." Legare means to bind together or unite. A religion should reunite us with reality, making it palatable and acceptable, with all its contradictions. It should unite people by raising their consciousness, as well as their spirit. It should also reveal the hidden harmony of things that seem to be in constant conflict. However, most religions alienate us from our selves and our reality. They teach us that we are born in sin and dump guilt feelings on us. They teach us not that the world is perfect just the way it is as God created it, but that it must be changed—"improved." They define God, and tell us what He approves and what He detests. They teach us what things He wants of us. They offer us a jealous and vindictive God. They tell us God is infinite, and then set limits on Him. They tell us He is nameless, and then name Him.

Christ said, "And ye shall know the truth, and the truth shall make ye free." (John 8:32). And the truth is that the world follows God's law, not man's, and there's nothing man can do about it, except to distort it to fit his own needs, deny it, accept it in resignation, or accept it in joy and good humor, as a liberation. Once you realize that things are the way they are, and that that is the way they are supposed to be, you are free.

Albert Einstein said (1979, p. 2):

In human freedom, in the philosophical sense, I am definitely a disbeliever. Everybody acts, not only under external compulsion, but also in accordance with inner necessity. Schopenhauer's saying that, "A man can do as he will, but not will as he will." has been an inspiration to me since my youth up, and a continual consolation and an unfailing well spring of patience in the face of the hardships of life, my own and others. this feeling mercifully mitigates the sense of responsibility, which so easily becomes paralyzing, and it prevents us from taking ourselves, and others, too seriously. It conduces to a view of life in which humor, above all, has its place.

Most religions are wrong in trying to impose meaning on the world. Chaos is not the enemy of the spirit, seriousness is.

Writer D. T. Suzuki (1971, p. 7) said, "I do not think theologians can ever laugh. They are too serious, too occupied in trying to identify themselves with the things of God, leaving no room for playfulness. For playfulness comes out of empty nothingness, and where there is something, this cannot take place."

Seriousness implies gravity; it is the concern with important, rather than trivial matters. Gravity is the force that pulls all things to the center. It is what keeps us from flying. It is the opposite of levity, which is the force that raises things and makes them light. Religion is supposed to free the spirit from gravity, raise it, lighten our loads, and enlighten our minds. But many religions are completely pessimistic, and try to convince their followers that there is no perfection on earth, and that heaven is theirs only after they die, that is if they are lucky enough not to have sinned too much, in which case, they can look forward to eternal damnation. These religions create gravity.

The earth creates the gravity that pulls on our bodies. Society creates the gravity that pulls on our minds. Both of them deny us freedom, which is what gives life its true meaning. Religion should help people realize their own true individuality and free them from the masses. The greater the mass, the greater the gravity, and the lower the spirit.

Here are a few comments on society by some knowledgeable men:

H. G. Wells said society is "The inertia, the indifference, the insubordination, and the instinctive hostility of the mass of mankind . . . "[1]

Thomas Browne said, "If there be any among those common objects of hatred I do condemn or laugh at, it is that great enemy of reason, virtue, and religion—the multitude: that numerous piece of monstrosity, which, taken asunder seem men, and the reasonable creatures of God, but confused together, make one great beast, and a monstrosity more prodigious than Hydra.[2]

According to Thoreau, "The mass never comes up to the standard of its best member, but, on the contrary, degrades itself to the level with the lowest."[3]

Emerson said, "Society everywhere is in conspiracy against the manhood of every one of its members. Society is a joint stock company, in which the members agree, for better securing of their bread, with each shareholder, to surrender the liberty and culture of the eater."[4]

According to the Dostoevsky (1880), the Grand Inquisitor said to Christ:

Thou wouldst go into the world, and art going with empty hands, with some promise of freedom which men, in their simplicity and their natural unruliness, cannot even understand, which they fear and dread, for nothing, has ever been more insupportable for man and human society, than freedom. But seest Thou these stones in this parched and barren wilderness. Turn them into bread, and mankind will run after Thee like a flock of sheep, grateful and obedient, though forever trembling, lest Thou withdraw Thy hand and deny them Thy bread.

Martin Luther said, "The mass is the greatest blasphemy of God."[5]

[1] As cited by Bartlett (1955) from *The Research Magnificent*.

[2] As cited by Bartlett (1955) from *Religio Medici* (Park 11, No. 1).

[3] As cited by Bartlett (1955) from *The Heart of Thoreau's Journal*, I. Shepard, Ed.

[4] As cited by Bartlett (1955) from *Self Reliance*.

[5] As cited by Bartlett (1955) from *Table Talk*.

Society instills the fear of God in all its members. God is one and indivisible. He is undefined and undefinable. He is amoral. He is His own boss. He has no authority above Him. He respects no law, is spontaneous and unpredictable. Fortunately for society, He is in heaven where He can't do any harm. But God forbid He were to materialize and take a human form and continue to behave like that. We would have to crucify Him and return him to His heaven.

We may be born in the image of God, but society makes sure we don't grow up in it. The few who try by breaking laws and not carrying I.D.s, ultimately get caught and are punished. Society wants you defined. It wants to know who you are, what you are, where you are, what you do, and for whom you do it—ad nauseam.

As soon as you are born, you are given a legal name, sexed, measured, weighed, and footprinted. There is no way society will let you slip away and grow up undefined. You are taught to expect, one day, to have to earn a living, at which time you will receive another, and a major, definition. You become named after what you do—a furrier, a salesman, a clerk, and so forth. At last you are really something.

Unfortunately for those who want absolute knowledge, these definitions prove to be pretty flimsy. Borders are used to define countries, cities, states, and counties, but there are always disagreements over them, if not actual wars. As a result, they change constantly. Some people, who have been defined men or women, have had their sexes changed and had to be redefined. Definitions divide but never really define. You can never know who you are, once and for all, no matter how well you are defined. That is why definitions, as well as the society that depends on them, are such great targets for comedy.

John Lilly (1975, p. 71) said:

> There are many ways in which one can objectify human life if he penetrates deeply enough inside his true self, and can abandon most of the usual identifications of self with the various programs and metaprograms which others have assigned him to identify with. Then he can realize his true self, as independent of the human condition, as generally presented. Humor, as a direct experience, then becomes more and more frequent.

Al Bernstein, a wealthy young man, was showing off his new yacht to his parents. He said proudly to them, "Well, what do you think of your son now? I am a captain. Did you ever think you would see the day when your little boy, Al, would be a captain?" "Listen," his mother responded, "to you, you are a captain; to me, you are a captain; and to you father, you are a captain; but to a captain, you're no captain."

One day, this very same Al Bernstein was shopping in a nautical supply store, when a big, burly man walked over to him, slapped him on his back, nearly knocking him over, and bellowed, "Jim Scott, you old son of a gun. The last time I saw you, you were bald, now you have a full head of hair, and you were much shorter, and you had a limp. Now look at you." Al Berstein replied, "I'm not Jim Scott. My name is Al Bernstein." The burly man slapped him on the back again and said. "How do you like that? You even changed your name."

When one removes himself from the usual consensus reality models and sits above the human condition, one can really appreciate the value of humor. Most of what the human race does is not only funny, but also totally ridiculous. The vast amounts of energy, money, time, and interest spent on useless activities—war, the development of new weapons, murder, suicide, the making of laws inappropriate to the human condition, sexual intercourse, for example—corroborate this. When one is disengaged from identification with these matters, when one is in a state of High Indifference, when he is objectively removed from the connection with these matters, he can appreciate the humor of the human condition (Lilly, 1975).

Herman Hesse (1929, pp. 62-63) said the same thing a little more poetically in his book *Steppenwolf*.

The lone wolves, who know no peace, these victims of unceasing pain, to whom the urge for tragedy has been denied, and who could never break through the starry space, who feel themselves summoned thither, and yet cannot survive in its atmosphere—for them is reserved, provided suffering has made their spirits tough and elastic enough, a way of reconcilement and an escape into humor. Humor has always had something bourgeois in it, although the true bourgeois is incapable of understanding it. In its imaginary realm, the intricate and many faceted ideal of all Steppenwolf's find its realization. Here it is possible not only to extol the saint and the profligate in one breath, and to make the poles meet, but also to include the bourgeois, too, in the same affirmation. Now it is possible to be possessed by God, and to affirm the sinner, and vice versa, but it is not possible for either saint or sinner (or for any other of the unconditioned) to affirm as well that lukewarm mean, the bourgeois. Humor alone, that magnificent discovery of those who are cut short of their calling to the highest endeavor, those who, falling short of tragedy, are yet as rich in gifts as in affliction, humor alone (perhaps the most inborn and brilliant achievement of the spirit) attains to the impossible, and brings every aspect of human existence within the rays of its prism. So live in the world as though it were not the world, to respect the law, and yet stand above it, to have possessions as though "one possessed nothing," to renounce as though there were no renunciation, all these favorite, and often formulated propositions of an exalted wordly wisdom, it is in the power of humor alone to make efficacious.

Lewis Thomas in an interview with Horace Freeland Judson said:

. . . and I think that one way to tell if something important is going on is by laughter. It seems to me whenever I've been around a laboratory at a time when something very interesting has happened, it has, at first, seemed to be quite funny. There's laughter connected with the surprise . . . and whenever you hear laughter, and somebody saying, "but that's preposterous", you can tell things are going well. (Judson, 1980, p. 69)

Sören Kierkegaard, a devoutly religious writer, had a dream when he was young:

> Something marvelous has happened to me. I was caught up into the seventh heaven. There sat all the gods in assembly. As a special grace, there was accorded to me the privilege of making a wish. "Wilt thou," said Mercury, "Wilt thou have youth, or beauty, or power, or long life, or the most beautiful maiden, or any other glorious thing among the many we have here-in the treasure chest? Then choose but one thing." For an instant, I was irresolute, then I addressed the gods as follows: "Highly esteemed contemporaries, I choose one thing, that I may always have the laugh on my side." There was not a god that answered a word, but they all burst out laughing. Thereupon, I concluded that my wish was granted, and I found that the gods knew how to express themselves with good taste, for surely it would have been inappropriate for them to answer me seriously, "This is conceited to thee." (van Hoboken, 1971, p. 6)

In conclusion, the world is divided like Humpty Dumpty, and in trying to put it together again, Einstein, one of the greatest minds of all time, spent the latter part of his life working on his Unified Field Theory, which had baffled him for more than a quarter of a century. He tried to set forth, in one series of mutually consistent equations, the physical laws governing two of the fundamental forces of the universe, gravitation, and electromagnetism—but failed.

Einstein got close.

Charlie Chaplin got closer.

As a religious comedian, what is my advise? If the world cannot be put together again, enjoy the pieces.

Does God, Himself, have a sense of humor? I can't answer, but the Bible says: "God hath chosen the foolish things of the world to confound the wise, and God hath chosen the weak things to confound the things that are mighty, and those things of the world which are despised, hath God chosen. Yea, and things that are not to bring to naught things that are, that no flesh should glory in His presence" (I Corinthians 1: 27-29). If that's not a sense of humor, I don't know what is.

"Let no man deceive himself. If any among you seemeth to be wise in this world, let him become a fool that he may be wise. For the wisdom of this world is foolishness with God" (I Corinthians 3: 18-21). I have taken this advice and have become a fool, professionally, religiously, and philosophically. I recommend it highly.

REFERENCES

Chuang Tzu. *Genius of the absurd* (C. Waltham, Arr.). New York: Ace Books, 1971.

Dostoevski, F. *The brothers Karamazov* (C. Garnett, Trans.). New York: Signet, 1957. (Originally published, 1880.)

Einstein, A. *The world as I see it* (A. Harris, Trans.). New York: Citadel Press, 1979.

Hesse, H. Steppenwolf (B. Creighton, Trans.). New York: Bantam Books, 1972. (Originally published, 1929.)

Judson, H. F. *The search for solutions.* New York: Holt, Rinehart & Winston, 1980.

Kepler, T. F. (Ed.), *Theologia Germanica.* New York: World Publishing, 1952.

Lao Tzu. *Tao te ching* (D. C. Lau, Trans.). Middlesex, Eng.: Penguin Books, 1963.

Lilly, J. *Simulations of God.* New York: Bantam Books, 1976.

Reps, P. (Ed.). *Zen flesh, Zen bones.* Tokyo: Chas. E. Tuttle Co., 1957.

Steinhart, P. "A larger stranger view of the universe is revealed." *Los Angels Daily News*, December 12, 1982, p. 1.

van Hoboken, E. *Sengai* (D. T. Suzuki, Trans.). Greenwich, Conn.: N.Y. Graphic Society, Ltd., 1971.

Chapter 3

Comic Creativity in Plays, Films, and Jokes

MAURICE CHARNEY

Comic creativity depends significantly on the involuntary nature of laughter. As physiologists are fond of pointing out, we cannot tickle ourselves and we cannot will to laugh. There must be a stimulus that seems to overcome us against our conscious will. Comedians try to *make* us laugh, and the communal setting of much stage comedy and entertainment provides a group persuasion to laughter. It is notoriously true that a drive-in movie is a bad place to see a comedy because the group supports are missing. Comedies and comedians need audiences; comedy is preeminently a form of social interaction. If laughter, like orgasm, is an involuntary muscle spasm, we should interest ourselves in what sort of creative genius it takes to produce laughter. I am using laughter as a convenient paradigm for comedy although I recognize that there are comic situations and comic literature that do not necessarily demand overt laughter. Perhaps we should say that comic creativity is designed to provoke laughter or its equivalent.

Jokes provide a handy testing ground for theories of comedy and especially of laughter. There is something teasing and explosive about jokes that offers instant gratification both to the teller and the listener. I can't guarantee to tell a joke that will make someone else laugh, but my own tried and true joke will certainly make me laugh. That may be enough for purposes of my theory. For example, a riddle joke in the question and answer format much favored by students: Question: "How does a nice Jewish girl [or, in other versions, a chorus girl] get a mink?" Answer: "The same way that minks get minks." Or: Question: "What did the elephant say to the naked man?" Answer: "How can you breathe through that little tube?" Or the Mae West joke exhaustively studied by psychoanalysis (Eidelberg, 1945): Mae West comes home after a long day and finds five sailors in her bedroom. She says: "I'm terribly sorry, but I'm tired. Two of you will have to go." These formulations may be too subtle for an academic audience, but there is a certain kick in jollifying an elite 2 or 3 percent and leaving the unenlightened mystified. There seems to be a general feeling that there is no comic creativity at all in jokes, but that, like folktales, jokes are merely varied from existing models and formulas. I would argue very vigorously against this assumption since the creativity lies not so much in the thematic materials as in the daring new combinations and stylistic experiments. It is not true that jokes, like matter, can neither be created nor destroyed, although they may be severely damaged in the telling.

In *Biographia Literaria* (1817/1906, p. 147), Coleridge speaks of "the willing suspension of disbelief that constitutes poetic faith." Some willing transformations must occur in the reader—some good will or commitment—for his disbelief or skepticism to be converted into poetic faith. In comedy I believe the process works somewhat differently. The involuntary nature of laughter demands an unwilling suspension of disbelief in the sense that our natural defenses against laughter are overcome, and we are plunged into comedy willy nilly. The comic faith would represent a willingness to go along with the transformation wherever it may lead. Once the barrier has been broken, we choose not to interrupt the flow of comic energy. If we believe in the workings of comic release, we feel a sense of power and mastery through overcoming our own restraints. To paraphrase Coleridge, we may speak of "the involuntary suspension of disbelief that constitutes comic faith."

Creativity in general is still a very inexact subject. In her essay in *Daedelus* Meredith Skura (1980) speaks of "Creativity as transgressing limits: the myth is as old as the idea of creativity itself," and she calls her essay, "Creativity: Transgressing the Limits of Consciousness." It is difficult to speak of creativity without invoking myth, folklore, and the magical powers usually attributed to the artist. For our present purposes, then, I would like to consider comic creativity in terms of various illusions created by comic characters or comedians. I use the word "illusions" to take account of a certain projection on the part of the comedian, a certain euphoria and self-magnification. I don't pretend to understand what really happens in comic creativity but only the ideal effects shared by speaker and audience. It seems to me that there are at least four illusions involved: omnipotence, unbounded energy, autonomous language, and perfect timing. These may all be considered aspects of omnipotence, but I think they are more appropriately illusions in their own right.

No comic illusion is more powerful than that of omnipotence, that confident feeling, often without any basis in fact, of absolute control over the audience (either the audience in the theater or the audience of other characters on stage). This fits nicely with the Superiority Theory of comedy because the comedian feels not only that he can do no wrong but also that he can improvise everything from the beginning, that everything that he encounters or that comes to hand will be useful to him. The illusion of omnipotence implies a wonderful sense of teleology; everything is purposive in some preordained way, nothing is purely random or accidental. This is not the hard and aggressive superiority theory of Hobbes, but it nevertheless depends upon a dreamlike state of perfect wish fulfillment. Nothing can go wrong because there is no resistance, no gravity, no physical or psychological obstacles—at least none that cannot confidently be overcome.

Charlie Chaplin was a master of this kind of omnipotence, which expressed itself in an uncanny superiority to all physical obstacles, including gravity. With balletic grace and total unconcern for danger, Chaplin skated blindfolded on the edge of an unprotected balcony in the department store in *Modern Times*. When he became aware of the danger, he reacted as any normal human being would, but this only emphasized the difference between the insouciant clown and the fearful mortal. Buster Keaton, too, glided through a world of resistances with seeming oblivion. He was not to be deterred by cannons, trains, waterfalls, collapsing houses, all of which were made to seem like innocuous toys. It is interesting that both Chaplin and Keaton were the acrobatic, thin man types, very different from fat clowns like W. C. Fields, Oliver Hardy, and Falstaff.

The characteristics of the clown as a comic type are already well established in the plays of Plautus, the Roman dramatist of the third and second centuries B. C. In *Pseudolus*, the title character is physically a clown, with "Red hair, pot belly, piano legs, big head, pointy eyes, darkish skin, red face, and whopping big feet" (Plautus, 1971 p. 145). Even though Pseudolus is a slave, he moves about in the play with perfect freedom, and in the final carousing scene, he triumphs drunkenly over his master. He is, in effect, the playwright in the play, so that his own ingenious plotting is like that of Plautus, and he is conscious that he can do whatever he pleases. In his address to himself and to the audience in Act I, he boasts of his omnipotence as plotter:

> You haven't even the shred of a plot in mind. You'd like to weave one, but you don't have a beginning to start from or an end to finish at. It's like being a playwright: once he's picked up his pen, he's on the hunt for something that exists nowhere on the face of the earth; yet he finds it anyway, he makes fiction sound like fact. I'll play playwright. . . . (p. 98)

This passage very self-consciously enunciates the aesthetic dimension of comic creativity: "I'll play playwright." The omnipotence of the comic hero is clearly identified as the power of the imagination.

The illusion of unbounded energy logically follows from a feeling of omnipotence. If the imagination is involved, it is fertile, abundant, copious, and overflowing. There is an illusion of hyperbole and excess. This is often expressed physically through the fat man type, who is bursting with flesh and comic invention at the same time. His body is emblematic of the comic spirit. The comic drunk, for example, like W. C. Fields, is made to float effortlessly on a sea of drink, which represents all the generous, flowing, loose, and unrestricted human impulses. W. C. Fields's wit flows without impediment or exhaustion; he is never at a loss for words, he can never be either dammed up or put down. His comic energy makes him omnipotent.

Shakespeare's Falstaff is also in the fat man, comic drunk type. The key to understanding his role is that he is inexhaustible. In his wit combats with Prince Hal, he is always triumphant as he must be to maintain his clown's superiority. His bigness is literally a source of verbal and imaginative vitality. The Prince inveighs against his large cowardice: "This sanguine coward, this bed-presser, this horseback-breaker, this huge hill of flesh" (1965, 2.4.241-243). But Falstaff lords it over smallness and pettiness in thundering hyperboles:

'Sblood, you starveling, you eel-skin, you dried neat's-tongue, you bull's pizzle, you stockfish—O for breath to utter what is like thee!—you tailor's yard, you sheath, you bowcase, you vile standing tuck! (1965, 2.4.244-48)

Thinness and miniaturization are offences against the generous comic spirit, and hyperbole, the figure of exaggeration, is the fat man's characteristic rhetoric. The fat man is a natural *miles gloriosus* or braggart soldier since all of his energy is expended on talk of war and doughty deeds.

One correlate of the illusion of unbounded energy is seen in stand-up comics. They need to dominate their audiences to such an extent that they seem to be indifferent to others and to create the illusion of being alone on stage and speaking to themselves. They are so totally committed to what they are doing that they don't need the audience at all to support them. Whether you laugh or not is your affair. The comedian seems in no way concerned because he knows full well that your laughter is involuntary and not freely given, that the only profound laughter is the one that comes of its own accord and has nothing to do with our conscious will. In the Richard Pryor in-concert movies (and also in *Live on the Sunset Strip*), the comedian creates the illusion of completely private and spontaneous conversation. It is not a memorized routine at all. The profusion of dirty words and invective more or less expresses a total indifference to the audience and their conventions, and we are forced to follow Richard Pryor's unbounded comic inventiveness and energy whether we want to or not. As audience, we are caught up in pressures and enticements that lie outside our conscious control. There is a wonderful insolence in the comedian's lack of concern for his audience. In Lenny Bruce it went even further to an active game of insulting and offending his listeners. This is the comedian working on the edge of chaos.

The illusion of autonomous language is a very comforting one indeed because it suggests that the comedian can make up a language of his own as he goes along or detach ordinary discourse from its conventional meanings. There is a link here between poetic and comic creativity. The great exemplar of autonomous language is Oscar Wilde's (1895/1958) play, *The Importance of Being Earnest*. The style is so consistently witty and epigrammatic that the characters can hardly be said to have any pretentions about communicating anything. The imperious Lady Bracknell functions as a display piece and her interview with Jack about his suitability as a husband for her daughter is more a comic turn than a vehicle for conveying information. It is a contest of wits in which Jack can only come off second best to the Grand Lady.

When Jack admits that he smokes, Lady Bracknell is pleased: "I am glad to hear it. A man should always have an occupation of some kind. There are far too many idle men in London as it is" (p. 302). "Occupation"—and all words relating to the utilitarian catalogue of the Puritan Ethic—are given a special aristocratic deflection that renders them inoperative except as puns and double entendres. Lady Bracknell's shock at Jack's origins is full of a very mannered theatricality: "To be born, or at any rate bred, in a hand-bag, whether it had handles or not, seems to me to display a contempt for the ordinary decencies of family life that reminds one of the worst excesses of the French Revolution" (p. 304). In what sense is Jack "bred" in a hand-bag, and how is it relevant "whether it had handles or not"? Lady Bracknell is doing her haughty turn, and poor Jack, so mysteriously cut off from his true origins, can hardly be guilty of "the worst excesses of the French Revolution." The language is autonomous in the sense that it is not closely applied to any particular meaning, but is rather flaunted about for effects of word play and verbal brilliance. Lady Bracknell "*sweeps out in majestic indignation*" after declaring her firm resolve not to allow her daughter "to marry into a cloak-room, and form an alliance with a parcel" (p. 304). How splendidly irrelevant all of this verbal exuberance is.

Shakespeare's early comedies also indulged a penchant for comic irrelevance that Hamlet inveighs against in his Advice to the Players: "And let those that play your clowns speak no more than is set down for them, for there be of them that will themselves laugh, to set on some quantity of barren spectators to laugh too, though in the meantime some necessary question of the play be then to be considered" (1963, 3.240-45). This good advice is rather hostile to the free spirit of comedy, which needs a lot of room to move around in. Hamlet the Purist does not necessarily represent the opinions of the author, and Shakespeare certainly shows a more mischievous and playful impulse in all of his clowns. They are primarily corrupters of words. In Launce's elaborate soliloquy (or is it really a mute dialogue?) with his dog Crab in *The Two Gentlemen of Verona*, the sad clown seems to have an unlimited amount of time to set on some quantity of barren spectators, while we gleefully lose sight of some necessary question of the play. In all the imagined turns of the dialogue, Launce is absolutely grave in defending himself against accusations directed to his dog, and he ends with a plaintive and unanswerable question: "When didst thou see me heave up my leg, and make water against a gentlewoman's farthingale? Didst thou ever see me do such a trick?" (1964, 4.4.38-40).

The recent absurdist drama has more vivid examples of language detached from meaningful communication and going its own merry way. Ionesco's (1958) *The Bald Soprano* is entirely devoted to this autonomous discourse, revivifying the dead clichés and frozen metaphors of conversation manuals. When the play opens, Mr. and Mrs. Smith, a typical English couple, are enunciating the stultifying platitudes of English domestic life: "There, it's nine o'clock. We've drunk the soup, and eaten the fish and chips, and the English salad. The children have drunk English water. We've eaten well this evening. That's because we live in the suburbs of London and because our name is Smith" (p. 9). The logic that underlies language has disappeared and in its place we have a bombardment of phrases without any roots in syntax. Everyone speaks either in slogans or orations. When the Martins and the Smiths thank the Fire Chief for "a truly Cartesian quarter of an hour," he replies with a mysterious allusion to the bald soprano. This produces *"General silence, embarrassment,"* relieved only by Mrs. Smith's judicious comment: "She always wears her hair in the same style" (p. 37). This is a comic routine unrelated to any of the burning issues of the play, and especially not to any of the burning issues proposed by the Fire Chief.

It finally remains to explain the illusion of perfect timing. Time can be interpreted as one of the physical barriers the comedian needs to overcome along with space, gravity, and physical limitations of any sort. Time is the medium in which comedy works. The ability to triumph over time is clearly another aspect of comic omnipotence. Performers are constantly speaking of timing as a relation between the person on stage and the audience. A stand-up comic will know how fast or how slowly to tell a story in relation to its effect on the hearers. One measure of his skill is the ability to tease the audience by either moving very quickly or very slowly to prove that he is not really dependent on the audience for setting the pace. Once again, the audience's involuntary responses are being manipulated in what can prove to be a daring display of control. Of course at some point the audience can rebel and insist on its own control of the timing. This is always harmful for a performer.

The great comedians we have been speaking of, both in literature and in life, are all masters of timing. The Marx Brothers, for example, tried to build a long sequence of jokes that came so fast that the audience never had time to settle back and make itself comfortable. The pace is furious and the effect of acceleration is one that can be almost painful in its intensity. We are literally worn out with laughter. This is the French idea of *fou rire*, mad, uncontrollable, prolonged, demonic laughter, an extraordinary tribute to the involuntary nature of laughter. Henny Youngman, a comedian who specializes in one-liners, may tell hundreds of separable jokes in 20 minutes, but the agglomeration feels like a logical sequence. The desired effect is endless laughter, in which all resistance to the joke teller disappears. In some literal sense, we are being assaulted by the jokes.

We experience the great comic characters of literature, and especially of drama, as those who triumph over time. The *quid pro quo, tu quoque*, or witty retort of the clown is a demonstration that his discourse is infinite, that he can never be put down. He must always have the last word, which is only last because no one chooses to challenge it. In this sense comedy avoids endings or finalities, which is why death is so important to tragedy and so antithetical to comedy. Thus Falstaff is always flexible in discourse, as if discourse had replaced the uncomfortable realities of the real world. The point of Gadshill and

Prince Hal's practical joke of robbing the thieves is that Falstaff is clearly a coward, a condition we never doubted from the start. Falstaff can shift out of responsibility and any imputation of lying by manipulating reality as an eternal present of discourse. When caught in an obvious lie—"Why, how couldst thou know these men in Kendal green, when it was so dark thou couldst not see thy hand?" (1965, 2.4.230-32)—he refuses to answer "upon compulsion." And when the Prince finally faces him down, Falstaff pleads that he was "a coward on instinct": "By the Lord, I knew ye as well as he that made ye. Why, hear you, my masters. Was it for me to kill the heir apparent? Should I turn upon the true prince?" (2.4.268-71). His timing is perfect, and he makes no unnecessary concessions to human frailty or error.

SUMMARY

We have been trying to explain comic creativity in terms of four illusions: omnipotence, boundless energy, autonomous language, and perfect timing. It is obvious that each of these illusions is part of all the others and they are all intricately intertwined. You cannot have perfect timing without an assumption of omnipotence that expresses itself with boundless energy and in a language that seems autonomous and sui generis and obviously separated from ordinary discourse. In this sense the comedian or the comic character is in a special protected status: He can do no wrong. If laughter is involuntary, we are surprised by laughter as much as we are surprised by sin. The comedian triumphs over our resistances and therefore we accord him a special licensed place as the holy fool. The ritual clowning in some societies very elaborately institutionalizes this function (Radcliffe-Brown, 1965).

It is important for our mental health and social well-being that we should indulge in the comic whether we consciously wish to or not. Thus the true goal of comic creativity is comic purgation. What are we purged of? Obviously not pity and fear as in tragedy, but more likely the kinds of anxieties, aggressions, and repressions that constitute the demons of daily life. Freud understood this purgation very compassionately in *Jokes and their Relation to the Unconscious* (1905/1963), and he associated the work of comedy very closely with the dream work of the *Interpretation of Dreams* (1900) and the daily clarifications of the *Psychopathology of Everyday Life* (1901). In this sense we all practice comic creativity as a necessary mode of self-preservation and survival.

REFERENCES

Coleridge, S. T. *Biographia literaria*. New York: Dutton, 1906. (Originally published, 1817.)

Eidelberg, L. A contribution to the study of wit. *Psychoanalytic Review*, 1945, *32*, 33-61.

Freud, S. The interpretation of dreams. In A. A. Brill (Trans.), *The basic writings of Sigmund Freud*. New York: Modern Library, 1938. (Originally published, 1900.)

Freud, S. Psychopathology of everyday life. In A. A. Brill (Trans.), *The basic writings of Sigmund Freud*. New York: Modern Library, 1938. (Originally published, 1901.)

Freud, S. *Jokes and their relation to the unconscious*. New York: Norton, 1963. (Originally published, 1905.)

Ionesco, E. *The bald soprano*. In D. M. Allen (Trans.), *Four plays*. New York: Grove, 1958.

Plautus, *Pseudolus*. In L. Casson (Trans.), *The menaechmus twins & two other plays*. New York: Norton, 1971.

Radcliffe-Brown, A. R. *Structure and function in primitive society*. New York: Free Press, 1965.

Shakespeare, W. *Hamlet*. E. Hubler (Ed.), *Signet Shakespeare*. New York: New American Library, 1963.

Shakespeare, W. *The two gentlemen of Verona*. B. Evans (Ed.), *Signet Shakespeare*. New York: New American Library, 1964.

Shakespeare, W. *Henry IV, Part One*. M. Mack (Ed.), *Signet Shakespeare*. New York: New American Library, 1965.

Skura, M. Creativity: Transgressing the limits of consciousness. *Daedelus*, 1980, *109*, 127-146.

Wilde, O. *The importance of being earnest*. In S. Barnet, M. Berman, & W. Burto (Eds.), *Eight great comedies*. New York: New American Library, 1958.

Chapter 4

Personality and Psychopathology in the Comic

SEYMOUR FISHER and RHODA L. FISHER

INTRODUCTION

The world's greatest humor experts are the comics. They do, after all, manage to make people laugh day in and day out. They must "know" a great deal about humor in order to invoke it so effectively. We may logically assume that one approach to learning more about the nature of funniness is to probe the comic. Actually, he is an intriguing character who has been around in different guises for a long time. He has variously been known as fool, clown, and court jester. It is almost impossible to find a culture in which he has not been an important figure. As will be seen, he has often occupied a curiously split role. At one level he is treated as the silly ridiculous one, but then he is also regarded as holding special powers. This is well illustrated by the position of the clown in many North American Indian tribes. As he participates in a religious ceremony, he many carry out certain priestly functions and yet simultaneously mock the whole thing. Willeford (1969, p. 96) noted: "Ceremonial clowns . . . are fun makers and . . . are yet awesome spiritual beings of fundamental importance to the culture and surrounded by taboos." We shall attempt to demonstrate that the comedians and clowns of today function in ways that are curiously similar to the ceremonial fools and clowns of old. It is strikingly apropos that Rogers (1979), an anthropologist, who became a participant observer of clowns in a modern circus, was impressed with the quasi-religious roles assigned to them (p. 92): "Every year when Ringling Brothers and Barnum and Bailey's trains pull out of winter quarters a priest blesses them—for a safe journey during the season. The priest is aided in his blessing by two clowns who serve as altar boys." She went on to say that "clowns are the soul of the circus" (p. 92) and thought of by other performers as having received "some kind of calling from heaven" (p. 92). In this chapter we have set ourselves the task of sorting out the scientific information that has accumulated concerning the behavior of professional humor producers. Who are the comics of the world? Where do they come from? What motivates them? Do they have identifiable personality patterns? Aside from laughter, what else might they be trying to evoke as they broadcast their funny signals?

ORIGINS

We would presume that comedians and clowns make up the bulk of the professional humor producers. It is possible that others might also fit this category, for example, comedy writers, cartoonists, and creators of comic strips. However, little or nothing is known about these latter groups (Cohen, 1981; Lanyi, 1977) and we will necessarily limit our discussion to comedians and clowns. Fisher and Fisher (1981) have presented particularly detailed information about the pathways to becoming a professional comic. They interviewed 43 professional comics and compared them with 41 professional actors. In addition, they reviewed the published biographies and autobiographies of another 40 comedians. They noted that a large proportion of the comics had originally come from families of lower socioeconomic status. Relatedly, Willhelm and Sjoberg (1958) reported, on the basis of a survey they undertook, that comedians are more likely to have grown up in broken families of a low socioeconomic level than other classes of actors and show people. Janus (1975, 1978) too reaffirmed the predominant lower socioeconomic origins of a sample of stand-up comedians he studied.

Fisher and Fisher discovered that few comedians enter directly into comedy as a vocation. They come to it gradually as they develop a focused awareness of their comic talent. On the average, comedians discover rather early in life that they are funny and can make people laugh. At school they are often class clowns and, as might be expected, do not usually do well academically. Aside from the fact that the schoolroom provides them with an opportunity to experiment with comic roles, they typically find the school experience painful and discouraging. Most of them initiated their entrance to a comic career by becoming involved in some other aspect of show business. For a large proportion this took the form of participating in a musical act or group. Many comics are excellent musicians. Well-known figures like Jimmy Durante, George Burns, Jack Benny, and Beatrice Lilly started out with musical acts. A common story told by comedians is that after they entered show business by playing and singing in some group, they gradually became aware that people laughed when they constructed funny bits in between musical numbers. As they learned they could be effectively funny, they were more and more pulled to try and make it as full-time comedians.

It is true that comedians have also diversely entered show business as actors, jugglers, rodeo performers, disc jockeys, and circus performers. Incidentally, Fisher and Fisher found that most comedians did not get much support from their parents for their comic ambitions. They were frequently quite bitter as they looked back on the intensity of parental opposition they had encountered. Professional clowns usually take a more direct pathway to their vocation. Fisher and Fisher included 15 clowns in their study. About 50 percent had fathers who were clowns and a large proportion grew up in circus families. At a relatively early age they knew they wanted to be clowns and seem rarely to have encountered parental opposition to their clown aspirations.

IS THERE A COMIC PERSONALITY?

Phrases like "comic personality" are loosely tossed about. There are widespread stereotypes about the "comic type." For example, there is the longstanding belief that comics are unusually prone to being "depressive personalities." However, even a superficial reading of a number of biographies and autobiographies of comics impresses one with the diversity of comic profiles rather than their similarity. To realize the extreme types represented one has only to compare the alienated Sid Caesar with the brash Mel Brooks or the self-depreciation of a Woody Allen with the forceful stance of a Dick Gregory, or the flamboyant style of Ernie Kovacs with the modesty of Jimmy Durante. Fisher and Fisher were extremely impressed with the fact that among the 43 comedians and clowns they interviewed, every conceivable form of personality structure was represented. Previous interviews of comedians by Wilde (1973), Fry and Allen (1975), Tynan (1979) and the participant observations of clowns by Rogers (1979) document a similar diversity.

Comics are not wrapped in an identifiable personality package. However, it should be added that when Salameh (1980) studied a group of stand-up comedians ($N = 20$) and administered the California Psychological Inventory to them, he found that they did differ from normal groups in the following respects: They were higher in dominance, social ambition, aggression, self-confidence, impulsivity, and verbal fluency. They were also more outspoken, self-centered, self-accepting, and inclined to individual achievement. Further, they depicted themselves as particularly flexible, psychologically minded, and more interested in feminine values. Salameh and Dudek (Note 1) conceptualized these findings as follows:

> In summary, the personality test findings give the general impression of intense, effective, independent and self-invested individuals whose primary allegiance is to their phenomenal world. They seem to be unhampered by social precepts, challenging

social assumptions and putting aside what is expected of them in favor of what they hope for; interested in genuinely communicating with others but not preoccupied with the impression they make on other persons. (p. 4)

However, although they differed from the normal population in the ways just enumerated, they did not differ significantly from a control group ($N = 20$) consisting of professional musicians, painters, and sculptors. Thus, one would have to say that their self-descriptions, as portrayed by their California Psychological Inventory scores, did not suggest a particularly unique profile. Comics simply matched a pattern common to all sorts of artistic and creative people. The pertinent literature indicates that it is fair to say that no one has been able to isolate or define a "comic personality" entity.

THEMES AND CONFLICTS

Evil versus Good

Fisher and Fisher (1981) did discover that comics are characterized by concerns about specific themes. In their study of 43 comics (28 stand-up comedians and 15 clowns) they obtained interviews and administered the Rorschach Inkblot Test and the Thematic Apperception Test. They also collected a series of Early Memories. There was a major control group comprised of 41 actors.[1] The mean age for the comics was about 47 and for the actors it was 37.[2] It was considered that the actors would control for the effects of such factors as identification with the role of the entertainer, being so often exposed to public attention, and having to cope with the problems of winning approval from audiences. The strategy used in the Fisher and Fisher investigations was first to explore the data from the first five comics and five actors collected in order to ascertain if there were detectable theme consistencies that could then be evaluated in the remainder of the samples. A number of such themes were, in fact, quickly spotted, and it was demonstrated that judges who were informed concerning them could use that information (on a blind basis) to discriminate significantly the Rorschach protocols of the comics from those of the actors.

---

[1] A special control group consisting of 17 entertainers (e.g., musicians, dancers) was also introduced late in the study, but played a minor part in the overall data analysis.

[2] About 33 percent of the comics and 50 percent of the actors were women. No significant sex differences within each group were observed for any of the measures administered. The educational levels of the comedians and actors were respectively 12.08 and 15.48 years. Religious representation in the two groups was such that the largest percent was Protestant, the second highest was Catholic, and the lowest was Jewish.

Among the various differentiating themes that emerged was one of central importance that concerned matters of evil versus virtue. At diverse response levels, it appeared that stand-up comedians and clowns are forever embroiled in an internal debate about their worth. They seem to alternate between picturing themselves as angels and devils. This lead was sufficiently promising that Fisher and Fisher went on to test it in the remainder of the sample of comedians and clowns. Using the clues provided by the first five exploratory cases they constructed objective scoring systems that were sensitive to preoccupation with good-bad themes, as they might appear in interview material and also in Rorschach and Thematic Apperception Test responses. Let us first consider what Fisher and Fisher discovered in their analysis of Rorschach inkblot imagery in the comics and the control subjects.

An inkblot good-bad scoring method was developed that considered the frequency with which direct references are made to good versus bad or indirect references to things and persons with morality connotations. Some examples of scorable responses follow: angel, saint, hell, heaven, church, judge, criminal, policeman. It was found that the comics produced significantly more such inkblot images than did the actors. One should add that no sex differences appeared, and this was consistently true in all of the data Fisher and Fisher collected with regard to comics. Salameh (1980) has reported a similar lack of sex differences for a variety of psychological measures in his study of stand-up comedians. But further with regard to the good-bad issue, it was found that the comics were unusually inclined to produce what Fisher and Fisher labeled "nice monster" responses. Typically, such responses involved first describing some bad, vicious, undesirable creature and then suddenly going into reverse and depicting the creature as friendly, nice, and good. Here are a few typical examples:

Faces. Evil looking—Mean mouth. Masculine—The evil is not very evil. A put-on. Pig-like—Ugly but yet somewhat endearing.

They can be scored with high reliability. The message conveyed by the "nice monster" image is that what appears to be bad is actually the opposite. It was found that the frequency of such inkblot images was significantly greater in the comics than in the controls. Quite the same result was obtained by Fisher and Fisher when the presence of good-bad themes in Thematic Apperception stories was measured with an objective scoring system. But the concern of the comic about his virtue was most directly highlighted when the statements he made during an approximate hour interview were analyzed for good-bad content categories.

It was observed, first of all, that comics were significantly more inclined than the controls to declare that the entertainment they provided had beneficial, curative intent (e.g., "My jokes heal people"; "I make people feel better"; "Comedy is a therapy. They pay me well. It's like being a surgeon"). Second, they were likewise more likely to make "good" remarks about themselves (e.g.,

"No one has a bad word for me." "I am quite religious, and I just feel that whatever God wants me to do He'll lead me"). Fisher and Fisher pointed out that preoccupation with "good-bad" can often be detected in the films of such well-known comics as Charlie Chaplin, Harold Lloyd, and Buster Keaton. Interestingly, the bespectacled young man that Harold Lloyd played so successfully evolved from the example of a "fighting parson" that Lloyd much admired. The good-bad preoccupation one finds in the modern comic coincides strikingly with the behavior of the earlier mentioned Indian ceremonial clowns who would act like bad, amoral boys and simultaneously perform holy, religious functions. Makarius (1970) refers to the ceremonial clown figure as an "amalgamation of power to do good with power to do evil—with the result that people turn to him for his capacity of healing, purifying, bringing happiness and luck, and at the same time recoil from him as from an unclean being, to whom every kind of impurity is assimilated and whose contact is defiling and baneful" (p. 57). Fisher and Fisher speculated that one of the prime goals of the comic, as he spins out his funny stuff, is to deny the possibility that he is a bad person. Humor is used to create an ambiance of relativity in which there is no absolute right or wrong, good or bad. The message is given that good and evil exist only in the eye of the beholder. Fisher and Fisher remarked:

> Presumably, when the comic appears before his audience he is a central figure in a quasi-morality skit. With the skills of the funny man he enacts the theme of evil and anti-evil and asks not only for absolution but also affectionate approval. Indeed, he asks too that we deny that there is any reliable way of determining what is good or bad. He is alternately the Devil, the Angel, and an Anarchist who denies that any meaningful standards about evil and virtue are possible. (p. 70)

Fisher and Fisher linked the comic's preoccupation with good-bad themes to certain socialization experiences he had. They were able to demonstrate from objective analysis of interview material that comics had, from an early age, been expected by their parents to take an unusual amount of responsibility. As children, comics had typically been called upon to be adult beyond their years; to begin earning money very early; to act as caretakers for siblings; and even to provide partial support for their parents. They were given the basic message that they were to grow up fast and that they did not have the right to experience the normal dependency and privileges that go with the status of being a child. They could win parent approval only by conforming to standards extremely difficult for a child to achieve or accept. Fisher and Fisher stated:

> One might say that, in essence, the comics' parents will give him approval only if he musters the special premature capacity they expect. Presumably, he earns the label good or the label bad as a function of getting or not getting such approval. It is the toughness of the parents' expectations that makes it difficult to win the 'good' label from them with any consistency. It is an arduous task to be good within their definitions of the term. So, we may theorize this is one source of the comic's chronic preoccupation with images of good versus bad. (p. 55)

In addition, Fisher and Fisher found that comics had significantly more positive attitudes than actors toward father and negative ones toward mother. Father was depicted in both interview protocols and Thematic Apperception Test stories as relatively good and virtuous. However, data from the same sources portrayed mother as critical, expecting too much, and set to punish wrongdoers. This attitude on mother's part was said to contribute particularly to the comic's concern about being a bad person and the necessity for taking on an unusual amount of responsibility.

Two previous investigators have looked at professional comics' perceptions of their parents. Janus (1975, 1978) published two brief notes based on interviews he carried out with 48 male and 14 female stand-up comedians, many of whom were nationally known. Incidentally, he administered the Wechsler Adult Intelligence Scale to all of the subjects and found the average IQ for males was 138 and that for females 126. He did anecdotally report that the male comedians regarded mother more positively than they did father but indicated that just the opposite was true in the case of female comedians. It will be recalled that Fisher and Fisher observed more negative feelings toward mother than father and there was no sex difference in this respect. Only Janus's findings for the female comedians match the Fisher and Fisher observations. It is not clear why his observations about his male subjects are so different from those of Fisher and Fisher. It is difficult, if not impossible, to explore the difference in view of the fact that Janus published his observations only in capsule anecdotal form. Another investigator, Salameh (1980), asked 20 stand-up comedians and 20 controls (viz., artists and musicians) to respond to a questionnaire that asked them to write descriptions of how much conflict they had had with each of their parents and their siblings during childhood. The descriptions were submitted to judges who rated them on a scale from low to high conflict. It was found that the comedians significantly exceeded the controls in amount of conflict reported with father: and while they also exceeded the controls in amount of conflict with mother, the difference was at a borderline level ($p < .10$). However, what needs to be clarified about these findings is that although they seem to show elevated conflict for the comedians, the actual mean levels were low (around 2 on a 4-point scale). The significant differences obtained were primarily a function of the extremely positive attitudes expressed by the control group subjects toward their parents rather than representing really negative feelings on the part of the comics. It should be added that the comedians depicted significantly more conflict as having occurred between their mothers and fathers than did the controls, but they did not indicate a noteworthy amount of conflict between their siblings and themselves. Obviously, the findings from the last three studies just cited are not in agreement. To reconcile the disparities is difficult because there are so many ambiguities and differences in approach. We have no information as to how Janus analyzed the interview data he obtained. Also, it is not clear what level of response Salameh tapped into when he asked subjects to write a response to a questionnaire that asked directly for a description of how much conflict one had had with one's parents. The fact that both the comedians and controls largely declared that all was well and that they had had little or no difficulty in relating to their parents suggests social desirability effects may have inordinately influenced the responses.

An opportunity to explore this issue further is supplied by previous studies in which attitudes of nonprofessional adult comics toward their parents have been evaluated. There have been three such studies (Bales, 1970; Block, 1971; Fisher & Fisher, 1981). They have employed diverse methodologies and populations. One (Block) involved a longitudinal sample. There is little agreement among the studies concerning the characteristics of fathers of nonprofessional comedic children or adults. However, all three did conclude that the mothers of comedic males are inclined to be nonmaternal and rather nonnurturant. This conclusion is, of course, congruent with the Fisher and Fisher formulation concerning the nonmaternal stance of the professional comic's mother. Although there are real differences in other respects between professional and nonprofessional comics, one cannot help but be impressed with the overlap of the findings concerning the mother in this instance. The idea has to be seriously entertained that the comedic style is linked to being reared by a mother who was relatively nonnurturant. As mentioned, Fisher and Fisher suggested that the nonnurturant mother gives her comic-to-be offspring the message that he ought to relieve her of her load, that he is a bad person because he expects "too much" of her, namely, that she should accord him the usual gratifications and privileges of the child.

The role of the nonmaternal mother in the development of the comic has been further highlighted in studies by Fisher and Fisher of children who get referred for treatment of a variety of maladaptive behaviors (e.g., doing badly in school, conflict with parents), but who have in common a "theatrical clumsiness, a clownish awkwardness, a schlemiel quality" (p. 109). Observations of such schlemiel children indicated that they often behaved like fools and were not infrequently class clowns. Although their parents did not think they were humorous, a detached observer could see that their behavior was absurd, ridiculous, and periodically quite funny. Fisher and Fisher determined that the Rorschach protocols obtained from such children were surprisingly similar to those typifying professional comedians and clowns. There was a similar unusual concern with good-bad themes and "nice monster" images. Other similarities also occurred that involved parameters that will be discussed at a later point in this chapter. In any case, Fisher and Fisher screened about 500 Rorschach protocols of children who had been referred for psychological treatment and isolated 31 (16 boys, 15 girls) that matched the typical comic inkblot pattern. A control group was also formed of children of equivalent age and sex, but whose Rorschach responses were clearly not of the comic variety. It was found that teachers rated the comic children as significantly funnier than they did the control children. Data had originally been gathered concerning the mothers and fathers of the children, including Rorschach protocols, the Study of Values (Allport, Vernon, and Lindzey, 1960), and the Parental Attitude Research

Instrument (PARI) that taps attitudes toward childrearing. In comparing the parents of the comic and control children, it was found that there were no differences between the fathers for any of the Study of Values scores. However, the mothers of the comics were significantly lower than the control mothers for the Social dimension, which is intended to measure the degree to which an individual's orientation is kind, sympathetic, and unselfish. That is, the mothers of the comics seemed to be less kind and more selfish in their orientation. When the parents' childrearing attitudes, as tapped by the PARI, were examined, it was discovered that the mothers of the comics were relatively inclined to see themselves as sacrificing too much for their children, and they tended to endorse the view that children should be urged to take responsibility for themselves as early as possible. The following are typical statements endorsed by the mothers of the comic children:

> The child who grows up with the idea that he will have to do almost everything for himself gets much further in life.
> A child will take care of himself much better later on if he never gets started in the first place expecting help from others.

The comic children's mothers were also noted to produce relatively low numbers of Rorschach inkblot images depicting close, intimate, "touching" attachments to others. The results obtained for the fathers of the comic children were spotty and did not add up in the consistent way they did with reference to the mothers. Obviously, the dominant theme that emerged for the mothers, across the findings from the Study of Values, the PARI, and the Rorschach, was a negativity toward being nurturant or close or maternal. This provides one more bit of evidence concerning the special message ("I expect you not to behave like a child") that comics seem so often to receive from their mothers. One should supportively add at this point that McGhee (1979), who studied a group of children longitudinally, found that those who were comically inclined had been reared by mothers who were rather nonmaternal and nonnurturant.

Size Imagery

When Fisher and Fisher originally inspected the Rorschach responses of the first five comics and first five actors they studied, they detected a distinct trend for the comics to be particularly preoccupied with images of reduced size. Significantly more often than the controls, the comics perceived inkblot figures as small. They seemed set to define things as tiny and diminutive. An objective scoring system for measuring number of inkblot references to smallness (e.g., small, tiny, dwarf) was devised; and when it was applied to comparing the remainder of the samples of comics and actors, the former were found to have produced significantly more such references. Fisher and Fisher conducted a series of studies to determine whether Rorschach images of smallness are linked to perceiving one's own body in analogous terms. It was demonstrated that the greater the number of inkblot references to smallness the more individuals underestimated their height and produced human figure drawings that were relatively small. So there was justification for concluding that the comic is inclined to perceive his own body space as reduced and squeezed in. Previous research (e.g., Wapner, Werner, & Krus, 1956; Shaffer, 1964; Dannenmaier & Thumin, 1964) indicated that sensations of body smallness are often linked with feelings of failure and inferior status. In these terms, the comics could be said to feel lowly and depreciated. Fisher and Fisher pointed out the fit between this finding and the inferior role usually accorded the comic fool. They note: "a sense of lowliness is ... the universal motif of the comic and his historical brother, the fool. All serious students of comedy have focused on the comic's basic declaration, which might be paraphrased: 'I am a silly nobody. I am foolish, little, childish and inconsequential' "[3] (p. 97).

But aside from the specific connotations of the "small" images present in the comic's inkblots, one may also consider that, at a more general level, they refer to the dimension of size. The size theme is found everywhere in comedy. Fisher and Fisher pointed out that comics are constantly building jokes on size contrasts. This can easily be seen in the comic images of Chaplin, Keaton, Laurel and Hardy, and Abbott and Costello. Or one can recall that Jimmy Durante endlessly commented about his big nose, Joe E. Brown about his huge mouth, and Woody Allen about his diminutive stature. Clowns too love to experiment with bigness and smallness. They are forever wearing huge gloves, getting into preposterously small cars, playing toy-like musical instruments, or exhibiting exaggeratedly large noses. Fisher and Fisher cited a good deal of psychoanalytic literature that has speculated about the relationship between comedy and size imagery. Dooley (1941) was one of the first to comment on the link between fantasizing smallness and being funny. In reference to a humorous patient she had had in therapy she noted:

> He (patient) saw himself as a little boy in a high chair in the kitchen, receiving all his mother's attention, and laughed over the diminutive creature's happiness and self importance ... He identified himself with the little children and at the same time acted the part of the superior grown-up person, who could treat them roughly and yet make laughter out of it for them and for himself. (p. 92)

Greenacre (1955), another psychoanalyst, focused strongly on the presumed tie between humor and preoccupation with body size. She sought to document the tie by minutely examining the work of two humorists, Jonathan Swift and Lewis Carroll. She pointed out that in *Gulliver's Travels* Swift created a hero whose adventures revolved about a series of episodes in which he encountered people

---

[3]Fisher and Fisher (1981) also reported that comics produce an unusual amount of Rorschach imagery in which there is a downward directionality (e.g., falling, diving, sitting down, underneath). Such "down" imagery was tentatively linked with feelings of alienation and failure.

and creatures whose bodies were either extraordinarily small or large. Relatedly, Carroll portrayed Alice (in *Alice's Adventures in Wonderland*) as experiencing an exotic round of body transformations, so that at times she was too small to reach a door handle and at other times her neck was so long as to be mistaken for a snake. Greenacre speculated that both Swift and Carroll had had traumatic childhood experiences that left them with a high level of body insecurity and a concern about potentially dangerous body changes. She wondered if there was a connection between feelings of body distortion and an interest in chopping up the world into humorous bits. Humor, she thought, had been used by Swift and Carroll as a means to project onto others their own feelings of body distortion. She noted that much of humor involves: "presenting people as physically bizarre, loathesome or ill-formed, or by so focusing on some body part that it appears out of proportion" (p. 271). Presumably the body incongruities experienced by comics motivate them to find and magnify the incongruities in others. Fisher and Fisher suggested that the specific preoccupation with sensations of body smallness present in the comics derives importantly from their early experiences with a mother whose nonnurturant attitude had a dwarfing, squeezing impact.

Concealment

Another theme that Fisher and Fisher found prominently in their comic sample had to do with concealment. This theme pictures the world as a place where true intentions are hidden and there is often a great deal going on beneath camouflaged exteriors. Fisher and Fisher developed objective criteria for scoring concealment imagery in both inkblot responses and Thematic Apperception stories. In both instances, concealment was scored whenever there were references to hiding, disguise, spying, plotting, camouflage, false impression, and other similar themes. It was demonstrated that the comics produced significantly more concealment imagery than did the actors in their inkblot responses and also more (borderline significant) in their imaginative stories. Fisher and Fisher indicated that in their interviews with comics they often found concern that things were not what they appeared to be. For example, one comedian said: "Be very careful about decisions. Things in this world are like an open book, but they're (really) like the C.I.A." (p. 75). He went on to say: "There is a little lie in everything" (p. 75). Another comic declared that deception was basic to all jokes. He thought that constructing a joke was "like catching your parents having an affair" (p. 76), and he indicated that when he is in front of an audience he feels like he is wearing a mask. Related kinds of comments were reported by Wilde who has interviewed many comics.

Wilde (1973) quoted Danny Thomas as saying: "Well, Gibran, in *The Prophet*, said it very succinctly: 'What is your sorrow but your joy unmasked?' You have *two masks*, that's a human being. Your joy is your sorrow *unmasked*. And vice versa" (p. 361, emphasis added). Wilde similarly reported that Shelly

Berman said, "I don't know what makes a man complain in a certain way, and generally a comedian has a complaint—a peculiar, oblique complaint *which he disguises in a specific way*" (p. 96, emphasis added). Wilde quoted Joey Bishop as saying, of his comedy: "*It's a camouflage.* Whatever success I've had in comedy is based on the fact that I don't look like I'm gonna say something that's terribly clever" (p. 106, emphasis added). Fisher and Fisher pointed out that many jokes evolve out of the discovery of concealed meanings that contrast with surface meaning. Comics like Charlie Chaplin and Woody Allen often treat objects as if they contain hidden within them qualities that are not at all apparent from their outward appearance. Chaplin was forever discovering that an alarm clock could be a can of tuna fish or a shoe was palatable and even delicious. Similarly, Woody Allen would recount how an innocent looking elevator could actually make anti-Semitic remarks to him. In speculating about the comic's preoccupation with concealment, Fisher and Fisher suggested that there were certain factors in their background that might be contributory. They felt that one important factor derived from the comic's chronic debate with himself as to whether he is a good or bad person. They noted:

> He is pulled back and forth by his ambivalence. We would speculate that a sense of disparity plagues him because he cannot balance his "I am good" and "I am bad" images. Simultaneously, as he reassures himself of his virtue, he is pricked by pangs of badness. We would suggest that this enduring disparity creates a sense of deception or covering up. Presumably, even as the comic reassures himself he is the good one, he feels like a pretender, like one who is camouflaging his badness. This sense of dissimulation could then become a powerful paradigm or frame of reference. It could persuade the comic that the world is constructed in an analogous fashion (pp. 78-79)

Fisher and Fisher proposed that a second factor in the comic's involvement with the concealment theme is that the fact that he often seems to have had contradictory experiences with his parents. More will be said about this matter of contradiction shortly, but in essence what has been observed is that when comics conjure up memories of their parents, there is an unusual amount of contradictory content. This could indicate that the comic experienced his parents' behavior as especially contradictory. If so, the comic might have had to learn that any communication from his parents should not be taken at face value and could shortly be succeeded by its opposite. He might have learned to look for the concealed because his parents habitually said or did one thing and actually meant something quite different.

Contradiction

When comics are asked to give early memories about their parents, they introduce an unusual amount of contradiction. Here are several illustrations:

My mother always *wanted to spank me* for something—she'd *start laughing* so hard

My father always had me *say my prayers.* He *wasn't religious.*

Even when my father *hit* me, I *loved* him. He was *God* . . . He's a *non-entity.* (Fisher and Fisher, 1981 pp. 129-130)

It was possible to show that such contradictions could be reliably scored, and a significantly greater number were found in the early memories of the comics than in those of the actors. The contradictions were detected only in the early memory reconstructions and were not present in any of the other types of material obtained during the interviews. This suggested that the memory inconsistencies owed their origin quite specifically to past contradictory experiences with one's parents. The findings concerning contradiction easily call to mind that a number of theorists have conceptualized humor as arising out of the integration of incongruity. Bergson (in Keith-Spiegel, 1972) traced the comic element to bringing together two independent things that can be interpreted quite differently at the same time. Similarly, Koestler (in Keith-Spiegel, 1972) portrayed humor as arising out of looking at an event in relation to two incompatible contexts. Perhaps the comic's familiarity with contradiction and incongruity in his own family gave him some of the expertise needed to master incongruity as it goes into constructing humor.

Salameh (1980) has recently thrown light on a specific aspect of the comic's involvement with contradiction. In his study of stand-up comedians (and artistic controls) he tested the hypothesis that when a comic is confronted with a tragic theme he is immediately motivated to conjure up an opposing comic theme and then to integrate them. The test was carried out by asking subjects to make up stories about pictures with tragic content. The stories were tape-recorded and judges later rated them as to the level of transformation of the picture's objective tragic or neutral content into comical content. There was a clearly significant result that indicated that the comics were more likely than the controls to achieve such transformations. In essence, the comics took the tragic and transmuted it into its opposite. This finding not only highlights a set on the part of the comic to think in terms of opposites but also supports Fisher and Fisher's hypothesis that comics have, from an early age, been inculcated with the responsibility to humor and soothe other people. As already indicated, many comics do see their comic role as one that calls for healing people and making them feel better. Fisher and Fisher also demonstrated that quite early comics feel the need to take heavy responsibility and to lighten the loads of their parents (especially mother). Fisher and Fisher proposed that the comic grows up in a family in which he is assigned the role of helping others to defend against their anxieties. They speculated:

. . . that the comedian learns as a child that by being funny and playing the part of the comic he gives his parents psychological support. His sense of obligation to them seems to get expressed, at least partially, in the feeling that he must create an

atmosphere that will blunt the impact of negative forces in the world. He probably
learns to stroke his parents with his funny role. (p. 71)

Apparently, so strong is his set to detoxify the bad or tragic that when, as in the
Salameh study, he is confronted with tragic themes, he automatically and
energetically turns to converting them to their opposite. Salameh and Dudek
(Note 1) broadly interpreted this behavior on the part of the comic "as a
preference for self creation over self-destruction, and as a symbol of the
continuity and resiliency of human existence" (p. 7).

COMPARISON WITH AMATEUR COMIC

Do professional and amateur comics resemble each other? Is the professional
simply a more extreme version of the amateur who, while he can be funny in his
social contacts with others, has simply not chosen humor making as a vocation?
There are some findings in the literature that might lead one to conclude that the
amateurs and professionals are quite similar. It will be recalled that when
Salameh (1980) administered the California Psychological Inventory to his
sample of stand-up comedians he found a pattern of scores that was different
from the average profile but similar to that characterizing artistic, creative
people. This pattern strikingly resembles that which has been found in a variety
of past studies of people who have shown themselves, in a purely amateur way,
to be funny.

Fisher and Fisher reviewed the pertinent literature and concluded that the
following attributes have been shown to be linked to the amateur funny person:
above average intelligence, verbal fluency, creativity, spontaneity, unconven-
tionality, leadership, aggressiveness, and favorable self-image. Just about every
one of these attributes appeared in the earlier cited list of attributes that
Salameh observed in his questionnaire approach to his stand-up comic group.
As mentioned, one could therefore conclude that the groups resemble each
other. However, when Fisher and Fisher approached the issue from quite
another perspective, they were not impressed that the amateurs and professionals were really alike in their personality dynamics. They administered a
Comic Questionnaire to 29 male college students and also obtained Rorschach
protocols from them. Only chance correlations were found between degree of
comic orientation and the various Rorschach variables that have been found to
characterize the professional comics. The Comic Questionnaire scores were not
correlated with good-bad images, "nice monster" responses, references to
"small," "down" responses, or concealment images. Thus, when the question
of whether amateur and professional comics are alike is asked in terms of
projective test criteria, the answer is negative. However, an approach based on
self-report questionnaires is more in the affirmative direction. How can this

apparent contradiction be resolved? First of all, one needs to underscore again that Salameh did not find the stand-up comedians to be different from the artists and musicians in the control group, and it is not unreasonable to assume that the typical amateur comic would likewise not be distinguishable from such controls.

The apparent resemblance between the professional comics in the Salameh study and the amateur comics in other studies has to do with their membership in a broad class of those who are spontaneous and creative. The differences found in the Fisher and Fisher study between comics and controls occurred under more stringent conditions. That is, the controls for the comics were not simply another group of the spontaneously creative, but also those who are professionally involved with audiences and the whole process of entertainment. Finally, it should be pointed out that several previous investigators have commented on the fact that questionnaires tap a different level (viz., self-report statements) than do projective or other perceptually oriented tests. Holtzman, Thorpe, Swartz, and Herron (1961) reported that questionnaire measures rarely correlate with inkblot parameters; Witkin, Goodenough, and Oltman (1979) elaborated on the fact that perceptual indicators of field independence-dependence correlate minimally with various questionnaire scores.

PSYCHOPATHOLOGY

As earlier noted, there is a widespread stereotype that comics are depressed people who are more psychologically disturbed than the average. The flamboyant self-destructive behavior of several nationally known comedians has certainly reinforced this stereotype. What do we find when we examine the pertinent scientific literature? There are really three sources of information: Janus (1975), Salameh (1980), and Fisher and Fisher (1981).

Janus's observations imply that comedians are rather disturbed people. Janus refers to their depressive tendencies, their instabilities, and the fact that 85 percent had at some time in their lives sought psychotherapeutic treatment. However, aside from the apparent high frequency of seeking psychotherapy, the other points mentioned by Janus are quite anecdotal and unsubstantiated. Salameh (1980) discovered that his stand-up comedians obtained significantly higher MMPI Depression scores than the general population, but not sufficiently high to be considered pathological. But to complicate matters, the comedians also obtained higher MMPI Ego Strength scores than the general population. It should be added that the comedians did not differ significantly from the controls (artists, musicians) with reference to either Depression or Ego Strength. Salameh had difficulty in reconciling the fact that the comedians were apparently more depressed and at the same time higher in ego strength than the general population. In one context, he and Dudek (Note 1) offered the following interpretation: "However, this pattern seems to reflect a creative responsiveness to reality in that the comedians' depression provides them with an emotional fabric, a raw material for artistic creation which their ego-strength allows them to circumscribe and productively utilize to create humanistic art" (p. 3).

Fisher and Fisher did note the special difficulties that comics have with their mothers, but were more impressed with their psychological resilience than their weakness. They pointed out that a majority grew up in difficult circumstances and had had to struggle with the vicissitudes of a particularly trying vocation, and yet managed to create reasonably sound identities and lives. At a more specific level, Fisher and Fisher made the following observations on the basis of their studies:

1. Interviews with a variety of comedians and clowns did not reveal the presence of an unusual amount of grossly visible disturbance.

2. Quantitative analysis of indices of pathology (e.g., anxiety, Pathognomic Verbalization) in the Rorschach responses of the comics did not indicate more than average psychopathology.

3. Measures of boundary articulation (as defined by the Fisher-Cleveland 1968 Barrier score) demonstrated that the comics have a greater sense of boundary security than is found in the average individual. To digress for a moment, note that this finding concerning body image would appear to contradict Greenacre's (1955) previously referred to conclusion that the humorous writers, Jonathan Swift and Lewis Carroll, whose lives she reviewed, had unusually high levels of body insecurity. A couple of explanations of the apparent contradiction come to mind. Perhaps comic writers are actually quite different from comics and therefore the body image insecurity Greenacre observed in them would simply not be applicable to comedians. On the other hand, if they are alike, it is conceivable that while Greenacre was correct in concluding that Swift and Carroll had a good deal of anxiety relating to the body as they were growing up, she might have underestimated how well they were able as adults to master, and compensate for, that anxiety. Perhaps the freedom they displayed as adults in experimenting with size changes in their literary fantasies might not have been possible if they had not first evolved a secure body image base. Analogously, it is conceivable that comedians do, early in life, find themselves confronted by serious body image conflicts, especially with reference to sensations of smallness, but that they emerge from the confrontation with strengthened compensatory defenses.

The three categories of observation just cited do not portray the comic as unusually disturbed or maladjusted. One can also say that the Salameh data present a similar relatively positive picture. It is further apropos that Fisher and Fisher found that those college students who describe themselves as comics are less likely to report the presence of physical symptoms serious enough to require treatment by a physician. Overall, one would have to say that in view of what we know at this point the burden of proof lies with those who would assert that comics are more disturbed than other people.

SUMMARY

While there are still few systematic studies of comics, enough information has accumulated to begin to give us a picture of some of their important attitudes and defenses. What stands in the foreground is their preoccupation with morality and a sense of obligation to do good. This preoccupation has been observed both in their consciously enunciated values and in their projective fantasies. When one considers that so many comics flaunt their naughtiness and go out of their way to focus aggressively and often approvingly on things considered to be bad and dirty, it is difficult to believe their concern about morality. One cannot but be skeptical that a comic who is gleefully reciting a list of four-letter words is actually preoccupied with "doing good." However, as we have seen, comics seem to be invested in describing themselves as good people and in depicting their comedy as having salutary, therapeutic effects upon audiences exposed to it. As Salameh has shown, when they encounter the tragic, they are highly motivated to negate it and to transmute it into something funny and pleasant. Their comedy can be seen, at one level, as a strategy for soothing people and for denying threat. One could say that as comics expose the potentially bad and dirty things in life, they make us laugh at these things and reassure us that they are not really as terrible as the culture assumes. Also, one can, as already noted, interpret the comics' line as an attempt to deny the reality of dependable standards of good and evil and thereby to cancel out sensations of unworthiness in themselves and others.

The comics' apparent need to play a soothing role may speculatively be attributed to early socialization experiences that emphasized taking responsibility and relieving one's parents (especially mother) of burdens. Comics were apparently, as children, reared by mothers who were not maternally inclined and who wanted their children to grow up as fast as possible. Fisher and Fisher (1981) have conjectured that comics' preoccupation with the absurd may have grown out of the fact that their mothers dealt with them in terms of the absurd expectation that they would not make the demands children are usually privileged to make. That is, comics' mothers seem to have communicated to them the puzzling notion that although they were children they were not to behave like children. Barchilon (1973) has suggested that when parents behave absurdly, their children inform them most directly of this fact by, in turn, behaving absurdly. The comics' devotion to absurdity might well represent just such a communique.

There is as yet no solid evidence that comics fit a certain personality pattern. Fisher and Fisher said, apropos of this point:

> The comic comes in many different forms. It is doubtful that anyone will ever succeed in compiling a neat trait profile of the professional comedian. What we have done is to establish that he has focalized areas of tension and doubt; certain attitudes toward his mother and father; and a number of beliefs about the demanding, contradictory,

deceptive nature of his environs. Within this psychological context many different trait patterns are possible and even probable. (p. 202)

This statement is, as already noted, apparently contradicted a bit by Salameh's observations that the stand-up comedians he studied showed trait patterns similar to those found in artistic creative populations. However, membership in a broad category like the "artistic creative" is hardly distinctive.

A final word should be said about the striking similarity between the role of the modern comic and earlier roles filled by the fool-priest and the court jester. They share the double quality of being simultaneously depreciated and yet possessed of special powers. The court jester was an object of ridicule and a funny scapegoat. However, he was, at the same time, considered to be in touch with a realm of irrationality and somehow in control of a magical supernatural stream. His presence was a form of insurance against the supernatural chaos "out there." He was perceived as having powers that helped to protect the king. Analogously, the modern comic plays the fool and the ridiculous one. But he dares to deal with all of the themes that are taboo and "off limits" and to do so in a way that serves to deny their threatening implications.

REFERENCE NOTE

1. Salameh, W. A., & Dudek, S. Z. *The personality and creative process of stand-up comedians*. Paper presented at the 89th Annual Convention of American Psychological Association, Los Angeles, 1981.

REFERENCES

Allport, G. W., Vernon, P. E., & Lindzey, G. *Manual for study of values*. Boston: Houghton Mifflin, 1960.

Bales, R. F. *Personality and interpersonal behavior*. New York: Holt, Rinehart and Winston, 1970.

Barchilon, J. Pleasure, mockery and creative integrations: Their relationship to childhood knowledge, a learning defect and the literature of the absurd. *International Journal of Psycho-Analysis*, 1973, *54*, 19-34.

Block, J. *Lives through time*. Berkeley, Cal.: Bancroft Books, 1971.

Cohen, J. S. Personality profiles of American comic art professionals. Unpublished doctoral dissertation, United States International University, 1981.

Dannenmaier, W. D., & Thumin, F. J. Authority status as a factor in perceptual distortion of size. *Journal of Social Psychology*, 1964, *63*, 361-365.

Dooley, L. The relation of humor to masochism. *Psychoanalytic Review*, 1941, *28*, 37-47.

Fisher, S., & Cleveland, S. *Body image and personality* (rev. ed.). New York: Dover Press, 1968.

Fisher, S., & Fisher, R. L. *Pretend the world is funny and forever: A psychological analysis of comedians, clowns, and actors.* Hillsdale, N.J.: Lawrence Erlbaum Associates, 1981.

Fry, W. F., Jr., & Allen, M. *Make 'em laugh.* Palo Alto, Cal.: Science & Behavior Books, 1975.

Greenacre, P. *Swift and Carroll.* New York: International Universities Press, 1955.

Holtzman, W. H., Thorpe, J. S., Swartz, J. D., & Herron, E. W. *Inkblot perception and personality.* Austin, Tex.: University of Texas Press, 1961.

Janus, S. S. The great comedians: Personality and other factors. *The American Journal of Psychoanalysis,* 1975, *35,* 169-174.

Janus, S. S., Bess, B. E., & Janus, B. R. The great comediennes: Personality and other factors. *The American Journal of Psychoanalysis,* 1978, *38,* 367-372.

Keith-Spiegel, P. Early conceptions of humor. Varieties and issues. In J. H. Goldstein & P. E. McGhee (Eds.), *The psychology of humor.* New York: Academic Press, 1972.

Lanyi, R. L. Comic book creativity as displaced aggression. Unpublished doctoral dissertation, University of California, Davis, 1977.

Makarius, L. Ritual clowns and symbolic behavior. *Diogenes,* 1970, *69,* 44-73.

McGhee, P. E. *Humor: Its origin and development.* San Francisco: W. H. Freeman, 1979.

Rogers, P. The American circus clown. Unpublished doctoral dissertation, Princeton University, 1979.

Salameh, W. A. La personnalité du comedien. Théorie de la conciliation tragi-comique. Unpublished doctoral dissertation, University of Montreal,, 1980.

Shaffer, J. P. Social and personality correlates of children's estimates of height. *Genetic Psychology Monographs,* 1964, *70,* 97-134.

Tynan, K. *Show people.* New York: Simon and Schuster, 1979.

Wapner, S., Werner, H., & Krus, D. M. The effect of success and failure on space localization. *Journal of Personality,* 1956, *25,* 752-756.

Wilde, L. *The great comedians.* Secaucus, N. J.: Citadel Press, 1973.

Willeford, W. *The fool and his scepter.* Evanston, Ill.: Northwestern University Press, 1969.

Willhelm, S., & Sjoberg, G. The social characteristics of entertainers. *Social Forces,* 1958, *37,* 71-76.

Witkin, H. A., Goodenough, D. R., & Oltman, P. K. Psychological differentiation: Current status. *Journal of Personality and Social Psychology,* 1979, *37,* 1127-1145.

Chapter 5

Humor in Psychotherapy: Past Outlooks, Present Status, and Future Frontiers

WALEED ANTHONY SALAMEH

Humor is the art of surfaces and linings, of nomadic singularities and of the ever transposed aleatory juncture, the art of static genesis, the savoir-faire of the naked event or "the fourth person singular"—all import, designation and manifestation suspended, all profoundness and elevation abolished.

Deleuze (1969)

The above quotation by the French philosopher Gilles Deleuze is a powerful description of the textures and graphics of humor that evokes various metaphors and parallelisms in the reader's mind. One can almost touch the surfaces and linings, roam the world of nomadic singularities, and live the naked event as one suspends all designations and manifestations to remember and enjoy a favorite humorous experience. If the reader is a clinician engaged in therapeutic work, he or she might want to enter into the quotation a little further by making a comparison between the world of humor as Deleuze depicts it and the world of psychotherapy: Can we not think of psychotherapy as the art of deciphering the surfaces and linings of another human being's psyche? Is it not a nomadic singularity that two persons who come from different pathways and have never hitherto met end up relating to one another at deeply meaningful levels? Does not psychotherapy require a maturational savoir-faire in the face of the naked events of the patient's life, a savoir-faire that requires therapists to suspend their profoundness and elevation, their value judgments, designations and manifestations, in order to understand the patient's* experiences from the patient's own vantage point? Finally, could we not posit that the intensity and the distinctive emotional and cognitive features of both therapy and humor set them apart from other everyday experiences and therefore place them in the original creative realm of "the fourth person singular"? The promising comparisons we undertook above might subsequently invite the metaphors of synthesis or integration, which leads us to the topic of this chapter: Is it possible to conceive of a fruitful alliance or, for the more reserved reader, of a productive relationship between therapy and humor, and if yes, under what conditions? Accordingly, this chapter will be divided into five sections: therapeutic theories explicitly incorporating humor, existing research on the therapeutic uses of humor, future research perspectives, ethical considerations, and humor as a therapeutic form.

THERAPEUTIC THEORIES EXPLICITLY INCORPORATING HUMOR

Humor is a human possibility (a "nomadic singularity") that is not restricted to any specific theoretical framework, therapeutic or otherwise. Many therapists who are humorously endowed therefore use humor in their daily therapeutic work naturally and implicitly without seeking further elaborations or theoretical justification for their humorous interventions. Yet other therapists have made humor an explicitly important cornerstone of their therapeutic work and have developed theories of psychotherapy in which humor plays a major role both structurally and operationally. The *Handbook of Innovative Psychotherapies* (Corsini, 1981) lists two such theories, "Provocative Therapy" and "Natural High Therapy."

Provocative Therapy

Provocative Therapy is a psychotherapeutic approach developed by Farrelly and his associates (Farrelly & Brandsma, 1974; Farrelly & Matthews, 1981). As the name implies, the stance of therapists within this approach is a provocative and self-disclosing one as they choose to transcend the traditional transference-countertransference model in favor of a full-fledged and intensely interactive relationship with the patient, using and humorously verbalizing their emotional reactions to the patient's style to provoke therapeutic change. An

---

*The words "patient" and "client" are used interchangeably in this chapter, without any implication regarding severity of symptoms, to describe people seeking therapeutic help. Nonetheless, this author usually prefers the word "patient" to "client" since it does not carry a business-like economical connotation and because its etymological root refers to a person in distress who is in need of help.

important theoretical assumption of Provocative Therapy is that patients are not as psychologically fragile as is usually assumed and that challenging the pathology patients exhibit can be a catalyst for their growth. The focus of Provocative Therapy is on current experiences and the content of the therapeutic process in terms of patient-therapist interactions, although childhood experiences are not ignored and may be explored if needed. Another assumption is that persons can achieve significant change if they so choose regardless of the degree of severity or chronicity of their illness, and that both they and their therapists underrate the degree of possible positive growth that can be achieved. Moreover, Provocative Therapy hypothesizes that when humorously provoked by the therapist and urged to continue their self-defeating behaviors, patients will tend to move in the opposite direction from the therapist's verbal definition of them, that is, in the direction of positive self-concept and self- and other-affirming behaviors.

Humor plays a central role in Provocative Therapy in the form of the techniques of exaggeration, mimicry, ridicule, distortion, sarcasm, irony, and jokes. These techniques seem to help in amplifying clients' maladaptive behaviors while simultaneously expressing clients' worst thoughts and fears about themselves, thereby depriving clients of their usual defensive ploys "The therapist will express the unutterable, feel the unfeelable, and think the unthinkable . . . often the therapist will overemphasize the negative, thus forcing the client to emphasize the positive aspects of his or her life" (Farrelly & Matthews, 1981, p. 686). But what about support, warmth, and acceptance of clients? Do these factors play a role in Provocative Therapy? Farrelly and his associates (1974, 1981) seem to address this concern with three clarifications: First, the provocative therapist is not ridiculing patients as human beings but is rather ridiculing their maladaptive behaviors in an effort to extinguish or countercondition these behaviors. Thus, irony and ridicule are usually not perceived by patients as destructive when used judiciously, specifically, and constructively by the mature therapist. Second, Farrelly would not deny that his techniques will initially provoke anxiety in patients as they discover that their defenses will be constantly confronted. However, the positive aspects and results of the confrontation are quickly visible: "Often in therapy, distinction must be made between short-term cruelty with long-term kindness versus short-term kindness and long-term detriment" (Farrelly & Matthews, 1981, pp. 683-684). Third, Farrelly argues that there is an equilibration between ironic verbal feedback and supportive nonverbal feedback in Provocative Therapy. The two different levels of therapist communication are postulated to provoke anxiety as well as the heightened client awareness necessary to initiate change.

Natural High Therapy

Another humor-based therapeutic perspective is O'Connell's Natural High Therapy (1977, 1981). O'Connell's approach seems to be a complex humanistic integration of Adlerian and Jungian approaches combined with Moreno's psychodrama techniques, with humor serving as a synthesizing factor as well as a central focus of the therapeutic process. O'Connell (1981) postulates the existence of three equally important and progressively related levels or dimensions of self-actualization in Natural High Therapy. Level 1 refers to the struggle to move from the external ego-attachments of "roles, goals, and controls" toward a healthy sense of self-esteem that is generated from within the person. Level 2 refers to the development of positive social interest in terms of fruitful relationships with others and the ability to encourage and be encouraged in dyadic interactions. Finally, level 3 corresponds to the maturation of transpersonal dimensions and the experience of spiritual communion, with the expansion of both self-esteem and social interest as the person transcends "ego-addictions" and gives up "demandements" to pursue the process (not the goal) of self-actualization.

Another theoretical tenet of Natural High Therapy is that the symptoms patients present to therapists are behavioral manifestations of displaced creative energies, indicating a high level of motivation to "search for power on the useless side of life" (O'Connell, 1981, p. 560). Consequently, symptoms are initially encouraged (in order to tap their energy) and brought out in various role-playing situations; yet at the conclusion of therapy, symptoms tend to be viewed by the patient as "an interesting side-show." Natural High Therapy uses a didactic-experiential format combining individual and group therapy to work with constrictions at the three levels of functioning described above. The therapeutic techniques used include psychodramatic and empty-chair techniques, role playing by both patient and therapist and dialogue with significant others, guided imagery, exercises to develop encouragement of self and others, and meditation techniques using breath-focusing and contemplation modalities. Throughout these exercises, patients are encouraged "to stroke the self for effort, never for perfection," while blaming behaviors are discouraged. Humor may be introduced at any point in the above situations since O'Connell (1981) considers it "the royal road toward actualization." O'Connell has also developed a specific therapeutic technique using humor that he calls "Humordrama." O'Connell defines Humordrama as follows: "A group method to teach and learn the sense of humor based on a psychodramatic format. Participants soliloquize their thoughts and feelings while playing their stressful situations. Doubles then use such techniques as brief sudden switches, employing verbal condensations, understatements, and overstatements to generate the humorous attitude" (1981, p. 923).

Other Therapeutic Systems Using Humor

Some psychotherapists have addressed the issue of humor and its use in their therapeutic work without necessarily building their theories around humor or making humor a cardinal underlying theme of their therapeutic systems. Frankl

(1966) uses a technique he calls "paradoxical intention" in his Logotherapy approach. It consists of encouraging clients to exaggerate their symptoms to the point of absurdity, which develops their ability to laugh at their neurotic constructions and subsequently to view their symptoms with the disinvested self-detachment necessary to extinguish symptom-associated behaviors.

Ellis (1977) uses puns, witticisms, evocative language, and other humorous techniques in his Rational-Emotive Therapy to facilitate clients' cognitive restructuring, self-acceptance, anti-absolutizing, and a responsible-pragmatic assessment of interpersonal and terrestrial realities. Greenwald (1975) uses humor in his Direct Decision Therapy to highlight clients' absurd decisions about their lives as well as to mirror or exaggerate maladaptive patterns and unveil new choices. Haley (1963) and Whitaker (1975) have used humor in the context of family therapy. Mindess (1971) uses situationally generated humor to encourage patients' movements toward an emotionally liberating and flexible mode of being. Grotjahn (1970) has discussed the use of humor in psychotherapy from a psychoanalytic perspective and has suggested that the therapist's use of humor is a sign of emotional freedom that provides a positive identification for the patient; as a form of interpretation, humor can "bypass the resistance" (Grotjahn, 1970, p. 62) and is therefore more acceptable to the patient. Other psychoanalytic therapists (Grossman, 1977; Zwerling, 1955) have used the patient's favorite joke as a projective diagnostic technique that can alert the therapist to important personality characteristics, dynamic conflicts, or central problem areas.

Integration

The foregoing perspectives on the therapeutic uses of humor offer both the clinician and the researcher some interesting insights concerning the diverse and promising horizons that humor can open up for the person employing it, enjoying it, or learning by it. however, the above psychotherapists' use of humor is based either on theoretical conceptualization or on experiential clinical validation but not on research findings in the strict and sometimes restrictive sense of the term "research" to denote the use of control groups, experimental manipulation of variables, and the numerical representation of findings.

Furthermore, with regard to the therapeutic systems proposed by O'Connell and Farrelly, it is evident that both clinicians are experienced psychotherapists drawing upon extensive exposure and skill in psychotherapeutic procedures. Their theories have evolved from their clinical experiences and their daily interactions with patients as well as from early influences of other theoretical frameworks; in Farrelly's case, the client-centered model and in O'Connell's case, the Adlerian/Jungian/psychodramatic models. Moreover, both clinicians have conducted numerous workshops and training experiences explicating their therapeutic approaches and teaching their techniques. A major criterion of the effectiveness of their therapeutic methods is the recognition that they have received from the students of their approaches, from other clinicians, and from the individuals who have worked with them as clients in psychotherapy. Nonetheless, as is the case with most other psychotherapies, neither Provocative Therapy nor Natural High Therapy has yet received a systematic research evaluation. Some interesting questions come to mind. For instance, how do Provocative Therapy and Natural High Therapy compare to each other? Are the two therapies similarly effective since they both center around the use of humor, or do they produce different treatment outcomes? How do these approaches compare with traditional psychodynamic therapies or with behavior therapy? How effective is either therapy in comparison to a waiting-list control group? Do the practitioners of either Provocative Therapy or Natural High Therapy possess specific personality traits (such as high flexibility, high levels of verbal expressiveness, playfulness, spontaneity, high levels of the therapeutic facilitative conditions, high self-disclosure, etc.) that distinguish them from the practitioners of other therapeutic modalities? How do patients react to the constant use of humor in these approaches? These questions will be further examined in the future research perspectives section. The preceding questions also trigger one more question, to be addressed in the following section: Is there any research regarding the use of humor in psychotherapy?

EXISTING RESEARCH ON THE THERAPEUTIC USES OF HUMOR

The Larger Context of Psychotherapy Research

Before discussing the existing research on the use of humor in psychotherapy, it seems useful to briefly contextualize research on the therapeutic uses of humor within the general backdrop of psychotherapy research. One comment we can make about the present status of research on psychotherapy is that it reminds us of what a gratefully anonymous author said about translations: The beautiful ones are not faithful, the faithful ones are not beautiful, and in looking for ones that are both faithful and beautiful you end up not getting married! In other words, it appears that certain "missing dimensions" in psychotherapy research have prevented this area of investigation from developing to its fullest and clearest potential.

What are some of these dimensions? First, one can observe a schism between the practitioners of psychotherapy and its researchers. The majority of the effective practitioners are fully engaged in their clinical work. They believe in the qualitative and artistic nature of the therapeutic experience and speak of it in experiential terms. On the other hand, good researchers want to categorize, classify, and objectify the therapeutic process. They approach the study of psychotherapy in quantitative and sometimes inflexible terms. Furthermore, those who practice both research and psychotherapy seem to have difficulty in maintaining excellence at both endeavors. Obviously, a missing dimension in this respect is the absence of a common language that would provide a meeting ground for the conceptualization and articulation of a research rationale and permit the adoption of mutually agreed upon terms, methods, and consensual criteria regarding therapeutic improvement. Such a rationale would take into account both the experiential complexity of psychotherapy and the need for standardized yet flexible research procedures.

A second missing dimension in psychotherapy research refers to some researchers' belief that a *single* scientific method can be applied to the study of the wide range of clinical phenomena occurring in psychotherapy. For instance, it seems evident that different research tools and varying methodologies are called for in researching the process versus the outcome of psychotherapy or patients' phobic reactions versus their depression. Similarly, a *combination* of research methods may need to be considered even within the same research study, depending on the nature of the specific variables under investigation.

The available methodologies in psychotherapy research include the clinical trials or extensive design using control groups (see Bergin & Garfield, 1971; Chassan, 1979; Garfield & Bergin, 1978; Kazdin, 1980), the intensive or analogue research design using one or few subjects (see same references as above), Carkhuff's training model for rating various levels of helper and helpee functioning (see Carkhuff & Berenson, 1967; Carkhuff, 1969), and the existential-phenomenological research method that has yet to be substantially applied to psychotherapy research (see Brian, 1978; Giorgi, Fischer, & Von Eckartsberg, 1971; Giorgi, Fischer, & Murray, 1975; Valle & King, 1978). Since this chapter is not intended for discussion of specific psychotherapy research methods, the interested reader is referred to the aforecited references on each method.

In conclusion, we can note that the field of psychotherapy research is still in its infancy or maybe latency stage and has not yet resolved its adolescent identity crisis, let alone firmly established its adulthood. We would therefore concur with Garfield (1981) who concluded his 40-year appraisal of psychotherapy as follows:

> Over the past 40 years, the number of psychotherapists has increased greatly, as has the number of psychotherapies. Research and research sophistication have also increased. . . . The issue of the effectiveness of psychotherapy has been questioned, debated, reformulated, defended, and still not conclusively settled. In spite of research studies and reviews supposedly showing that psychotherpy is more effective than no therapy, questions and criticisms remain. . . . Research to discover variables and procedures that are potent for particular individuals with particular problems is still sorely needed. (pp. 181-182)

Thus, research on humor in psychotherapy inherits the methods and problems, but also the promises inherent in the global spectrum of psychotherapy research, and we can certainly expect humor to be one of the new therapeutic variables Garfield alludes to in the above quote, a variable whose potency awaits corroboration within the next decades of psychotherapy research.

Two Trends of Humor in Psychotherapy Research

Keeping in mind the preceding considerations, we might now ask: Is there any existing research on the use of humor in psychotherapy? The first response to this question is that there is a clear dearth of research in this area. A notice by this author in the June 1982 *American Psychological Association Monitor* requesting published or unpublished studies dealing with the clinical uses of humor in therapy yielded only three responses! Nonetheless, an overview of the literature reveals two significant trends. The first trend predominates the literature until 1970 and continues up to the present (Bloomfield, 1980; Dewane, 1978; Klein, 1974; Poland, 1971; Schwarz, 1974). Many of the articles in this tradition are interesting yet at times are anecdotal and lacking either in methodological systematization or theoretical conceptualization. While acknowledging the usefulness of humor and its benefits as a therapeutic medium, these reports do not usually include specific directives or empirical data on how humor can be used in psychotherapy.

Furthermore, the few existing experimental studies before 1970 utilized cartoons or written jokes and thus could not be generalized to social or spontaneous humor. The literature on humor up to 1970 was also characterized by a preponderance of speculative articles dealing with the use of humor in psychotherapy from a psychoanalytic perspective whereby humor was invariably seen as a defense mechanism, an indirect expression of forbidden aggressive or sexual impulses, and a psychological back door used to deceive the strict superego into allowing repressions to go out for a quick walk and get some fresh air. This author espouses a clearly different perspective of humorous phenomena wherein therapeutic humor is seen as a creative growth experience that is more related to progression, expression, and conception than to regression, repression, and deception.

The publication of Goldstein and McGhee's (1972) *The Psychology of Humor* launched a new trend in the general field of humor research. This second trend was characterized by a fresh nonpsychoanalytic and empirical outlook that coincided with a similar empirical orientation in the study of various dimensions of therapeutic humor, resulting in the completion (between 1971 and 1980) of a small but important cluster of unpublished doctoral dissertations. We will now briefly review these studies.

Methodological and Theoretical Issues. In an exploratory study of the psychotherapeutic aspects of humor, Kaneko (1971) elaborated a research model to investigate the role of humor in psychotherapy and included suggestions for future research. Burbridge (1978) reviewed the literature regarding the use of humor in psychotherapy and the various interpretations of its therapeutic significance.

The Effect of Humor on Therapeutic Process.   Huber's (1974) research indicated that humor did not decrease tension related to discussing intimate topics in counseling, yet also suggested that the counselor's personality characteristics might affect clients' perceptions of their therapists' use of humor in conjunction with discussion of intimate topics. Killinger (1976) expanded Kaneko's (1971) research and carried out an innovative and systematic study to examine whether humor is facilitative of therapeutic process. Humor was defined in Killinger's study in terms of seven descriptive categories and was classified according to affect as laughter or nonlaughter humor. Humor incidents were extracted from audio-tapes of therapy sessions and rated by independent judges as to therapist intent in using humor and the facilitation of outcome for the client following therapist's use of one or more of the seven specific categories of humor. Nonhumorous therapy statements excerpted from the same therapy sessions were also rated to provide a control and comparison measure. The results revealed no significant differences in the frequency of the use of humor by therapists differing in levels of clinical experience, suggesting that the therapist's experience level is not the key factor in determining how often humor is used. Moreover, no increase in therapists' use of humor was observed between early and later therapy sessions. Results further indicated that the therapists' use of humor was usually focused on clients' problems while staying with the topic of interaction and communicating in a nondefensive manner. Humor was also found to be facilitative in promoting a positive therapist-client attitude and in furthering client self-exploration.

Client Reactions to the Therapeutic Use of Humor.   Labrentz (1973) found that clients who read and rated 25 humorous cartoons prior to an initial counseling interview tended to give the counseling relationship a significantly higher rating than clients who were not exposed to the same pre-interview treatment. Golub (1979) conducted a study to determine whether or not counselor's use of humor increased subjects' positive ratings of the counselor and the counseling session in which humor was used; she did not find a significant difference between subjects' evaluations of counselors based on the sole criterion of whether counselors did or did not use humor. On the other hand, both the most anxious and least anxious subjects rated counselors more positively than moderately anxious subjects. These results seem to corroborate Huber's (1974) results and again indicate that clients' evaluations of therapist humor could be affected both by the clients' anxiety level and by other therapist personality factors surrounding or coloring therapists' uses of humor.

Therapist-Related Variables in Using Humor.   Schienberg (1979) found that therapists' ego-permissiveness was positively related to their accuracy in predicting patients' funniness rating of and themes recognized in specific cartoons. Buckman (1980) conducted individual interviews with eight therapists to explore their views regarding the use of humor in psychotherapy and identify recurrent themes connected with therapists' use of humor.

Studies Investigating the Use of Humor in Group Therapy.   Childs (1975) found that use of targeted or directed humor in group therapy was the result of an attempt to comment on or control the behavior of other group members. Depending on the types of directed humor produced by the group, humor could either facilitate or disrupt group process. Furthermore, individual group members were shown to exhibit different characteristic uses of humor within the group, with males rather than females being the predominant initiators of humor.

Taubman (1980) found that in a group home treatment setting for male juvenile delinquents, a significant positive relationship existed between the youths' evaluation of the teaching-parents (child-care workers) and the degree to which the teaching-parents and youths matched on levels of successful humor. Further, behavioral matching between teaching-parents and delinquent youth on successful humorous behaviors was inversely related to youths' self-reported delinquency. Taubman concludes that high teaching-parents evaluation and low delinquency would occur in those treatment programs in which youths imitate the appropriate humor behaviors (and other socially appropriate behaviors) of teaching-parents.

Peterson (1980) investigated the role of laughter in group therapy by rating the therapeutic value of laughter-associated group interactions and concluded that laughter episodes may serve as signs of an ongoing or imminent shift in the direction and/or level of group interactions.

In summary, the above-cited studies are admittedly exploratory in nature, yet they generally share the characteristics of using empirically based approaches and focusing on specific identifiable dimensions of the role of humor in psychotherapy. These characteristics distinguish the second trend of humor in psychotherapy research from the first trend.

FUTURE RESEARCH PERSPECTIVES: A THIRD TREND

Our review of the literature in the previous section has identified two major trends in the work on humor in psychotherapy, the first trend being psycho-analytically oriented and speculative in nature and the second being non-psychoanalytic, empirically grounded, and introducing promising research possibilities. In this section, we will attempt to outline a third trend of future research perspectives that, together with the research already initiated by the second trend group of researchers, will hopefully contribute to the launching of new outlooks in research on humor and its therapeutic uses. In analyzing the various dimensions of the therapeutic experience, Levinson (1962) identified seven essential dimensions: characteristics of the therapist, characteristics of the patient, the therapist-patient pair, stages in the treatment career, influence of the institutional setting, social context of the patient's life, and overall treatment outcome. We will now attempt to explore how humor enters at each of the above levels, as well as at some other levels reflecting specific therapeutic properties of the humor experience.

Therapist Factors

Therapist factors are the personal characteristics that therapists bring into the psychotherapy session. Carkhuff and his associates (Carkhuff & Berenson, 1967; Carkhuff, 1969) have identified the following seven traits as being important core facilitative traits of the effective therapist: empathy, respect, genuineness, concreteness, self-disclosure, immediacy, and confrontation. Both the preliminary evidence presented in the previous sections of this chapter and clinical experience would allow us to postulate that humor is another core facilitative trait of effective therapists. This author has therefore constructed a 5-point *Humor Rating Scale* to rate therapists' use of humor in psychotherapy. Level 1 on the Humor Rating Scale refers to destructive humor, level 2 to harmful humor, level 3 to minimally helpful humor responses, level 4 to very helpful humor responses, and level 5 to outstandingly helpful humor responses. Each higher level is assumed to add to and surpass the lower preceding level on the therapeutic humor dimension. An illustrative clinical vignette is included for each of the five levels of therapist humor. The written version of these vignettes may not completely reflect their full "live" impact as they occurred during psychotherapeutic work and within the context of client statements, but it is hoped that the essential flavor of each interaction can still be conveyed. The Humor Rating Scale is presented in Table 5-1.

By using the Humor Rating Scale to rate live or videotaped segments of psychotherapy sessions, researchers can explore the various levels of therapist use of humor in psychotherapy and whether the higher facilitative levels of humor use are related to high levels of functioning for the other core facilitative conditions (or, conversely, whether nonfacilitative levels of humor abuse by therapists are correlated with low levels of functioning for the other facilitative conditions). Finally, the Humor Rating Scale could be used to assess the degree of improvement in therapist humor subsequent to training in the effective uses of therapeutic humor.

Researchers who may consider using this scale are referred to an article by Gormally and Hill (1974) addressing some of the salient methodological issues related to the use of rating scales in psychotherapy research.

Table 5-1. Humor Rating Scale

Level of Therapist Humor	Clinical Vignette

Level 1   Destructive Humor
Therapist humor is sarcastic and vindictive, eliciting client feelings of hurt and distrust. Therapist abuses humor to callously vent his/her own anger toward clients or the world and is consequently insensitive to and unconcerned with the impact of his/her humor on clients. Therapist humor may judge or sterotype clients; its caustic quality denigrates clients' sense of personal worth, leaving them with a typical "bitter aftertaste" reaction. Since the therapist's use of humor is destructive and retaliatory in nature, it tends to significantly impede client self-exploration and divert the thera-peutic process.

Therapist to client who reports feelings of inadequacy related to a negative self-image: "Well, you obviously have much to be modest about: your face could sink a fleet, and on top of it you have the I.Q. of a tree. On the other hand, being stupid could help you qualify for disability payments."

Level 2   Harmful Humor
Therapist humor does not manifest the blatant client disrespect found at level 1, but is still not attuned to clients' needs. Therapist mixes the irrelevant use of humor with its abuse, at times introducing humor when it is unapplicable to the issues at hand. The therapist may follow up his/her abuse of humor with a "redemptive communication" that essentially acknowledges the inappropriateness of the previous abusive comment and attempts to make verbal or non verbal amends for it. Overall, therapist humor is harmful and incapable of facilitating thera-peutic process since it is indiscrimi-nate and invalidated either by missed timing or by the attempt to redeem derisive comments.

Client states that he is confused about his goals in life and unable to understand him-self. Therapist replies "Here you go off on a fishing pole again! It's almost like your mind is full of wallpaper." Client, with a nervous titter: "So I guess I should be perfect! Asking confusing questions can lead me astray, right?" Therapist, now self-conscious: "well, uh, I'm like that too sometimes. Sometimes I can't think straight." Therapist goes on to explain about his own periods of confusion, indirectly apologizing. Attention is gradually shifted away from the client's experiencing.

Level 3   Minimally Helpful Humor Response
Therapist humor *does not* question the essential worth of individuals and is adequately attuned to clients' needs.

A married couple is reporting to the therapist that their sexual contacts have gradually decreased in frequency and are

Table 5-1 *(continued)*

Level of Therapist Humor	Clinical Vignette

Level 3   Minimally Helpful Humor Response

Therapist uses humor for and not against clients as a means of reflecting their dilemmas in a concerned yet humorous manner. Therapist humor promotes a positive therapist-client interaction, yet remains mostly a reaction to clients' communication rather than an active or preferred therapist-initiated mode of communication.

presently relegated to rare "special occasions" instead of being a continuous element of their relationship. Therapist: "So I guess it's (sexuality) now like the good old Christmas tree. It's a hassle to get it from the attic and set it up. It's nice while it lasts, but it only gets turned on once a year!"

Level 4   Very Helpful Humor Response

Therapist humor is substantially attuned to clients' needs and to helping them identify new options. Therapist humor may expose or amplify specific maladaptive behaviors yet simultaneously conveys a respect for clients' personhood. It facilitates clients' self-exploration while inciting them to recognize and alter dysfunctional patterns. The educational, confortable, and enjoyable nature of therapist humor stimulates a positive and candid client-therapist relationship. Nevertheless, therapist humor still lacks some of the intensity, timing, and graphic language characteristic of level 5 humor responses.

Client complains that she and her husband are always arguing, yet it becomes increasingly clear to the therapist that the client and her husband use arguing as an "exciting" (albeit offensive) conduit for expressing both their intellectual inquisitiveness and their emotional affinities toward each other. Client ends her story with: "It's funny, but after we argue I end up feeling both frustrated and aroused." Therapist replies: "You mean the rocks he throws fit the holes in your head?"

Level 5   Outstandingly Helpful Humor Response

Therapist humor conveys a profound understanding of clients, is characterized by spontaneity and excellent timing, and challenges clients to live to their fullest potential. Therapist humor reflects his or her emotional and cognitive freedom used to facilitate clients' emotional arousal and cognitive restructuring. It generates significant self-exploration and accelerates the process of client change by defining problems, condensing and symbolizing therapeutic

During a group therapy session, a manipulative client is recounting to the group his repeated failings at achieving honest non-manipulative communication with others. Although he tries, others don't seem to believe or respond to his "authentic" self-relevations. Therapist: "You know your situation reminds me of a corrida scene with the bull and toreador. We don't know whether you're the bull for whose slaughter we should feel sorry or the toreador whose courage we ought to

Table 5-1 *(continued)*

Level of Therapist Humor	Clinical Vignette
Level 5 Outstandingly Helpful Humor Response	
process material, identifying new goals, and promoting constructive alternatives. The creative nature of therapist humor can elicit decisive existential insights and encourages clients to develop their own humor along with other attitudinal changes.	admire." Another group member: "But he's really not the bull, he sets other people up as being bulls." Client, laughing: "So I end up being the toreador. I give my coup de grace and demand my Olé!" Group members, in unison: "Olé!"

Note: This author's observational data indicate that physical responses to levels 1 and 2 humor are usually characterized by a preponderance of giggling, tittering, forced laughter, or short anxious laughs. Levels 3, 4, and 5 humor usually elicits predominantly diaphragmatic or abdominal gut-level laughter.

Patient Factors

Patient factors refer to the personal characteristics, expectations, and unique conflicts each patient brings into therapy. These factors have been examined by Labrentz (1973) and Golub (1979). Again the Humor Rating Scale may be used to rate patients' use of humor in therapy and its relationship to their symptoms. For instance, does patients' general functioning improve as they reach a level 3 rating for their use of humor in therapy? At what level of humor use can one expect patients' symptoms to subside? Does a level 1 use of humor reflect an inability to be authentically humorous or a distortion of humorous abilities? Furthermore, Carkhuff and his associates (Carkhuff & Berenson, 1967; Carkhuff, 1969) have proposed that exploration, understanding, and action are important helpee dimensions that can facilitate the therapeutic process. They have developed 5-point rating scales to assess patients' level of functioning for each of these dimensions. It would be interesting to investigate the relationship between clients' level of functioning for the above dimensions and their level of humorous functioning as assessed by the Humor Rating Scale.

Matching Factors

These factors refer to the specific match of client and therapist and how it can affect therapeutic process. Huber (1974), Killinger (1976), and Peterson (1980) have already initiated research along these lines in connection with humor. Some interesting questions, however, remain unanswered: How does a level 4-5 humorous therapist respond to a client using level 1 or 2 humor (as rated by the Humor Rating Scale)? What happens to therapeutic process when a patient employing level 4 or 5 humor is matched with a therapist showing lower levels of humor use? How do humorous therapists respond to clients who are nonhumorous? Another interesting question in this respect is whether the use of ethnic humor by clients of various ethnic backgrounds is appropriately decoded by humorous therapists whose ethnicity is different from their clients' or whether therapists' humor is more facilitated by a client of the same sex, class, or ethnicity as the therapist. The influence of humor on therapeutic process can also be investigated by rating laughter-associated interactions and comparing them with nonlaughter interactions for client depth of self-exploration and level of insight achieved following the therapeutic use of humor, as well as for other process-related variables.

Technique Factors

Technique factors refer to the humorous techniques used by therapists during psychotherapeutic interactions. Various classifications of humorous techniques have been used by Killinger (1976), Browning (Note 1), and others. This author has developed his own classification of therapeutic humor techniques as specified in Table 5-2.

Research is needed to determine which of the foregoing humor techniques are more therapeutically facilitative, as well as which humor techniques are most appropriate for different client populations. Moreover, the technique categories may need to be modified or expanded as indicated by future research in this area. With respect to therapist variables, it would be important to determine if specific humor techniques are associated with specific personality traits of the therapist and whether therapists functioning at high or low levels on the humor scale typically use certain humor techniques to the exclusion of others. The issue of patients' use of specific humor techniques could also be examined in its relationship to their general level of functioning, which leads us to the next category of factors.

Diagnostic and Assessment Factors

The use of humor as a diagnostic and assessment tool was initiated by some psychoanalytically oriented therapists who would ask about their patients' favorite joke and subsequently analyze the various elements and content of the joke to detect diagnostic classification indices, major dynamic conflicts, and important personality characteristics (Grossman, 1977; Zwerling, 1955). The psychoanalytic interest in the diagnostic potential of humor stimulated the

Table 5-2. Therapeutic Humor Techniques

Therapeutic Humor Technique	Definition	Clinical Vignette
Surprise	Using unexpected occurrences to transmit therapeutic messages.	Drilling noise outside office. Patient is talking about his domineering wife. Therapist: "Your wife is talking to you *now!*"
Exaggeration	Obvious overstatement or understatements regarding size, proportions, numbers, feelings, facts, actions.	To patient who romanticizes his depression while refusing to consider alternatives: "I could help you, but I guess that wouldn't do any good anyway. You know we all die eventually."
Absurdity	That which is foolish, nonsensical, inane, irrationally disordered. That which *is* without having any logical reason to be.	A young businessman is spending inordinately long hours at the office and on business trips. He reports that his wife has complained about his increasing lack of interest in their sexual relationship. Therapist responds: "It sounds like the best way for you to get more invested in your sex life is to make it tax deductible!"
The Human Condition	Refers to problems of living that most human beings encounter, viewed from a humorous perspective to stress their commonality.	Therapist to a perfectionistic patient who worries that he is not being "totally honest" in communicating *all* his feelings to others: "As the holy books have indicated, it is difficult for mankind to be honest at all times. But if you want to be a phony, you should be honest about it."
Incongruity	Linking two or more usually incompatible ideas, feelings, situations, objects, etc.	Oppositional female patient reacts to therapist interpretation by stating that she "has already entertained that possibility." Therapist responds: "You've entertained it, but you didn't go to bed with it."

Table 5-2 (continued)

Therapeutic Humor Technique	Definition	Clinical Vignette
Confrontation/ Affirmation Humor	Confronts patients' maladaptive and self-defeating behaviors while simultaneously affirming their personal worth as individuals. Assumes that patient confrontation is best digested by patients when coupled with affirmation.	A patient in group therapy is confronted by other group members regarding his compulsive nose-blowing behavior. He passionately defends his need to "Breathe clearly." Therapist responds: "You know we can see that you've got a lot of intensity, but you don't have to blow it out your nose!"
Word Play	Using puns, double entendres, bons mots, song lines, and well-known quotes or sayings from popular culture to convey therapeutic messages.	Therapist to patient who keeps depriving himself of what he really wants: "You know what Oscar (Wilde) said, 'I can resist anything but temptation.' " To another man who prevents himself from enjoying life or other people because he refuses to take small acceptable risks.' "Mae West did say 'When I choose between two evils, I always like to take the one I've never tried before.' "
Metaphorical Mirth	The use of metaphorical constructions, analogies, fairy tales and allegories for therapeutic story-telling to help patients assimilate new insights or understand old patterns.	Patient is talking about how his interpersonal communication is becoming less confused as he really listens to others and gives relevant feedback. Therapist: "It's like that lion you see at the zoo who always growls at you but you don't know what he means. And one day you go to the zoo and he smiles and says, 'Hi there, I've been fixin' to talk to you.' And you talk to each other and become pen-pals."
Impersonation	Humorously imitating the typical verbal response or maladaptive style of patients and of significant others they may bring up in therapy.	Patient repeats a characteristic "Fssss" sound with his tongue whenever he experiences sadness or other "vulnerable" emotions, so as to block the expression of such feelings. Therapist imitates this

Table 5-2 *(continued)*

Therapeutic Humor Technique	Definition	Clinical Vignette
		"Fssss" sound when patient displays it. Patient gradually shifts from suppression to acknowledgement of his feelings.
Relativizing	Contextualizing events within a larger perspective such that they lose their halo of absoluteness. Relativizing gives the message that: "Nothing is as serious as we fear it to be, nor as futile as we hope it to be" (Jankelevitch, 1964).	Patient recounts his painful struggle with his "weight problem," even though his physician informed him he is only 3-5 pounds overweight. Therapist, "Well, I notice you've lost some weight behind the ears since last week."
The Tragi-Comic Twist	A delicate humor technique requiring almost surgical precision that consists of a transformation of patients' detrimental tragic energies into constructive comical energies. It begins with a well-timed implicit or explicit juxtaposition of the tragic and comic poles of a given phenomenon followed by a reconciliation of the two poles in a humoristic synthesis that triggers laughter.	Patient who has chosen depression and crying as a behavioral mode of response to any environmental stressor is crying during session about feeling rejected and tense. Therapist responds: "I guess you're trying to relax now." Patient's crying turns into frantic laughter as he replies: "That's one thing I do really well, I know how to cry." Therapist: "Maybe you can relax about crying." More laughter. Therapist asks patient why he is laughing. Patient: "I suppose there are other ways of releasing tension besides crying." The entire session then focuses on the above issue.
Bodily Humor	Using the entire body or specific muscle groups in physical activity aimed at imitating or creating non-verbal reflections of typical maladaptive mannerisms in order to encourage their extinction.	Patient exhibits a typical rotational hand movement to express disillusionment with others' behavior when it does not meet his "requirements." Therapist uses this same hand movement in therapy whenever patient is expressing disillusionment with therapist's behavior not meeting his expectations.

development of psychological tests specifically designed to assess the individual's personality structure based on his or her reactions to humorous stimuli. Such tests include Roback's *Sense of Humor Test* (1943), the *Mirth Response Test* (Redlich, Levine, & Sohler, 1951), the *IPAT Humor Test of Personality* (Cattell, Catell, & Hicks, 1952), and O'Connell's (1964) Story Test. This area of clinical humor research has not received much attention within the last decade, and none of the above-mentioned tests seem to have gained wide use in clinical practice. Further research is needed in this area to synthesize the existing studies on the clinical assessment properties of humor and to develop new testing measures that would simultaneously include several types (instead of a single type) of humorous stimuli such as jokes, cartoons, incomplete humorous sentences, and the rating of subjects' own humorous productions.

Problem Definition Factors

One of the important issues in any therapeutic interaction is the therapist's ability to define the patient's problems and develop goals of therapeutic action based on the demarcation of problem areas. Consequently, this author has repeatedly stated to patients, "We cannot defy your problems until we define them." In this regard, humor can be a potent communication tool to help define problems in a quick, flexible, economical, and easily retrievable format. Two clinical examples can help illustrate the potential of humor as a problem-definition modality. The first example has to do with a patient whose dynamics centered upon the theme of being rejected and feeling helpless about it. During his third therapy session, the patient was relating some material about feeling rejected by his peers and how this constituted a repetition of earlier life experiences. Suddenly a rattling noise could be heard outside the therapy room, at which point this author said, "Don't worry; you see, when people stop rejecting you the ghosts will," at which point the patient interrupted his favorite self-absorbed tirade and engaged in loud laughter. The aforementioned comment had defined his dynamic of constantly seeking rejection as well as creating rejection in situations where it did not exist.

Another patient seemed to be having difficulties in relating to women since he was so preoccupied with controlling people instead of being with them. This pattern caused considerable frustration and ultimately rejection in heterosexual relationships. The patient was relating his failure at "convincing" last night's date to have intercourse with him, to which this author retorted, "Listen, you can't possibly go to bed with her because *you* love to go to bed with power." This comment triggered the patient's laughter but also registered with him as a concise definition of his problem. Nine sessions later, the patient's opening statement at the beginning of the therapy session was, "Guess what, I didn't go to bed with power last night!," implying that he was able to enjoy sexual intimacy when he could give up his alienating obsession with control.

These two vignettes illustrate the economical and focusing properties of humor as a problem-definition tool. Some interesting research possibilities in this area include comparing the ordinary nonhumorous method of defining problems to a humorous problem definition format at the outset of psychotherapy then assessing patients' recollections of humorous and nonhumorous problem definitions at various junctures during the therapeutic process or at the conclusion of therapy. Another research possibility would be to ask patients to humorously depict (in cartoon, joke, or other format) the problems for which they are seeking therapy prior to the beginning of therapy, and then to evaluate their therapeutic progress in comparison with a control group who obtained a similar psychotherapeutic follow-up but was not exposed to the pretherapy humorous problem-definition treatment.

Environmental Factors

Environmental factors in psychotherapy refer to the affective and structural tones conveyed to clients by the setting within which psychotherapeutic services are rendered. It is apparent to us that the beneficial environmental effects of humor have yet to be used let alone researched by mental health professionals. This author uses the term "environmental humor" to refer to a therapeutic variety of humor that emanates from and grows within the environment in which individuals live. Environmental humor can then be seen as an organic humor, the humor of invitation, acquaintance, and dialogue. A short visit to any psychiatric ward or psychotherapy office would quickly confirm the impression that environmental solemnity, environmental apathy, or environmental depression have been preferred over environmental humor. New research is needed in this important area to specify the environmental benefits of humor. For instance, do those institutional settings where humor is introduced (via humorous wall posters and quotes, a weekly "humor enrichment day" using humorous films with humorous patient drawings and humorous lectures by staff, reinforcement for socially appropriate humorous behavior, etc.) show fewer daily accidental injuries, less physical illness, and higher levels of patient-staff interaction than other institutional settings where humor is disregarded? Second, what is the effect of environmental humor on patients' therapeutic progress?

Motivational Factors

Motivational factors in psychotherapy pertain to the level of positive motivational energies that both therapist and patient bring into the psychotherapeutic endeavor. These factors are summarily addressed when the clinican wonders after his or her initial interview whether the patient is well-motivated for psychotherapy. This author would propose that humor is a "motivational enhancement act"; in other words, persons who are humorous at level 3 and above on the Humor Rating Scale can be said to be characterized by constructive motivational energies. This hypothesis is corroborated by the work of Abraham Maslow and George Vaillant since both personality theorists have indicated that highly functioning or self-actualizing individuals tend to possess a healthy sense of humor. In this regard, it seems important to investigate the relationship between patients' motivational investment in psychotherapy and their development of a healthy sense of humor. Similarly, do patients who already possess a level 3 or above sense of humor at the onset of psychotherapy show a high level of motivation (no missed sessions, active participation in therapy, etc.) for psychotherapeutic work? Another interesting research potentiality would be to investigate the effect of using humorous materials (cartoons, jokes, staff humor, etc.) on the activation of constructive motivational processes in individuals suffering from severe or disabling physical illness.

Creativity Factors

One of the important goals of psychotherapy with regard to creativity factors is to help patients surpass their constrictions and develop a greater awareness of creative alternatives. Furthermore, an effective therapeutic intervention prepares clients to deal with life resourcefully by providing them with creative problem-solving mechanisms. In this respect, healthy humor can be considered as a creatively therapeutic problem-solving modality representing the human capacity for survival, continuity, and adaptation. Thus, the investigations conducted by Koestler (1966), Fry and Allen (1975), and Salameh (1980) have clearly substantiated the creative nature of the process of humor production and its similarity to the creative processes operating in other forms of artistic expression. These findings may have significant implications for psychotherapy. Evidently the therapist who uses humor is indirectly reinforcing the patient to learn to use humor creatively by identifying with or incorporating the therapist's own humorous perspective. Yet the question remains as to whether humor can be systematically used to directly teach creative problem-solving skills to various client populations (in-patients, day-treatment patients, out-patient populations, college students, etc.). This author espouses the view that individuals can be trained to use humor therapeutically and creatively in much the same format by which they can be trained to use empathy, hypnosis, psychodrama, or any other therapeutic modality. In this author's experience, individuals can be trained to use humor at least up to level 3 of the Humor Rating Scale. This author has developed materials for training therapists in the therapeutic use of humor (Salameh, Note 2) but has not yet researched the efficacy of his training methods. More research is needed to develop systematic and effective training models for training both patients and therapists in the many therapeutic, creative, and problem-solving dimensions of humor.

Outcome Factors

Outcome factors in psychotherapy pertain to the end result of a specific psychotherapeutic intervention. Some of the questions related to treatment outcome are: Did the treatment help the patient? To what degree? For how long do patients maintain their therapeutic gains after the termination of a specific treatment modality? How do various treatment systems compare to each other with regards to effectiveness? It has not been conclusively shown to date that therapeutic treatments explicitly or implicitly incorporating humor are either more *or* less effective than those treatments that do not use humor. One consideration with respect to this issue is that the effectiveness of humor-based approaches depends on the level of humor used by therapists applying a given approach. From what we have presented so far in this chapter we would assume that, in order to be effective in using humor, therapists would need to be functioning at level 3 or above of the Humor Rating Scale. Second, as the research by Huber (1974), Killinger (1976), and Golub (1979) may well be suggesting, it would seem that the therapist's maturity as well as the other personality variables and core facilitative skills surrounding therapist's use of humor can either subtract from or enhance the value of therapeutic humorous communications for clients. Another outcome issue pertains to the additive effects of all the factors we have discussed so far. Accordingly, it would be ideal to study client outcome for a humorous treatment approach used by a creatively humorous therapist with a humorously responsive patient to assess and define problems humorously in a humorous environment, but it would be realistic to focus on the additive effects of some of the factors mentioned above, such as the effect on outcome of a match between a humorous therapist and humorously responsive patient or a nonhumorous therapist and a nonhumorous patient. Finally, as has been pointed out earlier, it would be of interest to compare patient outcome for humorously based psychotherapies like Provocative Therapy and Natural High Therapy to the outcome of traditional psychoanalytic therapies or behavior modification therapy.

ETHICAL CONSIDERATIONS: WHAT HUMOR IN PSYCHOTHERAPY RESEARCH IS NOT ADVOCATING

In discussing the use of humor in psychotherapy and the possible research avenues in this virtually unexplored area, it seems important that some of the ethical implications of the use of humor in psychotherapy be addressed. Kubie's (1971) examination of this issue led him to conclude that humor has a destructive aspect that impedes its use in therapeutic interactions. He noted that the therapist's humorous remarks can block patients' self-disclosure and confuse them as to whether the therapist is "really serious or only joking."

Patients could also perceive the humorous therapist as mocking them, to which they may subsequently react either by reinforcing their own defenses against accepting the importance of their symptoms or by depressively joining the therapist's perceived invitation to engage in self-flagellation. Moreover, Kubie proposes that therapists can use humor to mask their own hostilities or anxieties toward the patient, to gratify their exhibitionistic needs for self-display, to avoid dealing with patients' painful experiences, or to block deeper therapeutic exploration of patients' conflicts. On the other hand, Kubie interprets the use of humor by patients as a ploy intended to seduce therapists out of their therapeutic role and lure them into a nonproductive playful role. In conclusion, Kubie argues that humor should be used in a limited fashion and only by experienced therapists during the later stages of the therapeutic process. However, he warns that the inexperienced therapist may be tempted to use humor too early in therapy, which would subsequently have detrimental consequences for clients. Two recurrent themes seem to characterize Kubie's article: The first is that he is discussing the abuse and not the use of humor, and the second is that he chooses to focus on the destructive deformation of humor instead of exploring its constructive facets. Nevertheless, Killinger's (1976) research suggests that therapists' level of maturity may be a more important factor than their level of experience with respect to determining how often humor is used. Killinger has also found that therapist humor usually focused on clients and their problems, stayed with the topic of interaction, facilitated client self-exploration as well as a positive therapist-client attitude, and communicated therapeutic messages nondefensively. All these findings tend to dispel Kubie's reservations about the use of humor in psychotherapy.

Kubie's comments would make more sense if we were to specify to whom he is referring since he seems to have accurately described the level 1 or 2 category of therapist humor as defined in the Humor Rating Scale, that is, the destructive and harmful humor response categories. These two categories refer to the abuse of humor that Kubie's article discusses at length. We would agree with him that humor, like hypnosis or role playing or any other therapeutic modality, *can* be abused. Yet we notice a significant difference in the *quality* of therapist humor at levels 3, 4, and 5. At these levels, therapists do not feel the need to express anger at their clients since they are not angry at themselves. They do not experience humor as a retaliatory maneuver but as a unique opportunity to facilitate clients' growth and expand their horizons. They use humor out of a sense of inner richness, not out of a feeling of depletion. They do not look at life or at interactions in terms of vengeance but in terms of gratitude and continuing self-exploration. Their humor is constructively vitalizing and not destructively undermining (especially at levels 4 or 5), which reflects the direction in which they have chosen to invest their energies. When these therapists use humor, their major ethical and professional concern is the patient and his or her welfare in answer to the question: What is the most beneficial response for the patient at this moment? Table 5-3 summarizes the characteristics of therapeutic versus harmful humor and may serve as an ethical guide for persons interested in

Table 5-3. Therapeutic versus Harmful Humor

Therapeutic Humor	Harmful Humor
Concerned with impact of humorous feedback on others	Unconcerned with impact of comments on others.
Has an educational, corrective message.	May exacerbate existing problems.
Promotes the onset of a cognitive-emotional equilibrium.	Prevents the onset of a cognitive-emotional equilibrium.
May question or amplify specific maladaptive *behaviors* but does not question the essential worth of all human beings.	Questions sense of personal worth, such as in racist jokes.
Implies self- and other-awareness.	Implies self- and other-blindness.
Has a gentle, healing, constructive quality.	Has a callous, "bitter aftertaste," detrimental quality.
Acts as an interpersonal lubricant; constitutes an interpersonal asset.	Tends to retard and confound interpersonal communication; constitutes an interpersonal liability.
Based on acceptance.	Based on rejection.
Centers around clients' needs and their welfare.	Reflects the perpetuation of personal dysfunctional patterns.
Strengthens, brightens, and alleviates.	Restricts, stigmatizes, and retaliates.
Aims to reveal and unblock alternatives.	Aims to obscure and block alternatives.

exploring the use of humor in psychotherapy, be they therapists, researchers, or observers.

CONCLUSION: HUMOR AS A THERAPEUTIC FORM

In the last 15 years, the field of psychotherapy has seen the emergence of new emphases such as short-term psychotherapy, cognitive behaviorism, and the emphasis on the psychology of the self within the psychoanalytic school. In this author's opinion, humor represents another new emphasis that would significantly benefit the field of psychotherapy and can be expected to make important contributions to the treatment of mental illness. The question posed at this juncture is not whether humor is a viable therapeutic modality, but rather in what form and dosage is it most therapeutic, under which conditions, for which therapist in interaction with which patient, in conjunction with which other therapist personality traits, and how therapists can be trained in its effective use. Fry and Salameh (Note 3) survey new developments in this area and provide the interested clinician with a comprehensive state-of-the-art exposure to the use of humor in clinical practice with different client populations.

Finally, the conclusion of this chapter takes us back to its beginning: Why does Deleuze call humor "the fourth person singular"? We believe that four therapeutic dimensions of the humor experience warrant this unique appelation, namely, passion, compassion, acceptance, and creativity. The passion of humor is its vitality, its intensity, and its commitment to affect life rather than passively watch it go by. The compassion of humor is its sagacious understanding of the human condition, its concerned yet zesty solace, and its affirmation that we are all travelers on the same sea. The acceptance of humor is its celebration of the continuity of life, its recognition of human finitudes, and its transformation of the human boundary into the human promise. The creativity of humor is that it is an artistic allegory of reality that extricates words and images from their constitutional configurations to place them in a new configuration wherein their initial signification is suspended in favor of a new signification. This new signification is simultaneously distinguished by its originality and its capacity to trigger laughter, which distinguishes it from other forms of artistic creation.

In the fortune cookie a minuscule fragment of wisdom read: "You cannot prevent birds of sorrow from flying over your head, but you can prevent them from building nests in your hair."

The statements contained in this chapter are entirely the author's and do not reflect the policies of either the California Department of Mental Health or Patton State Hospital.

REFERENCE NOTES

1. Browning, R. C. *Major elements of the sense of humor.* Paper presented at the Second International Conference on Humor, Los Angeles, Cal., 1979.
2. Salameh, W. A. *A training model for the clinical use of humor in psychotherapy.* Paper presented to the Riverside Psychiatric Group, Riverside, Cal., 1981.
3. Fry, W. F., & Salameh, W. A. (Eds.). *Handbook of humor and therapy.* Book in preparation, 1983.

REFERENCES

Bergin, A., & Garfield, S. (Eds.). *Handbook of psychotherapy and behavior change.* New York: Wiley, 1971.

Bloomfield, I. Humor in psychotherapy and analysis. *International Journal of Social Psychiatry*, 1980, *26*, 135-141.

Brian, B. C. A phenomenological investigation of the hysterical personality. Unpublished doctoral dissertation, California School of Professional Psychology, San Diego, 1978.

Buckman, E. S. The use of humor in psychotherapy. Unpublished doctoral dissertation, Boston University, 1980.

Burbridge, R. T. The nature and potential of therapeutic humor. Unpublished doctoral dissertation, Institute of Asian Studies, San Francisco, California, 1978.

Carkhuff, R. R., & Berenson, B. G. *Beyond counseling and psychotherapy*. New York: Holt, Rinehart and Winston, 1967.

Carkhuff, R. R. *Helping and human relations: A primer for lay and professional helpers* (Vol. I & II). New York: Holt, Rinehart and Winston, 1969.

Cattell, R. B., Cattell, A. K. S., & Hicks, V. *IPAT humor test of personality*. Champaign, Ill.: Institute for Personality and Ability Testing, 1952.

Chassan, J. B. *Research design in clinical psychology and psychiatry* (2nd ed.). New York: Irvington, 1979.

Childs, A. W. A tale of two groups: An observational study of targeted humor. Unpublished doctoral dissertation, University of Tennessee, 1975.

Corsini, R. J. (Ed.). *Handbook of innovative psychotherapies*. New York: Wiley, 1981.

Deleuze, G. *Logique du sens*. Paris: Editions de Minuit, 1969.

Dewane, C. Humor in therapy. *Social Work*, 1978, *23*, 508-510.

Ellis, A. Fun as psychotherapy. *Rational living*, 1977, *12*, 2-6.

Farrelly, F., & Brandsma, J. *Provocative therapy*. Cupertino, Cal.: Meta Publications, 1974.

Farrelly, F., & Matthews, S. Provocative therapy. In R. Corsini (Ed.), *Handbook of innovative psychotherapies*. New York: Wiley, 1981.

Frankl, V. *Man's search for meaning*. New York: Washington Square Press, 1966.

Fry, W. F., & Allen, M. *Make 'em laugh: Life studies of comedy writers*, Palo Alto, Cal.: Science and Behavior Books, 1975.

Garfield, S., & Bergin, A. E. (Eds.). *Handbook of psychotherapy and behavior change* (2nd ed.). New York: Wiley, 1978.

Garfield, S. Psychotherapy: A 40-year appraisal. *American Psychologist*, 1981, *36*, 174-183.

Giorgi, A., Fischer, W. F., & Von Eckartsberg, R. (Eds.). *Duquesne studies in phenomenological psychology* (Vol. I). Pittsburgh: Duquesne University Press, 1971.

Giorgi, A., Fischer, C., & Murray, E. (Eds.) *Duquesne studies in phenomenological psychology* (Vol. II). Pittsburgh: Duquesne University Press, 1975.

Goldstein, J. H., & McGhee, P. E. (Eds.). *The Psychology of Humor*. New York: Academic Press, 1972.

Golub, R. R. An investigation of the effect of use of humor in counseling. Unpublished doctoral dissertation, Purdue University, 1979.

Gormally, J., & Hill, C. E. Guidelines for research on Carkhuff's training model. *Journal of Counseling Psychology*, 1974, *27*, 539-547.

Greenwald, H. Humor in psychotherapy. *Journal of Contemporary Psychotherapy*, 1975, *7*, 113-116.

Grossman, S. The use of jokes in psychotherapy. In A. Chapman & H. Foot (Eds.), *It's a funny thing, humour*. London: Pergamon, 1977.

Grotjahn, M. Laughter in psychotherapy. In W. Mendel (Ed.), *Celebration of laughter*. Los Angeles: Mara, 1970.

Haley, J. *Strategies of psychotherapy*. New York: Grune and Stratton, 1963.

Huber, A. T. The effect of humor on client discomfort in the counseling interview. Unpublished doctoral dissertation, Lehigh University, 1974.

Jankelevitch, V. *L'ironie*. Paris: Flammarion, 1964.

Kaneko, S. Y. The role of humor in psychotherapy. Unpublished doctoral dissertation, Smith College, 1971.

Kazdin, A. E. *Research design in clinical psychology*. New York: Harper and Row, 1980.

Killinger, B. E. The place of humor in adult psychotherapy. Unpublished doctoral dissertation, York University, 1976.

Klein, J. On the use of humor in counseling. *Canadian Counsellor*, 1974, *8*, 233-237.

Koestler, A. *The act of creation*. London: Hutchinson, 1966.

Kubie, L. S. The destructive potential of humor in psychotherapy. *American Journal of Psychiatry*, 1971, *127*, 861-866.

Labrentz, H. L. The effects of humor on the initial client-counselor relationship. Unpublished doctoral dissertation, University of Southern Mississippi, 1973.

Levinson, D. J. The psychotherapist's contribution to the patient's treatment career. In H. H. Strupp & L. Luborsky (Eds.). *Research in psychotherapy* (Vol. II). Washington, D.C.: American Psychological Association, 1962.

Mindess, H. *Laughter and liberation*. Los Angeles: Nash Publishing, 1971.

O'Connell, W. Resignation, humor, and wit. *Psychoanalytic Review*, 1964, *51*, 49-56.

O'Connell, W. & Bright, M. *Natural high primer*. Houston: Natural High Associates, 1977.

O'Connell, W. Natural high therapy. In R. Corsini (Ed.), *Handbook of innovative psychotherapies*. New York: Wiley, 1981.

Peterson, J. P. The communicative intent of laughter in group psychotherapy. Unpublished doctoral dissertation, University of Tennessee, 1980.

Poland, W. S. The place of humor in psychotherapy. *American Journal of Psychiatry*, 1971, *128*, 127-129.

Redlich, F. D., Levine, J., & Sohler, T. P. A mirth response test: Preliminary report on a psychodiagnostic technique utilizing dynamics of humor. *American Journal of Orthopsychiatry*, 1951, *21*, 717-734.

Roback, A. A. *Sense of humor test* (2nd ed.). Cambridge, Mass.: Sci-Art Publishers, 1943.

Salameh, W. A. Personality of the comedian: The theory of tragi-comic reconciliation. Unpublished doctoral dissertation, University of Montreal, 1980.

Schienberg, P. Therapists' predictions of patients' responses to humor as a function of therapists' empathy and regression in the service of the ego. Unpublished doctoral dissertation, California School of Professional Psychology, Los Angeles, 1979.

Schwarz, B. E. Telepathic humoresque. *Psychoanalytic Review*, 1974, *61*, 591-606.

Taubman, M. T. Humor and behavioral matching and their relationship to child care worker evaluation and delinquency in group home treatment programs. Unpublished doctoral dissertation, University of Kansas, 1980.

Valle, R. S., & King, M. (Eds.). *Existential-phenomenological alternatives for psychology*. New York: Oxford University Press, 1978.

Whitaker, C. Psychotherapy of the absurd: With a special emphasis on the psychotherapy of aggression. *Family Process*, 1975, *14*, 1-16.

Zwerling, I. The favorite joke technique in diagnostic and therapeutic interviewing. *Psychoanalytic Quarterly*, 1955, *24*, 104-115.

Chapter 6

Pathological Disorders of Laughter

MICHAEL S. DUCHOWNY

BACKGROUND

During the latter part of the 19th century, clinical and pathological investigations of carefully selected case studies significantly increased our understanding of the brain substrates for normal and abnormal mental phenomena. For the first time, accurate localization of discrete anatomic pathways involved in language, voluntary movement, and spatial recognition became possible. However, equally clear explanations for the neural basis of emotional phenomena still proved elusive by these methods. By the beginning of the 20th century, no particular brain region could be shown to have special importance for the emotions, and all postulated mechanisms for experiencing or expressing emotions remained imprecise (Mills, 1912).

An initial insight into these problems followed from experiments by David Ferrier using galvanic stimulation at the cortical surface. Focal applications of electrical current were shown to induce contractions of facial musculature that closely resembled the voluntary act of smiling (Spillane, 1981). However, neither the corresponding emotion (i.e., joy or happiness) nor the corresponding behavioral motor response (i.e., laughter) could be produced by this technique. Facial muscle contractions thus appeared to be an isolated cortical response and only a component of a more complex emotional activities. This finding suggested a limited role for the cerebral cortex in the experience and expression of positive emotions.

Other anatomical studies confirmed these observations by demonstrating that cortical neurons do not project directly to autonomic centers participating in emotional responses. These conclusions were especially important since virtually all emotional characteristics were thought to have some cortical representation at that time.

Bard (1928) further clarified the contribution of noncortical regions by excising the cortex of cats and observing their behaviors. After recovery, these animals displayed a behavioral pattern that closely resembled the motor patterns for expressing anger (rage response) observed in the intact animal. The experimentally induced emotional response physiologically differed from the natural one only by its being triggered by relatively trivial exogenous stimuli—otherwise, animals were behaviorally indistinguishable. This experimental phenomenon was termed "sham rage" and was reliably induced in every operated animal.

It was later shown that subcortical centers for the emotions were organized into an elaborate system, residing in both cerebral hemispheres and possessing a rich network of interconnecting fiber tracts (MacLean, 1949; Papez, 1937). These anatomic structures constitute the limbic system, which is composed of highly developed integrative mechanisms for regulating the emotions. Through reciprocal connections with the cerebral cortex and lower autonomic and motor centers, emotional significance may be selectively attached to focused voluntary processes. Positive and negative emotions are represented (i.e., joy or sadness) and the activation of motor pathways in turn produces the corresponding motor acts of laughter or crying.

Clinical studies of disorders of human emotions have confirmed similar patterns of brain organization. A "sham" emotional state has been shown to follow surgery for deep cerebral hemisphere brain tumors that disrupt connections between the cerebral cortex and deeper structures (Alpers, 1940). Patients who acquire a complete paralysis of facial muscles for voluntary smiling may still activate the same muscles to express a full range of involuntary emotional responses (Monrad-Krohn, 1924). It would thus appear that, as in animals, the human limbic system is also able to analyze emotional cues and initiate a complete behavioral motor response independent of the cerebral cortex. In the case of a stimulus perceived as joyous or humorous, an involuntary motor act of laughter will follow, even if voluntary smiling is impaired.

Subcortical anatomic and physiological relationships were unknown during the 19th century and their relatively recent appreciation may help to explain why our knowledge of the neural basis of the emotions is only in its infancy. Studies of the limbic system are technically difficult because of their elaborate interconnecting pathways and depth below the cortical surface. Therefore, clinical observations are especially useful for increasing our knowledge of normal and abnormal limbic mechanisms.

Among noncortical brain disturbances, pathological disorders of laughter constitute a relatively common neurological symptom. Because of their atypical manifestations these conditions have traditionally aroused a high level of interest that has resulted in careful documentation. Aside from their value in revealing local disturbances of brain functions, these reports have provided insights into underlying patterns of brain organization for the expression of positive emotional experience.

WHAT IS PATHOLOGICAL LAUGHTER?

Pathological laughter may be defined as an abnormal behavioral response that superficially resembles natural laughter but differs by virtue of abnormalities of motor patterns, emotional experience, or appropriateness of social context.

Each of these disturbances may individually pose particular problems in recognition, requiring careful observation or post hoc analysis using movie film or videotape (Ames & Enderstein, 1975; Dreyer and Wehmeyer, 1977; Mutani, Agnetti, Durelli, Fasio, & Ganga, 1979). The social cues often lack humor and consist of little more than brief innocuous observations, recollections of past experiences or "personal secrets."

Ascertaining whether a patient experiences joy or humor during laughter may be especially challenging. Patients with pathological laughter may not necessarily feel inward joy or humor even though a euphoric mood is automatically assumed. Patients with preserved intellectual abilities are strikingly aware of this dichotomy, which results in management problems for friends, family, or caretakers who are unable to comprehend the absence of inner well-being. These circumstances may become further confused if different pseudo-affective responses occur during the same outburst. For example, smiling may precede weeping, or frowning may precede laughter.

Pathological laughter should not be confused with abnormalities of smiling or spasm of the facial muscles. The former is typified by stressed individuals who exhibit involuntary facial movements such as teeth grinding or curling the upper lip. These affectations may be voluntarily arrested by minor environmental modifications such as shifting the topic of conversation or changing the nature of a given task. The latter circumstance is characterized by tonic (i.e., continuous) contraction of the facial musculature as seen in conditions such as tetanus. An extreme muscular spasm can induce a characteristic "risus sardonicus" that is easily distinguished from the motor patterns of true smiling or laughter.

Examples of pathological laughter may be broadly subdivided into three major categories. Although some degree of clinical overlap will occur, these categories are thought to represent distinct manifestations and anatomic substrates. Table 6-1 illustrates patterns of similarity and distinctiveness for each category of laughter.

Excessive Laughter

This pattern of laughter is associated with a general state of emotional lability. Brain mechanisms for experiencing emotions and producing laughter both

Table 6-1. Clinical manifestations of pathological laughter.

	Excessive	Forced	Epileptic
Loss of consciousness	No	No	Yes or No
Emotional experience	Yes	No	No
Self-insight	No	Yes	Yes or No
Autonomic disturbance	No	Yes	Yes or No
Onset in childhood	No	No	Yes
Onset in adulthood	Yes	Yes	No
Association with structural damage	Yes or No	Yes	Yes or No

appear to be normal, suggesting that an overall failure of inhibitory mechanisms has occurred. In a sense, these patients have a pathological disturbance of humor as well since they perceive many nonhumorous situations and remarks to be extremely funny. They are further unable to inhibit their laughter and rarely manifest any insight into the nature of their circumstances. Affected individuals may be in near-permanent moods of euphoria of may fluctuate between mood extremes with remarkable sparing of their cognitive process.

In some patients, the degree of mood elevation approaches the manic or hypomanic states of psychiatric patients with bipolar affective disorders. During euphoric periods, considerable merriment is derived from relatively trivial humorous memories or ideas.

Excessive laughter typically occurs in an older population and is often associated with senile and presenile dementia. It was originally described in patients with tertiary syphilis who manifested a characteristic style of self-directed humor known as "Witzelsucht," in which complex parodies were made of one's own actions or words. Excessive laughter can always be differentiated from natural laughter by its lack of social context and because other listeners or participants never share the patient's sense of humor or enjoyment.

Forced Laughter

This group includes all patients who experience involuntary outbursts of explosive, self-sustained laughter. The laughter typically involves forceful, clonic movements of the facial and respiratory muscles in conjunction with autonomic disturbances of heart rate, vasomotor control, and sphincter tone. Disturbances of emotional response and mood are rare. The abruptness of onset, magnitude of the motor response, and lack of emotional disturbance closely resemble the sham rage of decorticate animals. For this reason, forced laughter has sometimes been termed "sham mirth" (Martin, 1950).

Forced laughter in man has been shown to result from bilateral interruption of descending voluntary motor pathways. This suggests that cortical areas mediating voluntary movement also inhibit subcortical centers mediating "emotional" motor responses (Kreindler & Pruskauer-Apostol, 1971). This disinhibition of subcortical motor centers leads to the involuntary stereotyped motor patterns observed in forced laughter. Involuntary relaxation of skeletal muscle tone and loss of tonic urinary sphincter tone also occur (Paskind, 1932; Rogers, Gittes, Dawson, & Reich, 1982), suggesting that a widespread disturbance of motor control has been induced.

Voluntary and involuntary motor responses may become dissociated in conditions such as Parkinson's Disease or facial diplegia (Haymaker, 1969; Wilson, 1924). In these disorders, inner emotional mechanisms remain intact, while voluntary motor mechanism for their expression are compromised. These conditions further underscore the existence of independent mechanisms for voluntary and involuntary motor expression.

Forced laughter is found almost exclusively in adults and is extremely rare before age 12. Although various explanations have been offered to explain this age specificity, none is fully satisfactory. Adult-onset degenerative diseases such as amyotrophic lateral sclerosis, multiple sclerosis, and cerebrovascular disorders are responsible for many instances of forced laughter (Davison & Kelman, 1939; Ironside, 1956; Poeck, 1969; Swash, 1972). Furthermore, forced laughter commonly begins during the course of multifocal cerebral diseases, which are more frequent in an older population.

Laughing (Gelastic) Epilepsy

Patients with paroxysmal disturbances of brain electrical activity may manifest laughter as a behavioral convulsive symptom. Manifestations of epileptic laughter are diverse, ranging from brief grins to prolonged and explosive outbursts of piercing screams (Jewesbury, 1954). Epileptic laughter is rarely an isolated behavioral manifestation; associated convulsive motor changes, eye movement abnormalities, and autonomic disturbances are the rule. Consciousness is usually lost during the seizure and patients remain unaware of their attack. It is important to be certain that an event is truly epileptic since nonepileptic disturbances of behavior and personality can also occur in patients with chronic temporal lobe seizure disorders (Bear & Fedio, 1977).

ANATOMICAL CORRELATES

Defining the anatomical substrates for pathological laughter may present methodological difficulties. Patients with primary brain disease often acquire multiple sites of damage; systemic disease producing neurological disturbance are also frequently associated with multifocal brain involvement. Anatomic correlation of solitary brain tumors may be imprecise because of tumor-related disturbances produced by surrounding cerebral edema. Furthermore, many patients with abnormalities of laughter have been treated with pharmacological agents with central nervous system actions.

Several brain loci are presently believed to function within an integrated system linking the emotional, motor, and autonomic components of laughter. Afferent and efferent pathways interconnect all areas and produce disturbances of laughter when these regions become primarily or secondarily involved. Three anatomic regions are of recognized importance.

Brain Stem

The brain stem contains nuclei of motor cell bodies with outflow to the facial, respiratory, and laryngeal musculature. Facial contractions during laughter are produced by branches of the facial nerve arising from the ipsilateral facial nucleus. The phonetic components of laughter result from coordinated, automatic contractions of laryngeal and respiratory musculature. Clonic (i.e., forceful) contractions of the respiratory musculature force air between the closed laryngeal folds. Absence of mental status changes, preservation of consciousness, and stereotyped expression are common characteristics of brain stem abnormalities in pathological laughter.

Primary dysfunction of brain stem structures is believed to be a rare cause of pathological laughter. This may be because processes disturbing the brain stem often interfere with respiration and are thus fatal. Centers controlling blood pressure and heart rate are also located adjacent to other nuclei in the brain stem so that even a small lesion would produce catastrophic disturbances. More commonly, brain stem dysfunction results from a release of brain stem nuclei from descending inhibitory control. Bilateral loss of descending cortico-bulbar pathways (i.e., cortical outflow regulating brain stem motor function) appears necessary to produce a permanently disinhibited state (Wilson, 1924).

Diencephalon and Limbic System

The hypothalamus and surrounding structures were originally thought to be of primary importance in pathological laughter. The hypothalamus is located in the diencephalic region, an area which encompasses contiguous structures in the wall and floor of the third ventricle. Abnormalities of the posterior hypothalamus or diencephalic region will result in outbursts of laughter or crying with prominent autonomic manifestations and absence of voluntary movements (Bender, 1952). Efferent fibers from the hypothalamus descend within the central gray matter of the midbrain and synapse with pathways mediating primitive behavioral responses. Efferent hypothalamic pathways also project to limbic nuclei and receive reciprocal limbic outflow.

The limbic system is composed of highly interconnected nuclei that analyze stimuli for emotional significance and initiate motor responses. These structures are arranged in circuits consisting of two rings with reciprocal connections. An inner, phylogenetically older ring includes the hippocampal formation, septal area, anterior perforated substance, olfactory tubercle, pyriform cortex, and amygdala. The outer ring is composed of orbito-insulo-temporal cortex, cingulate gyrus, entorhinal cortex, and the subiculum (Haymaker, 1969).

Limbic nuclei project to the neocortex and receive afferent input from diverse viscera having autonomic innervation. This widespread anatomic connectivity has suggested the term "visceral brain" to describe the complete limbic circuit (MacLean, 1949). Laughter produced by limbic activation is often found in connection with emotional and autonomic disturbances and complex behavior manifestations. Loss of consciousness and stereotypy are variably present.

Cerebral Cortex

The cerebral cortex is involved with organizing and integrating conscious experience with involuntary sensory and motor aspects of laughter (Ironside, 1956). Afferent and efferent cortical pathways are closely linked to subcortical limbic, diencephalic and brain stem centers subserving motor, emotional and autonomic components of laughter.

Two separate efferent cortical pathways controlling respirations have been described (Haymaker, 1969): a respiratory-arresting center within the inferior frontal lobe and a respiratory-accelerating pathway arising from parietal cortex with efferent connections to the striatum, globus pallidus, brain stem, and diencephalon. Additional anatomical studies demonstrate fibers of both pathways in close alignment in the region of the subthalamus. These pathways descend to the mesencephalic region and terminate in the medulla oblongata (Ironside, 1956).

Cortical neurons controlling voluntary facial expression and eyelid closure arise in the lower portion of the precentral gyrus of motor cortex. Efferent fibers descend in the genu of the internal capsule and basis pedunculi and synapse in the brain stem with the nuclei of the facial nerves. Fibers then course peripherally and branch to supply the ipsilateral muscles of facial expression. The upper face receives innervation from both cerebral hemispheres, whereas the lower facial muscles receive only contralateral innervation. The dichotomy of innervation results in a selective loss of lower voluntary facial movement following interruption of descending fibers.

Abnormalities of laughter produced by dysfunction of pathways at the cortical level rarely occur in isolation and coexistent defects of memory, attention, or perception are frequent. More extensive cortical involvement may result in dysphagia, dyspraxia, hemiplegia, or visual field defect. A dysfunction at several cortical sites may also be associated with subcortical involvement of the internal capsule or basal ganglia (Poeck, 1969).

Patients undergoing prefrontal leukotomy may develop pathological laughter (Kramer, 1954). This surgical procedure interrupts fiber tracts coursing through prefrontal white matter and disconnects prefrontal cortex from diencephalic structures. Following surgical disconnection, excessive laughter occurs in the immediate postoperative period along with other changes in behavior or personality. Outbursts of excessive laughter often persist during the first postoperative year and then gradually diminish. Pathological laughter continuing for 3 years has been described. All patients do not manifest excessive laughter after prefrontal surgery, but explanations for this variability are lacking.

Many different processes affecting the frontal and temporal lobes will result in pathological laughter (Daly & Mulder, 1957; Druckman & Chao, 1957; Gascon & Lombroso, 1971; Poeck & Pilleri, 1963; Sethi & Rao, 1976; Swash, 1972; Weil, Nosik, & Demmy, 1958). Both lobes are closely connected to diencephalic structures and the limbic system, with the frontal lobe being especially important for the organization of conscious exteroceptive experience. Frontal lobe lesions typically produce disorganized behaviors and thought patterns and compromise expressive language and praxis.

The temporal lobes are believed to be involved in the integration of interoceptive functions. Amnesia or distortions or emotional perceptions are common symptoms of temporal lobe dysfunction. Electrical stimulation of the human temporal lobe results in motor smiling and laughter and a feeling of joy (Sem-Jacobsen & Torkildsen, 1960). Bilateral temporal lobe excision eliminates normal emotional responsiveness in monkeys and man (Kluver & Bucy, 1939; Terzian & Ore, 1955). Rarely, occipital lesions will produce disturbances of laughter (Leopold, 1977), but the precise mechanisms and anatomical substrates are unknown.

PATHOPHYSIOLOGY

Neural circuits participating in laughter are activated in response to stimuli of positive emotional significance. Stimuli may consist of interoceptive signals arising from internal receptors mediated by ascending relay pathways through the brain stem and diencephalon, or may reflect activation arising from conscious voluntary activities of the cerebral cortex. All of these stimuli can be received and analyzed by the limbic system. If the degree of emotional significance (i.e., the amount of limbic activation) is sufficient to reach a predetermined threshold, it will trigger a coordinated motor response involving facial, respiratory, laryngeal, and autonomic functions. With pathological laughter, the threshold for inducing laughter appears altered. Excessive and forced laughter will result from a permanent lowering of threshold, whereas only a transient, reversible change occurs during gelastic seizures.

Abnormalities of laughter threshold are insufficient to explain all manifestations of pathological laughter. For example, an abnormal quality to the laughter would also suggest dysfunctional phonetic and respiratory mechanisms. For patients who are unable to inhibit laughter once it has begun, a defect in feedback inhibition is postulated. Abnormalities of local chemical mechanisms mediating respiration may also occur.

Interference with mechanisms for producing laughter may result from activation or destruction of various brain sites. Abnormalities of laughter are thus likely to reflect a dysequilibrium of excitatory and inhibitory factors.

Activation

Electrical stimulation applied to the motor strip of the frontal cortex induces mouthing and facial movements resembling smiling (Penfield, 1954). Awake subjects report that their induced facial movements occur in the absence of emotional experiences. Depth electrode stimulation of limbic system sites during evaluation for psychosurgery of intractable seizures produces pleasurable sensations and memories but no motor responses (Gloor, Olivier, Quesney, Andermann, & Horowitz, 1982, Sem-Jacobsen & Tokildsen, 1960). Several limbic sites including the septal region, hippocampus, and hippocampal formation play a role in positive mood changes, but stimulation of the overlying temporal cortex does not produce similar changes (Gloor et al., 1982).

Activation of the hypothalamus and diencephalic region is the most reliable method to produce pathological laughter. This effect was first observed during surgery for removal of a colloid cyst of the third ventricle (Foerster and Gagel, 1934). During the procedure, swabbing the floor of the third ventricle with a pledget repeatedly induced paroxysms of well-developed laughter. The relative ease with which hypothalamic stimulation can induce laughter has subsequently been confirmed in more recent studies (Dryer & Wehmeyer, 1977). Since the quality of laughter so closely resembles laughter occurring in a natural setting, several authors have postulated a specialized "laughing center" in the region of the hypothalamus (Foerster & Gagel, 1934; Ironside, 1956). However, direct cortical and limbic stimulation are also capable of activating laughter, so it is unlikely that a hypothalamic center plays a unique role. Laughter probably results from additional activation at several different central nervous system sites. The hypothalamus may possibly be of special significance as a relay center for widespread propagation of electrical activity or may influence laughter threshold.

Laughter has not been produced by brain stem activaton. This procedure is technically difficult to accomplish and has not been shown to produce interpretable results.

Gelastic Epilepsy

The first documented case of laughter as a seizure manifestation was published by Trousseau (1873); over 100 cases have now been described (Gason & Lombroso, 1971; Roger, Lob, Weltregnyi, & Gastaut, 1967). The term "gelastic" was first used by Daly and Mulder in 1957 and is derived from the Greek word "gelos" for mirth. Gelastic epilepsy is now considered to be the appropriate term for all convulsive seizures in which laughter occurs.

Neural centers for laughter endogenously activated by epileptiform discharges will transiently reach suprathreshold levels for laughter activation. An electroencephalogram (EEG) recorded during a seizure typically reveals generalized paroxysmal discharges or focal paroxysmal activity from the frontal or temporal regions (Gascon & Lombroso, 1971; Roger et al., 1967). In one gelastic seizure occurring in a naturalistic setting, paroxysmal discharges were recorded as soon as the laughter had begun (Arfel & Laurette, 1975).

Gelastic seizures characteristically are recurrent stereotyped events. They are usually brief and self-limited, with prolonged episodes rarely occurring (Gumpert, Hansotia, & Upton, 1970; Rogal, 1937) Most seizures occur spontaneously but may occur in response to a variety of stimuli. One patient experienced seizure onset on hearing the word "funny" (Mori, 1969); another could voluntarily elicit a seizure by hyperextension of the neck and truncal regions (Jacome, Maclain, & Fitzgerald, 1980). Walsh and Hoyt (1969) reported episodes of laughter triggered by lateral ocular gaze; laughter induced by gaze-associated pursuit or convergent eye movements has also been described (Leopold, 1977).

Gelastic seizures may begin at any age, but a childhood onset is quite common. Gelastic seizures occurring in the early newborn period have also been described (Sher & Brown, 1976). Neonatal onset is especially remarkable because it demonstrates that brain substrates for laughter are fully functional at birth. Mechanisms for the expression of emotion are thus mature at the same time that mechanisms for interpreting social cues are undeveloped. It thus appears that brain mechanisms participating in laughter are of special importance, possibly because these pathways are closely involved with processes necessary for the organism's survival (i.e., respiration and autonomic functions). Mechanisms for emotional experience are not immediately critical for the newborn organism and thus develop later. During postnatal brain growth, the ability to experience humor or joy develops coincident to pathways that link these responses to circuits involved with laughter.

Most reported cases of gelastic seizures are associated with structural brain damage and have a poor long-term prognosis, but benign outcomes have also been described (Mutani et al., 1979; Sher & Brown, 1976). Gelastic seizures may vary over time and shift in relation to other manifestations of the convulsive sequence. This process may reflect a dynamic "ripening" or maturation of neural pathways controlling the expression of laughter. Repeated brain stimulation has been shown to experimentally induce ripening of behavioral seizure manifestations (Goddard, McIntyre, & Leech, 1969). This maturational epileptic process, termed "kindling," is thought to involve both facilitation and antagonism of neural circuits (Duchowny & Burchfiel, 1981). Kindling has not been demonstrated in human epileptogenesis, although it is believed to be a factor in certain forms of epilepsy (Adamec, Stark-Adamec, Perrin, & Livingston, 1981).

Epileptic laughter may occur before, during, or after motor convulsive manifestations; isolated laughter without motor or behavioral abnormalities is unusual. Patients are usually unconscious during an attack and show a retrograde amnesia upon recovery. Patients rarely report a pleasurable aura before losing consciousness (Gascon & Lombroso, 1971). In a large series of gelastic seizures, Roger et al. (1967) were able to identify two individuals with preserved consciousness and memory function but neither experienced pleasurable sensation while laughing. However, most epileptic experiences are probably underreported in view of the associated amnesia.

The quality of epileptic laughter is quite variable. A variety of complex sounds may occur (Roubicek, 1946), or vocalizations may consist of rudimentary or guttural utterances (Bladin & Papworth, 1974; Gascon & Lombroso, 1971; Loiseau & Beaussart, 1973). Autonomic manifestations may include 1971 vascular flushing (Lehtinen & Kivalo, 1965; Money & Hosta, 1967), pallor (Druckman & Chao, 1957), penile erection, or incontinence (Wakoh & Washio, 1956). An association with hiccoughs has also been reported (Money & Hosta, 1967). Accompanying motor patterns range from elementary facial myoclonic twitching (Mori, 1969) to complex sequences consisting of "butterfly movements" (Gascon & Lombroso, 1971) or alternating upper extremity abduction and adduction (Ames & Enderstein, 1975). Laughter has also been reported to accompany massive myclonic spasms (Longo & Roses, 1964).

Despite these variable manifestations, clinicians have attempted to classify gelastic seizures according to characteristics suggesting primary hypothalamic or primary limbic involvement. Hypothalamic attacks typically consist of brief episodes of elementary laughter with loss of consciousness. There is retrograde amnesia for the event, and associated emotional or motor behavioral manifestations are unusual. Limbic seizures are more variable showing diverse behavioral manifestations and a variety of emotional sensations. Changes in consciousness and memory functions are also variable. Features of hypothalamic and limbic seizures are shown in Table 6-2.

The electroencephalogram is often helpful in differentiating limbic from hypothalamic onset. Seizures of limbic origin are accompanied by paroxysmal disturbances of the anterior and mid-temporal regions (Mutani et al., 1979; Weil, Nosik, & Demmy, 1958), whereas generalized discharges over the vertex of both hemispheres are noted with hypothalamic attacks (Arfel & Laurette, 1975; Gascon & Lombroso, 1971). However, a wide variety of EEG abnormalities have been described. Instances of both frontal and generalized

Michael S. Duchowny

Table 6-2. Gelastic seizures: Hypothalamic versus limbic.

	Hypothalamic	Limbic
Quality of laughter	Simple	Complex
Emotional correlate	Absent	Variable
Consciousness	Lost	Variable
Postictal amnesia	Yes	Variable
Autonomic dysfunction	Prominent	Variable
Associated behaviors	Rare	Running; crying
EEG	General Spike-wave	Focal temporal spikes

paroxysmal discharges have been observed in the same individual, which suggests that secondary activation may occur. The variability of patterns of the EEG has compromised some of its diagnostic utility.

Epileptic crying has also been described and may occur together with laughter in the same individual. An association of laughter and crying may also occur during forced laughter, which suggests that one final common pathway may be responsible for mediating the expression of a variety of emotional responses.

Epileptic running, a variant termed "cursive" epilepsy, can occur in patients with gelastic seizures. Gelastic and cursive seizures have been described after head trauma (Jandolo, Gessini, Occhipinti, & Pompili, 1977) and neonatal hyperviscosity (Sugimoto, Matsumura, Sakamoto, & Taniuchi, 1979). Patients with these symptoms show focal temporal paroxysmal abnormalities on their EEGs that presumably represent limbic activation (Sethi & Rao, 1976). While the occurrence of epileptic laughter and running is rare, the association suggests that seizure mechanisms can encompass a wide range of emotional expression (Dreyer & Wehmeyer, 1977; Lehtinen & Kivalo, 1965).

Some young children with gelastic seizures will also manifest a precocious onset of puberty. This unusual association is quite rare and is presumed to represent dysfunction of the posterior hypothalamus, a region of importance for both laughter and sexual maturation (Matustik, Eisenberg, & Meyer, 1981; Penfold, Manson, & Galdicott, 1978; Wakoh & Washio, 1956; Williams, Schutt & Savage, 1978). Gelastic seizures in these children resemble those associated with other causes, and autonomic phenomena, loss of consciousness, and generalized motor seizure activity occur commonly (List, Dowman, Bagchi, & Bebin, 1958).

Precocious puberty is characterized by a premature onset of secondary sex characteristics including external genitalia, breasts, pubic, and axillary hair. Excessive somatic growth and premature advances in bone maturation may also occur. Endocrinological manifestations of precocious puberty include a diagnostic rise in gonadotropins and growth hormone levels during the first few hours of sleep (Penfold et al., 1978), which is characteristic of an early pubertal rather than prepubertal phase of development. Increased levels of luteinizing releasing hormone (LHRH) have also been reported in cerebrospinal fluid (Bierich, Schonberg, & Blunck, 1967). A 2-year-old girl with precocious puberty has been effectively treated with a long-acting analogue of gonadotropin-releasing hormone (Crowley, Comite, Vale, Rivier, Loriaux, & Cutler, 1981), but there is no data regarding the effect of treatment on gelastic seizures.

Precocious puberty may begin at an extremely young age and several cases have been reported at birth (Penfold et al., 1978). These newborn infants presumably experienced activation of the hypothalamic-pituitary-gonadal axis in utero. Children with precocious puberty often become obese, which also points to an abnormality of hypothalamic regulation. Intelligence is usually preserved at the onset of sexual maturation but declines with advancing age. Extremes of behavior characterized by episodes of aggression and explosive anger or passivity and inertia occur commonly in these children (Money & Hosta, 1967).

Lesions

Pathological laughter may also accompany the destruction of neural tissue at several central nervous system sites. Rapid onset of pathological laughter occurs with a variety of cerebrovascular disorders including thrombosis (Davison & Kelman, 1939; Swash, 1972), embolus (Davison & Kelman, 1939), subarachnoid hemorrhage (Clarke, 1931), and hemorrhage into brain substance (Davison & Kelman, 1939). Pathological laughter may also constitute a prodromal warning of impending cerebrovascular catastrophe (Andersen, 1936; Badt, 1927). Féré (1903) termed this phenomenon "Le fou rire prodromique." In these cases, the laughter assumed a special macabre quality since affected individuals literally laughed at their own impending doom.

Pathological laughter has been described with a variety of brain tumors occurring at multiple loci (Achari & Colover, 1976; Cantu, 1966; Cantu & Drew, 1966; Dreyer & Wehmeyer, 1977; Gascon & Lombroso, 1971; Ironside, 1956). Tumors may arise in the cerebral hemispheres, diencephalon, or brain stem regions; malignant, benign, and congenital tumors have all been described (Dreyer & Wehmeyer, 1977; List & Bebin, Note 1). Other acquired pathological conditions associated with laughter include white matter diseases such as multiple sclerosis (Martin, 1950) and Schilder's disease (Davison et al., 1939), and motor neuron diseases such as amyotrophic lateral sclerosis (Davison & Kelman, 1939; Ironside, 1956). Pathological laughter has also been reported with degenerative syndromes of gray matter such as Wilson's disease, Neimann-Pick disease, retinitis pigmentosa, and dystonia musculorum deformans (Chen & Forster, 1973; Davison & Kelman, 1939; Gumpert et al., 1970). Rarely, onset may follow nervous system infection of meningitis or measles encephalitis (Chen & Forster, 1973). Cerebral atrophy (Gascon & Lombroso, 1971), head injury (Chen & Forster, 1973), and polycythemia (Sugimoto et al., 1979), have also been implicated.

An unusual variant of pathological laughter occurs in children with a particular form of facial anomaly and mental retardation termed the "happy puppet" syndrome (Angelman, 1965). "Puppet" children are characterized by severe cognitive delay and an unusual facial appearance with microcephaly, protruding jaw, frequent tongue protrusions, unsteady gait, and puppet-like arm movements. Myoclonic seizures and incomplete choroid and iris pigmentation have also been described. Puppet children also manifest habitual smiling, frequent laughter, and excessive giggling. Although extremely rare, additional children with these features have now been reported (Bower & Jeavons, 1967). Autopsy data is unavailable and the sites of central nervous system disturbance are unknown so that no explanation exists for the unusual somatic appearance or abnormalities of mood and laughter.

With the exception of one study noting an increased incidence of pathological laughter in Down's syndrome (Norris, 1971), there are no reports of pathological laughter in association with inherited conditions or chromosomal abnormalities. Pathological laughter thus appears to occur in response to an acquired rather than inherited disturbance of the central nervous system. Furthermore, since pathological laughter is rarely an isolated symptom and is much more likely to occur in association with other physiological or behavioral abnormalities, the neural substrates for laughter are likely to develop with other systems. They may be intimately related to other physiological processes and it is possible that more serious dysfunction of these mechanisms would be lethal. This would explain the absence of inherited disorders of laughter.

Recent studies of emotional expression suggest that when fully mature the mechanisms for emotional experience and laughter are asymmetrically represented in the cerebral hemispheres (Hall, Hall, & Lovoie, 1968; Gianotti, 1972; Kolb & Taylor, 1981; Sackheim, Greenberg, Weiman, Gur, Hungerbuhler, & Geschwind, 1982). Positive emotional experience and fits of laughter are both believed to be lateralized to the left cerebral hemisphere, whereas dysphoric mood shifts and possibly fits of crying are mediated by systems within the right cerebral hemisphere (Sackheim et al., 1982). A disorder of emotional experience and expression is thus believed to reflect a lateralized hemispheric imbalance resulting from activation of the ipsilateral hemisphere or disinhibition of contralateral hemispheric structures.

SUMMARY

Abnormalities of laughter are a rare but well recognized complication of central nervous system disease. The literature contains many documented examples with a variety of clinical characteristics. Excessive, forced, and epileptic laughter constitute the most prevalent clinical syndromes. Pathological laughter is the result of multiple etiologies, and their clinical manifestations suggest involvement at the cortical, hypothalamic-limbic, and brain stem levels. A localized "laughing center" does not appear tenable from the clinical evidence, although the hypothalamus has been postulated to be especially important. The neural substrates for the production of the entire repertoire of laughing are present at birth, prior to the development of mechanisms for their release. Further postnatal development then occurs.

Several hierarchical levels of the nervous system participate in an integrated fashion to produce laughter. Certain stimuli will be sufficient to activate a predetermined threshold for producing laughter. An abnormal lowering of this threshold level may explain many but not all cases of pathological laughter. Abnormalities of feedback inhibition and motor coordination may also occur. Under normal circumstances, a person reading a funny story, observing a cartoon, or hearing a joke would receive and process the visual or auditory information in the cortex. This information would then be relayed to the limbic system where it would be encoded into the appropriate emotional sensation (i.e., humor or mirth). A stimulus that is insufficient to trigger the threshold for laughter would induce a "silent chuckle" or fleeting feeling of happiness. If the laughter threshold is reached, a preset motor response is initiated and is spontaneously inhibited when the stimulus is removed.

Each brain region mediating laughter may be primarily or secondarily involved, and it may be difficult to distinguish regional characteristics from the clinical symptoms. Limbic circuits are particularly important for screening incoming stimuli for their emotional importance to the organism and generating positive and negative emotional responses (i.e., humor or fear). Limbic centers are also able to activate pathways producing coordinated motor responses for emotional expression (laughter or crying). Pathological laughter, crying, and running have all been observed together during the same outburst, which strongly suggests that a final common pathway may mediate many different emotional responses. Laughter and crying share strikingly similar facial, phonetic, and respiratory mechanisms and are usually differentiated by their social context. Mechanisms mediating laughter and crying have been shown to involve lateralized cerebral hemispheric structures.

Activation of the limbic system may occur via inputs from the cerebral cortex or from brain stem and diencephalic relay centers. The cerebral cortex is capable of analyzing conscious sensorimotor experiences; verbal and nonverbal sensory stimuli that are received and encoded by the cortex are relayed to the limbic system to be interpreted as humorous or pleasurable. Lower brain stem centers may also relay internal sensations to the limbic system for interpretation of emotional significance.

Evidence from clinical studies of patients with abnormalities of laughter suggests that brain pathways for expressing laughter are present in a mature form at birth and remain relatively intact throughout the life span. The presence of abnormalities of laughter at birth would additionally suggest that the intrauterine development of these pathways is vulnerable; acquired rather than genetic or inherited disorders appear to be responsible. Acquired conditions continue to play a significant role in postnatally acquired pathological disturbances of laughter.

By contrast, brain regions for analyzing sensory cues and attaching emotional significance are undeveloped at birth and undergo maturation postnatally. Inhibitory control mechanisms for laughter also mature at a relatively more advanced stage of development. With advancing age, these systems exert greater influence over mechanisms for laughter and are established in a hierarchical fashion. In the older child or adult, laughter may occur in response to a wider range of internal cues or external sensory stimuli. Disorders of inhibitory mechanisms are more likely to occur in older populations.

ACKNOWLEDGMENTS

The author wishes to express his gratitude to Ms. Mercedes Cazobon for her assistance in preparation of this chapter.

REFERENCE NOTE

1. List, C. F., & Bebin, J. Hematoma of the hypothalamus causing a syndrome of precocious puberty and petit mal epilepsy with paroxysmal laughter. Paper presented to the American Academy of Neurology, April 26, 1956.

REFERENCES

Achari, A. N., & Colover, J. Posterior Fossa tumors with pathological laughter. *Journal of the American Medical Association*, 1976, *235*(14), 1469-1471.

Adamec, R. E., Stark-Adamec, C., Perrin, R., & Livingston, K. What is the relevance of kindling for human temporal lobe epilepsy? In J. A. Wada (Ed.), *Kindling 2*. New York: Raven Press, 1981.

Alpers, B. J. Personality and emotional disorders associated with hypothalamic lesions. *The Hypothalamus: Procedures of the Association for Research in Nervous and Mental Diseases* 1940, *20*, 725-752.

Ames, F. R., & Enderstein, O. Ictal laughter: A case report with clinical, cinefilm, and EEG observations. *Journal of Neurology Neurosurgery and Psychiatry*. 1975, *38*, 11-17.

Andersen, C. Crise de rise spasmodique avant deces: Hemorragie thalamique double. *Journal Belge de Neurologie et de Psychiatrie*, 1936, *36*, 223-227.

Angelman H. Puppet children: A report on 3 cases. *Developmental Medicine and Child Neurology*, 1965, *7*, 681-688.

Arfel, G., & Laurette, G. Evolution of paroxysmal discharges, assessed by radio-telemetry, in an infant with "gelastic epilepsy." *Electroencephalography and Clinical Neurolophysiology*, 1975, *39*, 554.

Badt, F. Lachen als ersles Symptom eines apoplektischen Insulles. *Zeitschrift fur die gesamte Neurologie und Psychiatrie*, 1927, *110*, 297-300.

Bard, P. A diencephalic mechanism for the expression of rage with special reference to the sympathetic nervous system. *American Journal of Physiology*, 1928, *84*, 490-515.

Bear, D. M., & Fedio, P. Quantitative analysis of interictal behavior in temporal lobe epilepsy. *Archives of Neurology*, 1977, *34*, 454-467.

Bender, M. Myoclonus of the eye, face, and throat. *Archives of Neurology and Psychiatry*, 1952, *67*, 44-58.

Bierich, J. R. Schonberg, D., & Blunck, W. Pubertas praecox infolge vonhamar tomen des hypothalamus. *Symposium Der Deutschen Gesellschaft fur Endokrinologie*, 1969, *15*, 301.

Bladin, P. F., & Papworth, G. Chuckling and glugging seizures at night-sylvian spike epilepsy. *Proceedings of the Australian Association of Neurology*, 1974, *11*, 171-176.

Bower, B. D., & Jeavons, P. M. The happy puppet syndrome. *Archives of Diseases of Childhood* 1967, *42*, 298-302.

Cantu, R. C. Importance of pathological laughing and/or crying as a sign of occurrence or recurrence of a tumor lying beneath the brainstem. *Journal of Nervous and Mental Diseases*, 1966, *143*(4), 507-512.

Cantu, R. C., & Drew, J. H. Pathological laughing and crying associated with a tumor ventral to the pons. *Journal of Neurosurgery*, 1966, *24*, 1024-1026.

Chen, R. C., & Forster, F. M. Cursive epilepsy and gelastic epilepsy. *Neurology*, 1973, *23*, 1019-1029.

Clarke, A. Quoted under the Summary of Proceedings, Ninety-Ninth Annual Meeting of the British Medical Assoction, Section of Neurology and Psychological Medicine. *British Medical Journal* 1931, *2*, 209.

Crowley, W. F., Comite, N. D., Vale, W., Rivier, J., Loriaux, D. L., & Cutler, G. B. Therapeutic use of pituitary desensitization with a long-acting LHRH agonist: A potential new treatment for idiopathic precocious puberty. *Journal of Clinical Endocrinology and Metabolism*, 1981, *52*, 370-372.

Daly, D. D., & Mulder, D. W. Gelastic epilepsy. *Neurology*, 1957, *7*, 189-192.

Davison, C., & Kelman, H. Pathologic laughing and crying. *Archives of Neurology and Psychiatry*, 1939, *42*(4), 595-655.

Dryer, R., & Wehmeyer, W. Fits of laughter (gelastic epilepsy) with a tumor of the floor of the third ventricle. *Journal of Neurology*, 1977, *214*, 163-171.

Druckman, R., & Chao, D. Laughter in epilepsy. *Neurology* 1957, *7*, 26-36.

Duchowny, M. S., & Burchfiel, J. L. Facilitation and antagonism of kindled seizure development in the limbic system of the rat. *Electroencephalography and Clinical Neurophysiology*, 1981, *51*, 403-416.

Féré, C. Le fou rire prodromique. *Revue Neurologique*, 1903, *11*, 353-358.

Foerster, O., & Gagel, O. Ein Fall von Epedymcyste des III Ventickels: Ein Beitrag zur Frage der Beziehungen Psychischer Storungen Zum Hirnstamm. *Z Gesamte Neurol. Psychiatr.*, 1934, *149*, 312-344.

Gianotti, G. Emotional behavior and hemispheric side of the lesion. *Cortex*, 1972, *8*, 41-55.

Gascon, G. G., & Lombroso, C. T. Epileptic (gelastic) laughter. *Epilepsia* 1971, *12*, 63-76.

Gloor, P., Olivier, A., Quesney, L. F., Andermann, F., & Horowitz, S. The role of the limbic system in experiential phenomena of temporal lobe epilepsy. *Annals of Neurology*, 1982, *12*, 129-144.

Goddard, G. V., McIntyre, D. C., & Leech, C. K. A permanent change in brain function resulting from daily electrical stimulation. *Experimental Neurology*, 1969, *25*, 295-330.

Gumpert, J., Hansotia, P., & Upton, A. Gelastic epilepsy. *Journal of Neurology, Neurosurgery and Psychiatry*, 1970, *33*, 479-483.

Hall, M. M., Hall, G. C., & Lavoie, P. Ideation in patients with unilateral or bilateral midline brain lesions. *Journal of Abnormal Psychology*, 1968, *73*, 526-531.

Haymaker, W. *Bing's local diagnosis in neurological diseases*. St. Louis: C. V. Mosby, 1969.

Ironside, R. Disorders of laughter due to brain lesions. *Brain*, 1956, *79*, 589-609.

Jacome, D. E., Maclain, L. W., & Fitzgerald, R. Postural reflex gelastic seizures. *Archives of Neurology*, 1980, *37*, 249-251.

Jandolo, B., Gessini, L., Occhipinti, E., & Pompili, A. Laughing and running fits as manifestation of early traumatic epilepsy. *European Neurology*, 1977, *15*, 177-182.

Jewesbury, E. C. O. Some clinical epileptic oddities. *British Medical Journal*, 1954, *2*, 1518-1520.

Kluver, H., & Bucy, P. C. Preliminary analysis of functions of the temporal lobes in monkeys. *Archives of Neurology and Psychiatry*, 1939, *42*, 979-1000.

Kolb, B., & Taylor, L. Affective behavior in patients with localized cortical excisions: Role of lesion site and side. *Science*, 1981, *214*, 89-91.

Kramer, H. C. Laughing spells in patients after lobotomy. *Journal of Nervous and Mental Diseases*, 1954, *119*, 517-522.

Kreindler, A., & Pruskauer-Apostol, B. Neurologic psychopathologic aspects of compulsive crying and laughter in pseudobulbar palsy patients. *Revue Roumaine de Neurologie*, 1971, *8*(2), 125-139.

Lehtinen, L., & Kivalo, A. Laughter epilepsy. *Acta Neurologia Scandinavia*, 1965, *41*, 255-261.

Leopold, N. A. Gaze-induced laughter. *Journal of Neurology, Neurosurgery and Psychiatry*, 1977, *40*, 815-817.

List, C. F., Dowman, C. E., Bagchi, B. K., & Bebin, J. Posterior hypothalamic hamartomas and gangliogliomas causing precocious puberty. *Neurology*, 1958, *8*, 164-174.

Loiseau, P., & Beaussart, M. The seizures of benign childhood epilepsy with rolandic paroxysmal discharges. *Epilepsia*, 1973, *14*, 381-389.

Loiseau, P., Cohadon, F., Cohadon, S. Gelastic epilepsy: A review and report of five cases. *Epilepsia*, 1971, *12*, 313-323.

Longo, L. P., & Roses, A. O. Epileptic laughter. *Bol. Asoc. Med. de P. R.,* 1964, *56*(10), 424-432.

MacLean, P. D. Psychosomatic disease and the "visceral brain": Recent developments bearing on the Papez Theory of emotion. *Psychosomatic Medicine*, 1949, *11*, 338-353.

Martin, J. P. Fits of laughter (Sham mirth) in organic cerebral disease. *Brain*, 1950, *73*, 453-464.

Matustik, M. C., Eisenberg, H. M., & Meyer, W. J. Gelastic (laughing) seizures and precocious puberty. *American Journal of Diseases of Childhood*, 1981, *135*, 837-838.

Mills, C. K. The cerebral mechanism of emotional expression. *Trans. Coll. Physicians Phila*, 1912, *34*, 147-178.

Money, J., & Hosta, G. Laughing seizures with sexual precocity: Report of two cases. *Johns Hopkins Medical Journal*, 1967, *120*, 326-336.

Monrad-Krohn, G. H. On the dissociation of voluntary and emotional innervation in facial paresis of central origin. *Brain*, 1924, *47*, 22-35.

Mori, K. Precocious puberty with fits of laughter and with a large cystic mass on the floor of the third ventricle (case report). *Archives Japonica Chirugia*, 1969, *38*(5), 800-801.

Mutani, R., Agnetti, V., Durelli, L., Fasio, F., & Ganga, A. Epileptic laughter: Electroclinical and cinefilm report of a case. *Journal of Neurology*, 1979, *220*, 215-222.

Norris, D. Crying and laughing in imbeciles. *Developmental Medicine and Child Neurology*, 1971, *13*, 756-761.

Papez, J. W. A proposed theory of emotion. *Archives of Neurology and Psychiatry*, 1937, *38*, 725-744.

Paskind, H. A. Effect of laughter on muscle tone. *Archives of Neurology and Psychiatry*, 1932, *28*, 623-628.

Penfield, W., & Jasper, H. *Epilepsy and the functional anatomy of the human brain*. Boston: Little Brown, 1954.

Penfold, J. L., Manson, J. I., & Caldicott, J. M. Laughing seizures and precocious puberty. *Australian Paediatric Journal*, 1978, *14*, 185-190.

Poeck, K., & Pilleri, G. Pathologisches Lachen und Weinen. *Schweizer Archiv Fur Neurologie und Psychiatrie*, 1963, *92*, 323-370.

Poeck, K. Pathophysiology of emotional disorders associated with brain damage. P. J. Vinken & G. W. Bruyn (Eds.), *Handbook of Clinical Neurology* (Vol. 3). Amsterdam: NorthHolland, 1969.

Rogal, O. Lauchanfalle als epileptisches. *Aquivalent Nervenarzt*, 1937, *10*, 93-95.

Roger, J., Lob, H., Weltregnyi, A., & Gastaut, H. Attacks of epileptic laughter. *Electroencephalography and Clinical Neurophysiology*, 1967, *22*, 279.

Rogers, M. P., Gittes, R. F., Dawson, D. M., & Reich, P. Giggle incontinence. *Journal of the American Medical Association*, 1982, *247*(10), 1446-1448.

Roubicek, J. Laughter in epilepsy, with some general introductory notes. *Journal of Mental Science*, 1946, *92*, 734-755.

Sackheim, H. A., Greenberg, M. S. Weiman, A. L. Gur, R. C., Hungerbuhler, J. P., & Geschwind, N. Hemispheric asymmetry in the expression of positive and negative emotions. *Archives of Neurology*, 1982, *39*, 210-218.

Sem-Jacobsen, C. W., & Torkildsen, A. Depth recording and electrical stimulation in human brain. In E. R. Ramey & D. S. O'Doherty (Eds.), *Electrical studies on the unanesthetized brain*. New York: Hoeber, 1960.

Sethi, P. K., & Rao, T. A. Gelastic, quiritarian, and cursive epilepsy. *Neurology, Neurosurgery and Psychiatry*, 1976, *39*, 823-828.

Sher, P. K., & Brown, S. B. Gelastic epilepsy: Onset in neonatal period. *American Journal of Diseases of Childhood*, 1976, *130*, 1126-1131.

Spillane, J. D. *The Doctrine of the nerves*. Oxford University Press, Oxford, 1981.

Sugimoto, T. Matsumura, T., Sakamoto, Y., & Taniuchi, K. Running and laughing fits as the sequelae of the neonatal hyperviscosity syndrome. *Brain and Development,* 1979, *1*(4), 323-326.

Swash, M. Released involuntary laughter after temporal lobe infarction. *Journal of Neurology, Neurosurgery and Psychiatry,* 1972, *35,* 108-113.

Terzian, H., & Ore, G. D. Syndrome of Kluver and Bucy reproduced in man by bilateral removal of the temporal lobes. *Neurology,* 1955, *5,* 373-380.

Trousseau, A. De L'Epilepsie. *Paris, Clinique Mediale de l'Hotel-Dieu de Paris,* 1873, *2,* 409.

Wakoh, T., & Washio, S. A case of precocious puberty with epileptic seizure. *Folia Psychiatrica et Neurologica Japonica,* 1956, *9*(4), 329-340.

Walsh, F. B., & Hoyt, W. F. *Clinical neuro-ophthalmology* (Vol. 1). Baltimore: Williams & Wilkins Co., 1969.

Weil, A. A., Nosik, W. A., & Demmy, N. Electroencephalographic correlation of laughing fits. *American Journal of Medical Science,* 1958, *235,* 301-308.

Williams, M., Schutt, C. O., & Savage, D. Epileptic laughter with precocious puberty. *Archives of Diseases of Childhood* 53-965-966, 1978, *53,* 965-966.

Wilson, S. A. K. Pathological laughing and crying. *Journal of Neurology Neurosurgery and Psychiatry,* 1924, *4,* 299-333.

Chapter 7

Humor and Health

VERA M. ROBINSON

A merry heart doeth good like a medicine: but a broken spirit drieth the bones.
Proverbs 17:22

INTRODUCTION

The association of humor and laughter to health and longevity and the belief that humor is necessary to human survival has been expressed by many. Yet, scientific research in the area of health-related humor has been sparse.

Until the last two decades, the lack of scientific technology to study the biochemical and physiological effects of humor has been one factor, but the focus on disease and illness and the "seriousness" of health care within the health care system has been the major obstacle. Although for both patients and staff humor has always been a form of communication, it has not been an "expected occurrence." Therefore, it has been largely ignored as a therapeutic mechanism and often negated, when it did occur, with, "This is not a laughing matter!" As a result, the concept of humor and its planned use in the healing process has not traditionally been included in the education of the health professional (Emerson, 1963; Robinson, 1977, 1978; Scheff, 1979, Moody, 1978; Cousins 1979a).

Negative emotions and their effects on health have been the emphasis in health research. Psychosomatic illnesses, both from the psychoanalytic and physiologic points of view have been studied extensively, but only recently has the effect of positive emotions on health or "psychosomatic health" been considered. However, there is a shift in health care to a health promotion framework. With biochemical studies of positive emotions, scientific evidence of the interrelatedness of mind and body, and an impetus in society towards self-care and holistic health, the phenomenon of humor has become a much more accepted area for study and research in the health disciplines.

A change in the education of the health professional's communication patterns toward a humanistic approach to the patient has also enhanced the use of humor. The focus is on openness, empathy, expression of feelings, and confrontation rather than the traditional socialization process of "distancing" (Scheff, 1979), of suppressing emotions, of maintaining that air of detached concern, objectivity and professionalism. In the past, humor was often used as a coping behavior by staff and clients, individually and indirectly, but without sanction by "the system."

Another factor contributing to the limited amount of research in this area is the difficulties associated with the observation and collection of data in the natural settings. The paradoxical nature of humor, its "thoughtfulness-spontaneity" balance (Fry, 1963), the increase or decrease in humorous occurrences when being observed, the hazards of being a participant-observer, the variations in humor response influenced by individual perception, the length of time necessary to collect meaningful data, as well as the lack of reliable methodological tools for studying spontaneous humor are some of the issues, (Emerson, 1963; Robinson, 1977; Goldstein, 1978). Laboratory studies of humor are often viewed with some reservation because of the lack of a data base of the natural settings. Laboratory studies measure response to humor rather than naturally created humor (McGhee 1978).

Laughter: The Healthy-Unhealthy Controversy

Another dilemma in research has been the controversy of what constitutes "healthy" humor and laughter, from both the psychological and physiological perspective. The healthiness of ridicule, sarcasm, black humor, and sick jokes in relationship to hostility and denial of reality is questioned. Concern is expressed about the nonhumorous, uncontrollable laughter of anxiety and hysteria, inappropriate laughter of the mentally ill, the cruel laughter at "funny" behavior and deformities, as well as laughter as a result of various diseases, neurological disorders, and lesions of the brain. Fear is expressed regarding the abuse and destructiveness of humor.

Although his message about humor is positive, Moody (1978) spends the greater portion of his book discussing the pathology of laughter and contra-indications for the use of humor by the physician because of its harmful effects. Perhaps the need to dispel the physician's predilection for disease was his motivation since he closes with the exhortation that health-care professions tend to take themselves too seriously. He distinguishes healthly use of mirth from unhealthy. The differential diagnosis? To be healthy, he says, mirth must occur within the context of understanding, love, and support, and must include the patient in the laughter.

That humor produces healthful results has been supported by armchair theorists over the centuries. Kant, as early as 1790 proposed that laughter and jokes furthered the "vital bodily processes" which had a "favorable influence on health". And, in the past several decades, research of the biochemical and physiological effects of laughter have validated their assumptions.

The controversy also exists in the mental health field. Does humor reveal health or serious problems? Keith-Spiegel (1972) raises this question: Does the laughing, joking person indicate that: (1) he is physically healthy and/or mentally well balanced or (2) divulging his innermost hang-ups, therefore indicating deep-seated problems, or (3) since he is laughing, handling his mental conflicts in a healthy manner?

Certainly, there has been much support for the emotionally therapeutic value of humor as an adaptive, coping behavior, as a catharsis for and relief of tension, as a defense against depression, as a sign of emotional maturity, and as a survival mechanism. But others have stressed the destructive aspects of humor: the sadistic, masochistic, guilt, and anxiety producing effects and its inappropriate use in psychotherapy (Brody, 1950; Grotjahn, 1957; Kubie, 1971), even while attesting to its benefits. The response to this negative posture has been refuted with the observation that if humor has been abused or has produced nontherapeutic results, the fault lies with the professional who is meeting his own needs (Levine, 1969; Rose, 1969; Poland, 1971; Mindess, 1971, 1976).

This issue of healthy versus unhealthy laughter is comparable to the years of struggle to define health and mental health, somehow denying the fact that perfect health or mental health is an illusion. Rather, there is a continuum on which health and mental health range and "health" becomes an individual state of optimum functioning. Humor in its complexity ranges also on such a continuum from healthy to unhealthy (Robinson, 1977).

Analyzing the function and purpose for humor in any situation, determining whose needs are being met, differentiating the laughter of disease and illness from health-producing laughter must be some of the considerations of the health professional. Research in the application of humor as a positive tool in the psychological, social, and physiological healing processes and in the education of the health professional is still sorely needed. But, despite this typical humor scholar's apologia syndrome for why it has not been done, there is some evidence that laughter and humor are "good for you."

A Perspective of the Literature

A brief overview of the literature before a discussion of the research itself might put into perspective some of the issues. The literature related to health and humor is disproportionate. There is much more literature related to mental health (encompassing psychological, sociological, developmental, and anthropological perspectives) than that related to physical health. Even less research analyzing humor in health-care settings has occurred. Behavioral scientists have focused on the broad perspective of mental health and on basic research in the physiology, biology, and developmental origins of humor. (These will be well documented in other chapters of the Handbook and will only be discussed here in relation to the application of humor to health and health care.) The application to health and health care itself has not had a similar direct focus.

Of the studies of humor in health-care settings, three of the earliest studies were sociological investigations in which humor and health were only serendipitous (Coser 1959, Fox 1959, Emerson 1963). Coser (1959) set out to study the social structure of a hospital ward and the patient role. Her observatons of humor led to her analysis. Fox's (1959) study was designed to investigate the social process on an experimental metabolic ward. She discovered that humor and joking was one of the major mechanisms utilized by both physicians and patients for coming to terms with the stresses of decision making and facing death in the experimental processes. The third study by Emerson (1963), although conceived as an investigation in the sociology of humor, was not concerned with hospitals or health as a major focus. Rather, her goal was to show that the nature of humor is related to the structural problems of the setting in which it occurs. She selected a general hospital simply as the natural setting because it was a large organization with a distinct status hierarchy and structured interaction, and focused on two major health areas: the pelvic examination and death.

The first direct application was a study of the use of humor in nursing (Robinson, 1970/1978). The functions of humor in health settings were identified, some observational data collected, and application to nursing care and nursing education was made. Subsequent research (Robinson 1977) provided beginning guidelines for cultivating the use of humor in health care and the education of health professionals. Case studies or anecdotal accounts of humor during hospitalization comprise the only other literature, although unpublished master's theses and doctoral dissertations dealing with the subject are on the increase.

In psychiatric settings, the studies, research, and literature related to psychotherapy and group psychotherapy are numerous and are reviewed in other chapters, but again descriptions of humor in natural settings are few. An analysis of laughter in psychiatric staff conferences and between psychiatric colleagues, a study of the humor on an open psychiatric ward, and examples of humor in nurse-patient relationships with psychiatric patients have been reported. An unpublished doctoral study (Zalis, 1980) looks at the role of humor in manic-depressive disorders, as a defensive, adaptive function in maintaining psychological equilibrium.

The literature describing the biological and physiological aspects of laughter, smiling, and humor in the prescientific period were speculative, descriptive, and philosophical. For example, the smile as an evolutionary process from the "baring of teeth" as an animal's defense to the smile that says one can "relax in safety" (Hayworth, 1928) and the relationship of tears and laughter (Hazlitt, 1819/1960; Koestler, 1964) as a human condition was noted. Scientific studies of the effects of laughter began in the late 1950s but have primarily described the physiology rather than application. The "healing" properties of laughter in disease and illness again have been speculative. We "knew" good humor and the will to live had a positive effect on getting well. We saw patients live when all evidence organically pointed to their demise. Conversely, there were those who "willed" themselves to die. There has been only one documented report of healing through laughter (Cousins, 1977, 1979a,b), although others have been narrated from personal experience (Moody, 1978; Walsh, 1928; Cousins, 1979a) and are reported to be occurring in various health settings, utilizing holistic health approaches.

Biochemical studies currently being conducted at the University of California at Los Angeles and not yet published incorporate all of the positive emotions (Cousins, 1982). Laughter is closely related to hope, the will to live, trust, faith, joy, and love, all of which mobilize the natural defense mechanisms of the body and have biochemical effects not only on the immunological system, but the endocrine, respiratory, cardiovascular, neurological, and musculo-skeletal systems as well, which are reputed to be both healing and health producing.

With this perspective, the research that has been completed is reviewed in the remainder of this chapter in reference to both the client and the health-care professional.

FUNCTIONS OF HUMOR IN HEALTH: THE CLIENT

Within the unique world of health and illness, humor is an indirect form of communication, one that both patients and professionals bring with them. Humor conveys messages, facilitates social relations, and manages the "delicate" situations that occur. Humor serves as a coping mechanism to deal with external pressures as well as the internal stresses related to health and illness. In addition to its communication function, humor serves social, psychological, and physiological functions.

Humor as an Indirect Communication

Humor has been described as a form of indirect communication that conveys, quickly and indirectly, messages that are usually emotionally tinged, and might be unacceptable if expressed or acknowledged directly. It may be a message of anxiety, fear, embarrassment, anger, or apology, or of warmth, love, support, hope, or trust. In times of illness, crisis, and stress, strangers (patient and professional) are suddenly thrust into intimate and somber contacts. There is not time to build a relationship, yet there is an expectation of trust and cooperation. The patient must submit to invasive, foreboding procedures and is expected to reveal intimate personal information and his innermost thoughts and feelings, all without question. Emerson (1963) found that a form of interaction that quickly provides this sense of familiarity, does not offend, and is easily facilitated was needed. Humor met these criteria and, because of its "joke-frame," provided the flexibility for easily terminating the interaction or moving into a serious discussion. The humor usually took the form of bantering, pleasantries, and jocular talk.

Fry (1963) first described the play-joke framework that not only provides for the "face-saving" quality and the quick resolution of the feelings behind the implicit message (Freud's psychic economy) but also for backing off with "It was just a joke" if the listener reacts negatively. Emerson (1963) found that humor was permissible in almost any situation in the hospital, was initiated by all categories of persons, and not many unsuccessful "jokes" occurred. When joking was unsuccessful, it was because "some implicit message not suitable for direct communication is stripped of its camouflage" (p. 150). When humor is used as a "trial balloon" to open up a serious discussion, there are cues for negotiating this transition (Emerson 1969). Indirect communication is valuable "in promoting the continued harmony of a social relation at the same time that important messages are conveyed" (1963, p. 47).

Sociological Functions: Coping with External Pressures

The health-illness setting is one in which many of the rules of normal society are disrupted, violated or suspended. Humor provides a mechanism for coping with these socially disruptive acts. It assists in establishing the patient-staff relationship, reduces tension from social conflicts, promotes solidarity, provides for social control, and "manages the delicate situations" created by illness and the health care system. It can be an agent for social change and has survival value (Robinson, 1977).

Coser (1959) found that patient's humor on a hospital ward decreased social distance, socialized other patients into the society, provided an outlet for hostilities and discontent, and allayed anxiety. Jocular talk, mostly jocular griping, related to three areas: anxiety about self, submission to a rigid authority structure, and adjustment to a rigid routine. The humor became a "safety-valve." Coser says the contribution humor makes to "social economy" as well as "psychic economy" should be stressed.

Kaplan and Boyd (1965) described the social functions of humor on an open psychiatric ward in a VA Hospital. The humor created a feeling of intimacy and provided a means of winning social approval. The need to adapt to the staff and the outside society, to restrain disruptive tendencies of the group, to alleviate personal anxiety, and to maintain a sense of solidarity was evidenced. Humor revolving around overdependency, sex, and deviant behavior served a social control function in providing a leveling mechanism with staff and a negative sanction for patients as well as providing group support. Self-deprecating humor permitted the patient to take a detached view of himself. The authors felt this was the "sine qua non" of the therapeutic process.

Under the "Medical Aegis" rules in society about social conduct and behavior regarding our bodies, bodily functions and intimate behaviors are often violated or ignored. In fact, the rules of the game are that neither the patient nor professional is to show embarrassment. Rather, each is expected to assume an air of detachment and nonchalance. Emerson (1963) found one of the greatest areas of social conflict to be the pelvic examination, a routine procedure that is the "ultimate invasion of privacy that a conscious patient experiences" (p. 167). It was usually the staff, most often the male doctor, who initiated the humor. The joking seemed to be an "institutionalized way the staff coaxed the patients to put up with affronts to their dignity" (p. 212).

Jokes around bedpans, bodily functions, and sex abound as a way of coping with or forestalling embarrassment. The male patient, placed in a dependent role, his male image threatened, may use humor as a form of social control and a leveling mechanism (Robinson, 1977). The use of humor in embarrassing interactions has been discussed by others. Fink and Walker (1977) found more laughter between persons of equal status and when large numbers of others were present, more laughter occurred and less embarrassment. The "joking relationship" in various cultures has also been recognized by anthropologists as a way to channel taboo sexual and aggressive drives in acceptable ways (Levine, 1961, 1968, 1969).

As an avenue for survival within the organization, for easing tensions, frustrations and anxieties, and expressing concerns about the current state of the health care system, humor is used in a variety of ways by the consumer. The jocular talk, cartoons, jokes, and get-well cards reflect society's decreasing confidence in the competency of the health professionals, frustration over the increased bureaucracy of the system, and anger and concern about the sky-rocketing costs of health care. To be openly hostile or questioning would alienate the system upon which the client is depending for care. Humor serves to facilitate expression yet maintain relationships and the functioning of the organization. "The doctor stops in to see me everyday and feels my purse." One patient gave his surgeon a cartoon of two "angels" sitting on a cloud. One says to the other: "The last thing I heard was my doctor saying 'Oops'!"

Humor can serve as an agent for social change and reform of the system. The use of humor as a reflection of societal anxieties, values, and need for change and reform has been documented by many (Bergson, 1900/1960; Stephenson, 1959; Boskin, 1979).

Psychological Functions:
Coping with Internal Stress

The intrapsychic stresses related to illness, health maintenance, and hospitalization are many and are often created by external forces. Robinson (1977) summarized the functions of humor as: a coping mechanism to relieve anxiety, stress, and tension; an outlet for hostility and anger; an escape from reality and a means of lightening the heaviness related to crisis, tragedy, chronic illness, disabilities, and death.

Anxiety is one of the most common sources of discomfort that prompts the use of humor. Coser (1959) found in her study that patients' anxiety centered around fears about themselves and the strange and unknown environment and the rigid structure of the hospital. The patients felt apprehensive, insecure, and a loss of control. The jocular talk served to allay this anxiety, recalling Freud's observation: "Look! here is the world, which seems so dangerous! It is nothing but a game for children—just worth making a jest about!" (Freud, 1927/1961, p. 166).

The stress level regarding the seriousness of the illness, permanent disabilities, pain, and threats of impending death is high. When anxiety level is too high, humor may "fall flat" or not occur until the crisis has passed or the anxiety has reached a moderate level (Freud, 1905/1960, Levine, 1956, Fine, 1977). Thurber once defined humor as "emotional chaos remembered in tranquility."

Hostile humor also occurs frequently in the health care setting. Expressions of anger, hostility, and frustration are perhaps the most constructive functions of humor, yet one of the most difficult for people to accept. It creates as much conflict in our society as sex! The anger at their illness, the rigidity of the institution and the dehumanizing aspects of the health-care delivery system are vented through the use of humor which serves also as a complaint (Coser, 1959; Robinson, 1977). Kaplan and Boyd (1965) observed the psychiatric patient's use of humor to express hostility. When directed at the staff, it served as a morale booster; when expressed against "civilians" it decreased the distance; and when expressed toward other patients, it forestalled deviant behavior.

The relationship between humor and aggression has been described by Fry (1963) in analyzing the "punch line" and the "pecking order" in jokes: by Lorenz (1963), "laughing men hardly ever shoot"; and by Mikes (1971), "make fun, not war." Humor provides a "safety valve" both emotionally and physiologically. Rage is the opposite of laughter. Laughter diminishes skeletal muscle tone and conforms to appeasement behavior so that the body as well is less able to function aggressively (Fry, 1977a).

Anger and anxiety often lead to denial of reality. Humor serves a very useful purpose in easing the way to dealing with the painful realities of illness or threats of disability or death. Freud (1927) stated that unlike other mechanisms for denial of reality, namely neuroses, psychoses, and alcoholism, humor does not "overstep the bounds of mental health" (p. 163). Mindess (1971) speaks to humor as an escape from reality in freeing us from the constrictive forces of society.

In times of tragedy, crisis, and death, humor is a technique for neutralizing this emotionally charged area. For that moment, the burden of the reality is forgotten. The humor provides for the retention of hope. Patients faced with disabling and disfiguring accidents, injuries, and illnesses use humor to put others at ease by their jokes or one-liners related to their stigma (Moody, 1978).

A bravado in the face of death was described by Fox in her sociological study of an experimental metabolic ward (1959). She found that both patients and staff used joking, but rarely did this humor cross the status line. The patients' humor focused on the problems and stresses they shared. They joked about their inactivity, incapacity, and isolation. They made jokes about the experimental surgery, the drugs and their roles as human subjects. Jokes about their symptoms and "death jokes" also occurred. These were the "most frequently made and most relished of all" (p. 173), "laughing at their hopes about getting well, made it easier for them to come to terms with the fact that, actually, this might never be possible" (p. 176). It was an attempt to make sense out of their predicament, yet express their anger and defiance. Emerson (1963) observed that death was a topic to be avoided and threat of death was not acknowledged in staff-patient interactions. However, most humor about death occurred among the staff, sometimes between staff and patients, but none between staff and visitors of terminal patients. Mikes (1971) points out that the literature is full of funny deaths and funerals and that laughing at death gives triple pleasure: the joke itself, the joy of laughing at death's expense, and the pleasure of taming death (p. 40).

Physiological Functions

Man has long affirmed laughter as necessary for biological survival and recognized that the absence of laughter and humor and play impaired physical and psychological health (Berlyne, 1969).

In Medieval physiology, humor was described as the four principal fluids of the body: blood, phlegm, color, and melancholy. A balance made for "good humor." Spencer (1860) described laughter as the discharge of excess nervous excitement. Darwin (1872/1965) stated that with laughter derived from the excitement of pleasure, "circulation becomes more rapid; the eyes are bright and the colour of the face rises. The brain being stimulated by the increased flow of blood, reacts on the mental powers" (p. 32). McDougall (1903/1963) defined laughter as an instinct that has "survival value," it "seems to quicken the respiratory and circulatory processes and . . . to produce a general sense of well-being or euphoria" (p. 388). It was nature's antidote for man's sympathetic tendencies.

The use of "humor therapy," "court jesters," and the recognition of the benefits of humor by physicians in the Middle Ages and through 19th century is described by Moody (1978) and also in a classic book by a physician, James Walsh (1928). Walsh "gives the reasons why the cultivation of a habit of laughter is a potent factor for health" (p. viii). The principal physical agent he says is the diaphragm and since all the other organs are just above or below, they are "massaged" in such a way as to modify their circulation of blood. He describes the effects upon the lungs, the increase in oxidation of the blood that accomplishes "the same thoroughgoing stimulation of inspiration as exercise with sport" (p. 37). He describes the relationship of laughter to all the other organs, to the mind, and to surgery, providing astute observations, many of which have been confirmed by the scientific studies that followed.

Koestler (1964) described laughter as a reflex. Humor is the "only domain of creativity where a stimulus on a high level of complexity produces a massive and sharply defined response on the level of physiologic reflexes" (p. 31). Laughter, like tears, he said, seems to have no biological function, yet produces such obvious relief that can hardly be called a "luxury reflex."

Fry's research of the physiological effects of laughter has been the most comprehensive (1969, 1971, 1977a,b, 1979). He studied the effects of mirthful laughter on heart rate, oxygen saturation levels of peripheral blood and respiratory phenomena. The physiologic impact of humor is as complex as the psychological. He found that both the arousal and cathartic effects of humor are parallelled in the physiological. Laughter, in contrast to other emotions, involves extensive physical activity and thus the results are comparable to that of physical exercise. It increases respiratory activity and oxygen exchange, increases muscular activity and heart rate, and stimulates the cardiovascular system, the sympathetic nervous system, and the production of catecholamines (which stimulate the production in the brain of endorphins, the body's natural pain-reducing enzyme).

The arousal state is followed by a relaxation state in which respiration, heart rate, and muscle tension return to below normal levels. The oxygen saturation level of peripheral blood is not affected during this relaxation state, blood pressure is reduced and a state similar to the impact of hearty exercise exists. The value of exercise has been well documented. Fry points to the value of humor and laughter in physical health, specifically in the prevention of heart disease, cerebral vascular accidents, cancer, depression, and other stress-related conditions (Fry, Note 1).

Bushnell and Scheff (1979), claimed support for the catharsis theory of laughter in the demonstration of physiologic relaxation and reduction of muscle tension during hearty laughter. Svebak (1975, 1977) investigated the respiratory phenomenon in laughter. He found that variability in the tonus of abdominal muscles of women during the inspiratory-expiratory cycle of "belly laughs" facilitated more frequent and enduring laughter responses. No such correlation was found in men. Later research (Svebak, Note 2) investigated the appreciation of humor in terms of hemispheric dominance through electro-physiological studies of brain activity. His findings indicated that laughter stimulated both hemispheres at the same time, coordinating all the senses and producing a unique level of consciousness and a high level mode of brain processing. The brain is essentially at its fullest capacity with the right and left brain functioning simultaneously. In relation to psychotherapy, it affords the client the ability to see both the logical, concrete and the abstract or subtle nuances of his problem, thus having significant therapeutic value.

Other research has investigated aspects of physiologic responses to humor, although not in direct application to health. Averill (1969) (as cited in Godkewitsch, 1976) found increased heart rate associated with mirth and concluded that the humor experience results in arousal of the sympathetic nervous system. Schachter and Wheeler (1962) found that an increase in arousal was a necessary condition in the appreciation of humor. Subjects injected with epinephrine were more amused than control subjects injected with saline or a third group injected with chlorpromazine. Goldstein (1970), recording skeletal muscle response (reaction time) found that latencies of overt humor responses were shorter for more humorous cartoons. Langevin and Day (1972) found that galvanic skin response amplitude was positively correlated with humor appreciation. Godkewitsch (1976) concluded that arousal, as indexed by heart rate and skin conductance, increases with the intensity of the humor response. Gardner (1981), in studying brain-damaged patients for linguistic abilities, found that only when both hemispheres of the brain are working together can the punch line of a joke be appreciated. The left hemisphere has been considered the dominant agent in linguistic functioning, but right-hemisphere damaged patients not only crack jokes at inappropriate times, but have difficulty getting the sense of jokes as told by others. The chemical properties of tears (tears of laughter as well as grief), are currently being investigated at the University of Minnesota, theorizing that emotional tearing is a unique exocrine response to stress similar to other excretory functions of the body (Frey, 1980).

The physiologic and biochemical research on humor that has occurred is an exciting breakthrough in documenting the "healthful" properties of of laughter. More research of its "healing" properties also needs to be done. The only documented report of healing is that of Norman Cousins (1979), a personal account of events that took place in 1964. Cousins' use of programmed sessions of laughter to induce pain-free sleep, lower the sedimentation rate, decrease paralysis and assist in his recovery from a collagen disease, ankylosing spondylitis, has been widely discussed (1979a,b; Goldstein, 1982). His present work at UCLA School of Medicine demonstrating the use of positive emotions and holistic health approaches with clients has been reported by him in the *Saturday Review* between 1977 and 82.

FUNCTIONS OF HUMOR: THE HEALTH PROFESSIONAL

The health professional's need for humor is as great as that of the client. Humor is of value in the stresses of education, the "reality shocks" experienced in initial clinical experiences, as well as the ongoing stresses of the day-to-day practice of the health professional. Humor in these contexts serves the same communication, social, psychological, and physiological functions described above for the client. The external pressures and the internal stresses in coping with the professional role are many. In addition to those stresses related to establishing an identity, maintaining collegial and collaborative relationships with other disciplines, and surviving in the health care organization, the internal stresses related to the constant life-death decisions, tragedy, crises, and death have created a preponderance of Gallows humor, which Fox (1959) dubbed "medical humor".

Medical Humor

Fox (1959), in her study of an experimental metabolic ward, and later study (1974) found that physicians utilized a highly patterned and intricate form of humor to deal with the constant possibility of death and failure, the uncertainty, and the trial and error method of treatment. As one physician said, "Our humor is a protective device. If we were to talk seriously all the time and act like a bunch of Sir Galahads . . . we just couldn't take all this" (1959, p. 76-77). Fox found in other observations of the socialization of the physician that in their medical training they "learn that an effective and appropriate way to handle their reactions . . . is to joke with their colleagues about them in a look-it-in-the-face-and-laugh manner" (1959, p. 81).

"Medical" humor extends to all health professionals facing the same stresses, and this gallows, macabre type of humor has been documented and seen also in many situation where considerable stress occurs: tragedies, wars, concentration camps, oppressed countries, and the black humor of fiction (Obrdlik, 1942; Frankl, 1963; Hill, 1968; Schulz, 1973). The crucial issue in health care is recognizing whose needs are being met when both patients and staff are utilizing gallows humor. Is the use of gallows humor appropriate in patient-staff interaction, particularly since the patient is the object of the tragedy? Coser (1959) suggested that humor across status lines may well take other forms and have other functions than humor among status equals. Emerson (1963) stated that more watchfulness is necessary in regard to humor because by its very nature, humor is always toeing the line between divergence and defiance, tottering on the verge of going too far.

The paradox is that medical humor brings the health professional closer to his colleagues, sharing in the realization that he is not perfect, and still human. Yet the patient is expecting and paying for seriousness, miracles and godliness (Robinson 1977). In the TV series, *M*A*S*H*, this fine line seems to be achieved. The staff's need for humor to survive is evident, yet the patient is never the victim of their humor, as zany and grotesque as it may be.

Communication Among Colleagues

Humor as a form of communication among health care professionals has been a long-standing occurrence, evidenced by observations, initiation rites of new students or staff, traditional student skits, the cartoons in *Medical Economics* and in *RN* magazines, and the "Time off" page in the *American Journal of Nursing*, among others. Investigation of the use of collegial humor, however, is meager. Goodrich, Henry, and Goodrich (1954) analyzed laughter in psychiatric staff conferences, in regard to the content and form. The major forms were disparagement and incongruity and the content was aimed at physicians and patients. There was a heartiness of laughter at death and a low percentage of laughter at sexual themes. It provided for group solidarity and a safety valve, but the disparagement of patients seemed to cause the personnel to lose sight of the patient's problems and was deemed nontherapeutic by the observers.

Coser (1960) also studied the social functions of humor among the staff of a mental hospital during staff meetings. She found those high in the hierarchy made the most witticisms while those low in the hierarchy made the fewest. The humor was usually directed at some target. Senior staff wit was directed toward junior members, while junior members directed their humor at patients, relatives, or themselves. The self-deprecating humor served to decrease the social distance, and the laughter of the senior members granted them belongingness to the group. The humor, Coser found, was used as a device for lending support and asking for support, to live up to role expectations, and to overcome and survive in the complex social structure of the organization.

In health-care areas where stress is high, such as the operating room, critical care units, and the emergency room, humor has been a traditional pattern. An anecdotal accounting of humor in the emergency room was reported by Lindsay and Benjamin (1979).

Education of the Health Professional

The planned use of humor in the educational process, as content in the curriculum, and as an intervention tool to be used in health care is still not a common occurrence in the educational programs of the health professions. Research regarding the positive value of humor in learning is still equivocal, despite the general belief that what is "learned with laughter is learned well" (Grotjahn, 1957; Eble 1966, McLuhan, 1967, Rogers 1969, Ziv 1976, Robinson 1977, 1978; See Chapter 10 by Zillmann and Bryant). Davies and Apter (1980) state that the idea that humor should be taken seriously in teaching children is widely accepted, and there is much anecdotal evidence, but comparatively little research, as to whether it actually helps children to learn.

In health education, there are anecdotal accounts also, and many have urged the inclusion of humor in the teaching-learning process and in the scientific writings related to health and science (Baker 1963, 1967; Bornemeier, 1960;

Reese, 1967; Roland, 1971; Cousins 1979; Moody, 1978.) Robinson (1977) suggested that the health educational system must consider the use of humor in four interrelated aspects: enhancing the learning process itself through humor, facilitating the process of socialization, teaching the concept of humor as a communication tool and modeling the use of humor as a vehicle for facilitating the other three.

A pilot study was conducted utilizing a guide for incorporating humor into the teaching-learning process (Robinson, 1977, pp. 176-181). Nursing instructors were asked to use the guide, students were asked to evaluate the instructors' performance, and materials and tapes from lectures were analyzed. Although the collected data were too few for statistical analysis, there was an overall positive response from students and a change in the attitude of the instructors from their initial skepticism. Most of the humor used was of the spontaneous-situational type, but formal jokes, humorous poems, and other canned humor were also used.

Coser (1960) in the study of laughter among colleagues observed that the use of humor between senior and junior staff served as a teaching device that not only helps the student to resolve the paradoxical role of both student and professional care-giver, but also serves as an informal process of socialization into the profession. O'Connell & Covert (1967) in a study of first-year medical students, comparing their future specialty choices with their attitudes toward death and humor appreciation, suggests that potential psychiatrists may need education toward increased empathy and humor to make death concerns a professional asset. The effectiveness of humor in the health professional's education and the impact on the health care-giver's role and on the quality of health care are much needed areas for investigation.

CULTIVATING HUMOR AS A TOOL
IN HEALTH PROMOTION

Recognizing the value of humor in health, the question is raised of how one goes about cultivating that sense of humor, that humorous attitude, and incorporating the humor into the therapeutic, healing, and health promoting process. Again, there is theorizing, suggestions, individual applications, and anecdotal accounts, but little scientific research on the process itself and in the clinical application of humor. As Levine (1980) observed, "the recent upsurge of interest in humour has had little impact upon its clinical applications, perhaps because most of the research and theorizing has been concerned with the essence of humour rather than its uses" (p. 255). According to Levine, the extensive work on the origins and development of the sense of humor (McGhee, 1971; 1979) and other studies of children's humor have contributed to two primary clinical areas: developmental assessment and psychotherapy with children.

In adult psychotherapy, much study and theorizing has also occurred regarding the therapist-patient relationship and the therapeutic use of humor in the one-to-one situation. Some models for clinical application, for example, Frankl's (1963) logotherapy, O'Connell's (1976) Natural High therapy, Farrelly's (1974) Provocative therapy, could be transposed to the general psychiatric setting or to other helping interactions with nonpsychiatric patients. Lamb (1980) describes the use of paradoxical intention (Frankl, 1963) in counseling a student with test-taking anxiety. However, research on the clinical application of humor for disease prevention and health promotion, the cultivation of a sense of humor, and the use of humor by the individual as a tool in stress reduction and day-to-day health practices has been negligible.

Mindess (1971) in a classic work aimed at demonstrating that humor can be cultivated, does so through describing the inner obstacles that block the unfolding of the humorous potential and then points out possibilities for overcoming them. His contribution has applicability to both professional and consumer in developing that humorous attitude. Robinson (1977) set out to provide some guidelines for the cultivation of humor in the health professional's intervention with clients, identifying four levels in the process: (1) the knowledge level about the concept of humor; (2) the acceptance level, acknowledging its value, being open to it and encouraging its use; (3) development of his/her own humorous attitude; and (4) application and creation of humor in interventions with clients. Utilizing the problem-solving framework, she made suggestions for assessing the usefulness of humor, its appropriateness for the patient, and then planning and evaluating the intervention.

There are many variables to be considered in a successful interaction, one of which is the culture of the patient. Since there were no studies related to the use of humor in times of illness in specific cultures, a study was made of three cultures: Black-American, Spanish-American and Southwest Indian (Robinson 1977, p. 107-128.) This exploratory study collected humorous incidents in health settings involving patients from these cultures. The results indicated that there was a difference related to cultural beliefs about health, minority group status, and whether the professional was from a different culture.

In the assessment process, Moody (1978) offers to the physician a "humor history" (p. 119). Emerson (1963) advises when humor might be used in preference to other forms of communication (p. 164) and describes cues for when the serious impact of humor might be transposed to a serious discussion (Emerson 1969).

Case studies or anecdotal accounts of the use of humor in health settings are few. Robinson (1970/1978) describes the planned use of humor with a patient following a cholescystectomy and the milieu of the ward that contributed to its success. Powell (1974) describes how children have used humor in hospital settings and how hospital personnel might encourage it. Wessell (1975) describes the use of humor by an adolescent girl hospitalized and immobilized for treatment of a severe scoliosis. Jaffe (1976), a professor of social work, describes how the use of gallows humor helped her and her family throughout her terminal illness. Hutchison (1976) described the application of humor she observed in nurse-patient relationships in a psychiatric setting, defining the level of intervention according to three categories: comic/non-verbal, wit, and humor. Accounts of the healing process in cancer and other diseases and the use of humor by clowns and hospital chaplains have also been described (Damsteegt 1975; Moody, 1978; Cousins, 1979a,b). Individual incidences have been noted of the "prescription" of humor and laughter in VA Hospitals, prisons, retirement homes, and to various groups in lectures, workshops, speeches, and articles, but research to document this application is not recorded.

So much more investigation and research is needed in the application of humor to health, not only to interventions in mental health, but to the healing process in disease, in the prevention of disease, and in the promotion of health. It is an overwhelming but an exciting prospect.

REFERENCE NOTES

1. Fry, W. F., Jr. *Using humor to save lives.* Paper presented at American Orthopsychiatric Association, Washington, D.C., April 1979.
2. Svebak, S. *Biological precursors of laughter.* Paper presented at Second International Conference on Humor, Los Angeles, August 1979.

REFERENCES

Averill, J. R. Autonomic response patterns during sadness and mirth. *Psychophysiology*, 1969, 5, 399-414.

Baker, R. A. *Psychology in the wry.* Princeton: Van Nostrand, 1963.

Baker, R. A. *A stress analysis of a strapless evening gown and other essays for a scientific age.* Englewood Cliffs, N.J.: Prentice-Hall, 1967.

Bergson, H. Laughter. In J. J. Enck, T. Forter, & A. Whitley (Eds.), *The comic in theory and practice.* New York: Appleton-Century-Crofts, 1960. (Originally published, 1900.)

Berlyne, D. E. Laughter, humor and play. In G. Lindzey & E. Aronson (Eds.), *Handbook of social psychology* (Vol. 3). Reading, Mass.: Addison-Wesley, 1969.

Bornemeier, W. C. Sphincter protecting hemorroidectomy. *American Journal of Proctocology*, 1960, *11*, 48-52.

Boskin, J. *Humor and social change in twentieth century America.* Boston: Trustees of the Public Library, 1979.

Brody, M. The meaning of laughter. *Psychoanalytic Quarterly*, 1950, *19*, 192-201.

Bushnell, D. D. The cathartic effect of laughter in comedy. Unpublished doctoral dissertation. University of California, Santa Barbara, 1978.

Bushnell, D. D., Scheff, T. J. The cathartic effects of laughter on audiences. In H. Mindesc & J. Turek (Eds.), *The study of humor.* Los Angeles: Antioch University, 1979.

Coser, R. L. Some social functions of laughter. *Human Relations*, 1959, *12*, 171-182.

Coser, R. L. Laughter among colleagues. *Psychiatry*, 1960, *23*, 81-95.

Cousins, N. Anatomy of an illness. *Saturday Review*, 28, May 1977, 4-51.

Cousins, N. *Anatomy of an illness*. New York: Norton, 1979. (a)

Cousins, N. Why laughter is good medicine. In H. Mindess & J. Turek (Eds), *The study of humor*. Los Angeles: Antioch College, 1979 (b)

Cousins, N. Back to Hippocrates. *Saturday Review*, February 1982, 12.

Damsteegt, D. Pastoral visits to presurgical patients. *Journal of Religion and Health*, 1975, *14*, 43-49.

Darwin, C. *The expression of the emotions in man and animals*. Chicago: University of Chicago Press, 1965. (Originally published, 1872.)

Davies, A. P., & Apter, M. J. Humour and its effect on learning in children. In P. E. McGhee & A. J. Chapman (Eds.), *Children's humour*. London: Wiley, 1980.

Eble, K. *A perfect education*. New York: Macmillan, 1966.

Emerson, J. P. Social functions of humor in a hospital setting. Unpublished doctoral dissertation. University of California, 1963.

Emerson, J. P. Negotiating the serious import of humor. *Sociometry*, 1969, *32*, 169-181.

Emerson, J. P. Behavior in private places: Sustaining definitions of reality in gynecological examinations. In T. P. Dreitzel (Ed.), *Recent sociology* (No. 2). New York: Macmillan, 1970.

Farrelly, F., & Brandsma, J. *Provocative therapy*. Cupertino, Cal.: Meta, 1974.

Fine, G. A. Humor under stress: No laughing matter. *Humor Research Newsletter*, State University of New York at Albany, 1977, *2* (1).

Fink, E. L., & Walker, B. A. Humorous responses to embarrassment. *Psychological Reports*, 1977, *40*, 475-486.

Fox, R. C. *Experiment perilous*. Glencoe, Ill.: Free Press, 1959.

Fox, R. C., & Swazey, J. P. *The courage to fail: A social view of organ transplants and dialysis*. Chicago: University of Chicago Press, 1974.

Frankl, V. Man's search for meaning. New York: Washington Square Press, 1963.

Freud, S. Jokes and their relation to the unconscious. In J. Strachey (Ed.), *The complete psychological works of Sigmund Freud* (Vol. VIII). London: Hogarth Press, 1960. (Originally published, 1905.)

Freud, S. Humor. In J. Strachey (Ed.), *The complete psychological works of Sigmund Freud* (Vol. XXI). London: Hogarth Press, 1961. (Originally published, 1927.)

Frey, W. H., II., Not so idle tears. *Psychology Today*, 1980, January, 91-92.

Fry, W. F., Jr. *Sweet madness: A study of humor*. Palo Alto, Cal.: Pacific Books, 1963.

Fry, W. F., Jr. The appeasement function of mirthful laughter. In A. J. Chapman & H. C. Foot (Eds.), *It's a funny thing, humour*. Oxford, Pergamon, 1977 (a).

Fry, W. F., Jr. The respiratory components of mirthful laughter. *Journal of Biological Psychology*, 1977, *19*(2), 39-50 (b).

Fry, W. F., Jr. Humor and the human cardiovascular system. In H. Mindess & J. Turek (Eds.), *The study of humor*. Los Angeles: Antioch University, 1979.

Fry, W. F., Jr., & Stoft, P. E. Mirth and oxygen saturation levels of peripheral blood. *Psychotherapy and Psychosomatics*, 1971, *19*, 76-84.

Gardner, J. How the split brain gets a joke. *Psychology Today*, February 1981, 74-78.

Godkewitsch, M. Physiological and verbal indices of arousal in rated humor. In A. J.

Chapman & H. C. Foot (Eds.), *Humour and laughter: Theory, research, and applications*. London: Wiley, 1976.

Goldstein, J. H. Humor and time to respond. *Psychological Reports*, 1970, *27*, 445-446.

Goldstein, J. H. In vivo veritas: Has humor research looked at humor? *Humor Research Newsletter*, State University of New York at Albany, 1978, 3(1).

Goldstein, J. H. A laugh a day: Can mirth keep disease at bay? *The Sciences*, 1982, *22* (Aug./Sept.), 21-25.

Goldstein, J. H., & McGhee, P. E. *The psychology of humor*. New York: Academic Press, 1972.

Goodrich, A. T., Henry, J., & Goodrich, D. W. Laughter in psychiatric staff conferences: A sociopsychiatric analysis. *American Journal of Orthopsychiatry*, 1954, *24*, 175-184.

Grotjahn, M. *Beyond laughter*. New York: McGraw-Hill, 1957.

Hayworth, D. The social origins and functions of laughter. *Psychological Review*, 1928, *35*, 367-384.

Hazlitt, W. Wit and humor. In J. J. Enck, E. T. Forter, & A. Whitley (Eds.), *The comic in theory and practice*. New York: Appleton-Century-Crofts, 1960. (Originally published, 1819.)

Hill, H. Black humor: Its cause and cure. *Colorado Quarterly*, 1968, *17*, 57-64.

Hutchison, S. A. Humor: A link to life. In C. Knuse & H. Wilson (Eds.), *Current perspectives in psychiatric nursing: Issues and trends*. St. Louis: Mosby, 1976.

Jaffe, L., & Jaffe, A. Terminal candor and the coda syndrome. *American Journal of Nursing*, 1976, December, 1938-1940.

Kaplan, H., & Boyd, I. H. The social functions of humor on an open psychiatric ward. *Psychiatric Quarterly*, 1965, *39*, 502-515.

Keith-Spiegel, P. Early conceptions of humor: Varieties and issues. In J. H. Goldstein & P. E. McGhee (Eds.), *The psychology of humor*. New York: Academic Press, 1972.

Koestler, A. *The act of creation*. New York: Macmillan, 1964.

Kubie, L. S. The destructive potential of humor in psychotherapy. *American Journal of Psychiatry*, 1971, *127*, 861-866.

Lamb, C. S. The use of paradoxical intention: Self-management through laughter. *Personnel and Guidance Journal*, 1980, December, 217-219.

Langevin, R., & Day, H. I. Physiological correlates of humor. In J. H. Goldstein & P. E. McGhee (Eds.), *The psychology of humor*. New York: Academic Press, 1972.

Levine, J. Responses to humor. *Scientific American*, 1956, *194* (February), 31-35.

Levine, J. Regression in primitive clowning. *Psychoanalytic Quarterly*, 1961, *30*, 72-83.

Levine, J. Humor. *International Encyclopedia of the Social Sciences* (Vol. 7). New York: Macmillan, 1968.

Levine, J. *Motivation in humor*. New York: Atherton, 1969.

Levine, J. The clinical use of humor in work with children. In P. E. McGhee & A. J. Chapman (Eds.), *Children's humour*, London: Wiley, 1980.

Lindsey, D., & Benjamin, J. Humor in the emergency room. In H. Mindess & J. Turek (Eds.), *The study of humor*. Los Angeles: Antioch College, 1979.

Lorenz, K. *On aggression*. New York: Harcourt, Brace & World, 1963.

McDougall, W. *An introduction to social psychology.* New York: Barnes & Noble, 1963. (Originally published, 1908.)

McGhee, P. E. Development of the humor response: A review of the literature. *Psychological Bulletin,* 1971, *76,* 328-348.

McGhee, P. E. Creating versus responding to humor. *Humor Research Newsletter,* State University of New York at Albany, 1978, *3*(1).

McGhee, P. E. *Humor: Origins and development.* San Francisco: Freeman, 1979.

McLuhan, M. *The medium is the massage.* New York: Bantam, 1967.

Mikes, G. *Laughing matter.* New York: Library Press, 1971.

Mindess, H. *Laughter and liberation.* Los Angeles: Nash, 1971.

Mindess, H. The use and abuse of humour in psychotherapy. In A. J. Chapman & H. C. Foot (Eds.), *Humour and laughter: Theory, research, and applications.* London: Wiley, 1976.

Moody, R. A. *Laugh after laugh.* Jacksonville, Fla.: Headwaters Press, 1978.

Obrdlik, A. J. Gallows humor: A sociological phenomenon. *American Journal of Sociology,* 1942, *47,* 709-716.

O'Connell, W. E. Freudian humor: The eupsychia of everyday life. In A. J. Chapman & H. C. Foot (Eds.), *Humour and laughter: theory, research, and applications.* London: Wiley, 1976.

O'Connell, W. E., & Covert, C. Death attitudes and humor appreciation among medical students. *Existential Psychiatry,* 1967, *6,* 433-442.

Poland, W. S. The place of humor in psychotherapy. *American Journal of Psychiatry,* 1971, *128,* 635-637.

Powell, B. S. Laughter and healing: The use of humor in hospitals treating children. *Association for the Care of Children in Hospitals Journal,* 1974, November, 10-16.

Reese, R. L. Does humor have a place in scientific writing? *American Medical Writers' Association Bulletin,* 1967, *17,* 11-13.

Robinson, V. M. Humor in nursing. In C. Carlson & B. Blackwell (Eds.), *Behavioral concepts and nursing intervention* (2nd ed.). Philadelphia: Lippincott, 1978. (Originally published, 1970.)

Robinson, V. M. *Humor and the health professions.* Thorofare, N.J.: Chas. B. Slack, 1977.

Rogers, C. *Freedom to learn.* Columbus, Ohio: Merrill, 1969.

Roland, C. G. Thoughts about medical writing. Can it be funny and medical? *Anesthesia and Analgesia: Current Researches,* 1971, *50*(2), 229-230.

Rose, G. J. King Lear and the use of humor in treatment. *Journal of the American Psychoanalytic Association,* 1969, *12,* 927-940.

Schachter, S., & Wheeler, L. Epinephrine, chlorpromazine and amusement. *Journal of Abnormal and Social Psychology,* 1962, *65,* 121-128.

Scheff, T. J. *Catharsis in healing, ritual and drama.* Berkeley: University of California Press, 1979.

Schulz, M. F. *Black humor fiction in the sixties.* Athens, Ohio: Ohio University Press, 1973.

Spencer, H. The physiology of laughter. *Macmillan's Magazine* 1860,*1,* 395-402.

Stephenson, R. M. Conflict and control functions of humor. *American Journal of Sociology,* 1959, *56,* 569-574.

Sully, J. *The psychology of laughter: A study in social adaptation.* New York: Gamut, 1963. (Originally published, 1902.)

Svebak, S. Respiratory patterns as predictors of laughter. *Psychophysiology*, 1975, *12*, 62-65.

Svebak, S. Some characteristics of resting respiration as predictors of laughter. In A. J. Chapman & H. C. Foot (Eds.), *It's a funny thing, humour*. Oxford: Pergamon, 1977.

Walsh, J. J. *Laughter and health*. New York: Appleton, 1928.

Wessell, M. L. Use of humor by an immobilized adolescent girl during hospitalization. *Maternal-Child Nursing Journal*, 1975, *4*, 35-48.

Zalis, T. A. A. The incidence and role of humor in hypomanic reactions. Unpublished doctoral dissertation. Long Island University, Brooklyn Ctr., 1980.

Ziv, A. Facilitating effects of humor on creativity. *Journal of Educational Psychology*, 1976, *68*, 318-322.

Chapter 8

Humor and Popular Culture

LAWRENCE E. MINTZ

Popular culture studies is a vaguely defined area of interest that includes the popular arts—that is, film, television, comic strips, cartoons, popular books, magazines, newspaper columns, popular theater, public entertainments of all sorts, and popular music, to list the most prominent of them—and the popular artifacts of everyday life, commonplace design, including housing, transportation, personal appearance, decorative art, *kitsch* collectables, and so forth. The study of popular culture embraces virtually all of the disciplines of the humanities and the social sciences. It encompasses all of the method for textual analysis—structuralism, content analysis, formalism, semiotics, and the more traditional discussion of plot, theme, character, style, images, myths, and symbols—along with methods for the consideration of the contexts of production, distribution and consumption—that is, who is using what for what purposes? Humor is very evident in all of the manifestations of popular culture, artifact as well as art. And popular culture clearly offers more material for the study of humor than any other category of subject-source (e.g., Chaney, 1979; Davison, Meyersohn, & Shils, 1978, 1980, 1981; Kando, 1980).

The following resources should be helpful in studying popular culture. *American Humor: An Interdisciplinary Newsletter* publishes an annual article checklist that provides a good example of the range of topic and method in the field and of the kinds of sources of information available to the student of humor in popular culture. The checklist includes references to articles in the popular press as well as to professional journals. The *Journal of Popular Culture* is the major journal in the field, but articles on humor and popular culture can be found in the *Journal of American Culture, American Quarterly*, and in literally dozens of journals in folklore, history, ethnic studies, literature, and all of the other topics, genres, and disciplines discussed above. The Center for the Study of Popular Culture at Bowling Green State University in Ohio maintains a museum and archives for popular culture studies, and the Library of Congress, Smithsonian, National Archives, and Vivian Beaumont Library are among the institutions with general collections. In addition there are dozens of more specific library and institutional collections such as the tv materials at UCLA and the Schubert theater materials at NYU as well as the several private collections of graphic arts materials.

This chapter seeks to outline the connection between humor and popular culture by noting some parallels in theory, method, and subject matter, by providing a generic overview of the common areas of expression of humor in the popular culture, and by providing a brief historical account of some of the recurring issues that a survey of humor in American popular culture might suggest.

Humor studies and the study of popular culture have much in common. Until recently, popular culture was a suspect and neglected source for all but a few adventurous sociologists and historians; working with it elicited raised eyebrows, snickers, and overstated, aggressive theoretical and methodological objections that perhaps developed from the insecurity with which scholars confront "nonserious" or allegedly frivolous activity in the sanctuaries of the intelligentsia. As is the case with humor research, popular culture studies are often "covered" by more respectable endeavors, hidden from public scrutiny, described with defensiveness and apology, or justified with ponderous counterattack, with language and structure designed to out-do the most sober, most elevated intellectual speculation.

The investigation of popular culture is gaining respect for the same reason that humor research forges on; both humor and popular culture are so central to virtually every culture and society, so omnipresent, powerful, and broad-based, that it is absurd to try to explain a culture or a society without reference to both of them (Bouissac, 1976; Mintz, in press). The pronouncements of the artistic and social elites, and spontaneous folk expressions are simply too much the tip of the iceberg, too few and small in importance, to be used as exclusive indices of belief and behavior or to be seen as primary influences in the determination of personality, acculturation, and social development. The popular arts, including such mass media as broadcasting, film, journalism, popular literature, the graphic arts, and advertising, and quasi-folk art (popular cultural manifestations, such as bumperstickers, imprinted T-shirts, graffiti, popular joke-cycles, public entertainments and celebrations) are, collectively, at the very least, as important as any other social institution (e.g., church, school, family) in determining and revealing who and what we are. Popular culture, like humor, deals with every important feature of our culture, including sex, violence, politics, and social class distinctions, racial, ethnic and regional differences, and the values, attitudes, dispositions, and concerns that characterize and unite us as well. Its consumption is a basic opportunity for us to communicate, to articulate, reify, and distill our vague, abstract sentiments, and to celebrate, acknowledge, and affirm in ritual the inchoate emotions of personality and culture. By examining popular culture we get closer to the day-to-day concerns of the public, in contrast to the portrait presented in the formal history and literature of the elite.

Since the late 1960s, a considerable scholarly apparatus has emerged to coordinate in part the various endeavors in the study of popular culture. This is quite a problem in popular culture studies as, again, with humor studies since the scholarly disciplines involved include virtually all of the social sciences— psychology, sociology, anthropology, cultural geography, the humanities, including literature, history, and art history, and the newer fields defined by genre or topic rather than by discipline, such as communications, film and broadcasting studies, women's studies, black studies, American studies, and so forth. The variety of approaches and the breath of activity have been of enormous importance in moving the study of popular culture from the descriptive and the appreciative, and from the primitive aesthetic debates over its quality and nature, to the genuinely analytic (e.g., Bigsby, 1977; Browne, 1980; Dunlop, 1975; Fine, 1977; Gans, 1974; Gillespie, 1972; Landrum, 1975; Zinsser, 1966). Modern popular culture studies has moved beyond collecting and classifying "because it's there" to considering texts and artifacts with a sophisticated bag of tools, including structuralism and other linguistic methodologies, phenomenological inquiry, computer-aided content analysis, and exegisis based upon a vastly expanded data base rather than upon highly selective, subjective isolation of predetermined elements. Of equal or perhaps greater importance has been the increased emphasis on the importance of *context*, particularly in the matters of production and distribution and of audience-related research. Popular culture scholars are more conscious than ever of the questions of *who* consumes what, how access to the artifacts was created or encouraged, and what the possible effects upon the audience might be. Questions about the motives (commercial, to be sure, but others, as well) and methods of the creators and distributors are explored with the recognition that popular culture is an industry and a public enterprise as well as an artistic phenomenon.

RELATIONSHIP BETWEEN HUMOR AND POPULAR CULTURE

The relationship between humor and popular culture deserves attention not merely because the history of the study of their manifestations is parallel or because both are multigeneric, multidisciplinary subjects for consideration. The two have been inseparable, everywhere and always. Most of the manifestations of humor are in popular culture arenas, or folk culture arenas. The more serious, formal avenues of expression have been devoid of humor, for the most part (there are some glaring exceptions, of course, such as ritually sanctioned, highly formal opportunities for public expression of humorous sentiments), and many, though by no means all or even most, of the expressions of popular culture are humorous simply because humor is a *popular*, that is, well-liked, well-received, and publicly protected, mode in which cultural expressions may be presented and entertainment achieved. The relationship between humor and popular culture is present, as I have suggested above, virtually everywhere one looks, past and present, but the examples with which I will view some of its manifestations will be from American culture, the area with which I am most immediately familiar.

We cannot discuss American humor without first saying something about humor generally, or at least humor that is . . . well, un-American. Try to detect which of the following jokes and anecdotes are American in origin and which are not:

1. Man was created a little lower than the angels, and has been getting a little lower ever since.
2. A fellow hears that one of a pair of twin brothers has died. When he meets the other twin on the street, he asks " Was it you who died or your brother?"
3. A bore is defined as a person who talks when you wish him to listen.
4. A gentleman, noted for his ability to make puns, was asked one night in company to make a pun. "Upon what subject?" he asked. "The King," answered the other. "Why, the King, Sir," said the punster, "is no subject."
5. An old man out riding on his old mare, just shy of being ready for the glue factory, met another man on a fine horse. The old man dismounted, approached the other and his fine steed, and said, "Would you like to change your horse for mine?" The man, looking with disdain at the old mare, said "Are you a fool?" "No," said the old man, "but I thought you might be."
6. " . . . he got me so mad I threw him so high in the sky he died of starvation before he ever hit the ground."

It is not always easy, once the language is updated, to know the origin of a joke or story. Of these six, only the first and third are American in origin, the first a saying of Josh Billings (Henry Shaw), and the second a definition from Ambrose Bierce's *Devil's Dictionary*. The joke about the twins was elaborated upon in a story by Mark Twain in 1882 (*The Stolen White Elephant*) but can also be traced back to some 19th century American joke books, to an 1880 version of *Joe Miller's Jests* published in London and, if we can rely on Blair and Hill (1978), first appeared in ancient Greece. The joke about the punster can be found in the original 1739 version of *Joe Miller's Jests*. The old man who wished to trade his mare is a variation on an ancient Oriental tale, and the braggart who threw his enemy into the sky, first appeared in a 16th century English joke book.

What we often think of as American products, such as the Paul Bunyan tales, were borrowed from our neighbors, in this instance, from French Canada.

Folklorists often note that a joke has been around for centuries, modified and updated in circumstance and language, and passed off as original. Of course, this is true of many jokes. Mark Twain often said that all he did was modify old stories and tales and relate them in an artful way. He has his Connecticut Yankee, Hank Morgan, revert to Camelot. At King Arthur's Court, Morgan reports having listened to a court jester.

> I think I never heard so many old played-out jokes strung together in my life. . . . It seemed peculiarly sad to sit there, 1300 years before I was born and listen again to poor, flat, worm-eaten jokes that had given me the dry gripes when I was a boy 1300 years afterwards. It about convinced me that there isn't any such thing as a new joke possible. Everybody laughed at these antiquities—but then they always do; I noticed that, centuries later.

Of American humor and its originality, Twain also noted that "Americans are not Englishmen, and American humor is not English humor: but both the American and his humor had their origin in England, and have merely undergone changes brought about by changed conditions and environment."

If Twain borrowed, however intentionally, from the work of others, it is possible to see parallels between more contemporary American comedians and much earlier work (Charney, 1977). I do not mean to suggest that Abbott and Costello borrowed consciously from the early Greeks (they did not) or that the Marx Brothers modeled themselves after a Commedia del Arte troupe, but the similarities are there, nevertheless.

Here is a brief bit of dialogue from *Cyclops*, a play by Euripides, written about 400 B.C.

CYCLOPS:	I was battered by Nobody.
CHORUS:	Then nobody touched you.
CYCLOPS:	Nobody blinded me.
CHORUS:	Then you can see. . . . What? Blinded by nobody?
CYCLOPS:	. . . Where's Nobody?
CHORUS:	Nowhere, of course.

And compare that with perhaps the most famous of all Abbott and Costello routines. Abbott notes the lineup of their baseball team. Who's on first base, What's on second, and I Don't Know's on third. Costello is bewildered.

ABBOTT:	I say Who's on first, What's on second, I Don't Know's on third . . .
COSTELLO:	Yeah, do you know the fellow's name?
ABBOTT:	Yes.
COSTELLO:	Well, who's on first?
ABBOTT:	Yes.

COSTELLO:	I mean the guy playing first.
ABBOTT:	Who.
COSTELLO:	The fellow playing first.
ABBOTT:	Who.
COSTELLO:	The first baseman.
ABBOTT:	*Who!*
COSTELLO:	The guy playing first.
ABBOTT:	Who is on first!
COSTELLO:	Well, what are you asking *me* for?

In the end, the exasperated Costello gives up, shouting, "I don't give a damn!" Abbott replies, "He's our shortstop."

We often think of the zany antics of the Marx Brothers as a purely American form of chaos. But they do not differ in many important ways from the early Commedia del Arte troupes that toured southern and central Europe in the 16th and 17th centuries. There were stock characters, identifiable by their masks and costumes, who were consistent in all of the more or less spontaneous, uncomplicated plays they performed. Commedia stories were simple, easy for the generally illiterate and uneducated audiences to follow. They were often obscene and scatological. Their characters were gross exaggerations of real life types. Likewise, Groucho, Chico, and Harpo are stock comic types, always wearing the same "masks," whether they are at the races, the opera, or in a department store, and always involved in a plot of gross simplicity, serving primarily as a vehicle for these stock characters to perform their unvarying routines. Of course, puns, many written by S. J. Perelman, are uniquely American and require a considerable knowledge of idiomatic American English and American customs. The point, however, is that the basic structure of American comedy is not unlike the structure of comedy at other times and in other places, while the particulars of our humor—the situations that arise and the settings in which they occur and the words used to poke fun at them—these may be seen as uniquely American.

It has often been said that no humor that is distinctly American existed until the Jacksonian era, in the 1830s. Even as late as 1840, Charles Dickens, describing a visit to America, noted that "Americans certainly are not a humorous people, and their temperament always impressed me as being of a dull and gloomy character." This changed following the Civil War.

HUMOR IN AMERICAN POPULAR CULTURE

Literature and Journalism

Students of American literature commonly assert that the comic mode is central to our national activity in that genre, and it is important to note that a considerable part of that comic literature can be described as popular culture. To be sure, many of our writers have been elevated to a "serious" or "classical" status, but their work was often originally commercially oriented and received by a large, diverse public. Mark Twain, for instance, conceived his comic masterpieces such as *Huckelberry Finn* as a popular work, and the writing in *Roughing It* and *Innocents Abroad*, to cite but two examples, originated in commercial journalism. Many of our major writers who are routinely described as "comic" are not really humorists, however, despite the technical accuracy of that term to describe the structure and tone of their work (e.g., Hemingway, Faulkner, Melville, Fitzgerald, Malamud, Bellow, Updike), and a case could be made that they are not really "popular" despite their hardbound best-seller list status. Book-length literature is a source for humor in the popular culture—Max Shulman, Peter DeVries, Philip Roth, for example—but our best comic writers are far too esoteric to be classified as popular (e.g., Robert Coover, Donald Bartheleme, Ishmael Reed, Thomas Pynchon).

However, humorous journalism, the shorter forms ranging from comic stories to columns and nonfiction features, is indeed the arena in which comedy and popular culture comfortably (and profitably) coexist. The almanac was one of the earliest and most important publications in America, serving as a communicator of news, practical information, and cultural expression, and not surprisingly, humor was one of its principle features. Anecdotes, folktales, aphorisms, and jokes made the almanacs entertaining and allowed for a humor-mediated discussion of the emerging American culture and personality. Benjamin Franklin, of course, became the best-known master of this light, but meaningful humor; however, he was but one of many successful practitioners of the art. Franklin and other early newspaper publishers used humor as an integral element of their journalism, developing the popular Brother Jonathan, a commonsense philosopher who represented the democratic philosophy that the simple, untutored farmer might indeed be the *wise* fool, a laughably unsophisticated but basically honest, shrewd, decent citizen. The humorous magazines of the early national period developed this device further, using it for topical commentary as well as for amusement. By the early 19th century, humor was the most prominent aspect of our national self-scrutiny, poking fun at and laughing with the archetypal comic common man. Newspaper columnists such as Seba Smith and later, Artemus Ward (Charles Farrar Browne), Petroeum V. Nasby (David Ross Locke), Bill Nye, and Mark Twain among countless others, contributed to a virtual national mythopoeia with laughter as a palliative and a mediator for dealing with the very real and delicate question of the viability of democracy (cf. Schutz, 1977).

By the late 19th and early 20th centuries, the humor magazines had emerged as a specialty genre (e.g., *Puck, Judge, Life*), and by the so-called "golden age" of American humor (roughly from the late 19-teens through the early 1930s) there was a plethora of them, particularly if one includes the omnipresent college magazines and the anthology, *College Humor*. The twenties produced *The New Yorker* more essentially a humor magazine then than now, and led to the prominence of humor in virtually all popular publications from newspapers to family-oriented domestic magazines. Writers such as James Thurber, Robert Benchley, Dorothy Parker, E. B. White, Don Marquis, Ring Lardner, and S. J. Perelman, to name but a few, generated a humorous popular culture of unprecedented and unequalled quantity and quality (Bier, 1968; Blair & Hill, 1978; Rubin, 1973).

The traditions of humor in popular journalism continue to survive even if the activity in the genre is less prominent today. The humor magazines have dwindled in number, but *Mad* and the *National Lampoon* carry on amidst a flotilla of shorter-lived, less successful endeavors; one finds humor of various kinds in magazines not exclusively or primarily humorous (e.g., *Playboy*, *The New Yorker*) and columnists such as Art Buchwald, Russell Baker, and Arthur Hoppe continue to present humorous writing in the manner of their predecessors.

Graphic Arts

Closely allied with humor in journalism, of course, is its expression in the graphic arts, and again the history is significant (e.g., Glanz, 1973). Political cartooning in America is properly traced to our earliest popular publications (again, Franklin is often cited as the founding father) through such influential figures as Thomas Nast who is often given (too much) credit for the public outcry that unseated the notorious Tweed Ring to later artists such as Herbert Block (Herblock) and Bill Mauldin. More recently there has been a veritable renaissance of political cartooning as evidenced not only by the work of a dozen or so well-known artists (MacNelly, Wright, Conrad, Oliphant, Auth, and others) but by another few dozen less prominent, but admirable, effective workers. Social satire in cartoon form is of equal importance, from John Held, Jr. to the cartoonists of the popular magazines in the "golden age" and in the offerings of the contemporary artists in *Playboy*, *The New Yorker*, and many other current periodicals. The comic book, not primarily a vehicle for humorous graphic art, has also contributed to the genre, particularly in the underground "comix" of the late-1960s and continuing to the present.

Comic strips are also an important popular culture expression for humor, beginning with the anarchical humor of *The Yellow Kid* at the turn of the century, the abstract and surreal humor of Herriman's *Krazy Kat* and Windsor McKay's fantasies, and continuing through the domestic "little man" humor of *Mutt and Jeff, Bringing Up Father, Caspar Milquetoast, Andy Gump, Blondie*, and the score of other jaundiced representations of American family life. Again the more modern representations of the art might legitimately be termed a renaissance, going back to the 1950s for *Pogo* and *Peanuts* and forward to such contemporary examples of brilliant graphic art humor as *Doonesbury, Tank McNamara, The Wizard of Id, BC, Broom Hilda, Cathy, Bloom County*, and many more. These comic strips are deceptively simple:

upon closer examination they yield a modern social humor in a form that allows us to laugh at our cultural foibles, to identify in an often-profound way with caricatured representations of ourselves (Berger, 1973; White & Pendleton, 1977).

Public Entertainment

Another expression of humor in popular culture with a long history is the broadly defined area of popular, public entertainments. The theater, per se, is the most formal arena for public entertainment, and comedy has been central, particularly to the *popular* theater since the 18th century (Gilbert, 1940). The first truly American theatrical performance (an American company performs an American play) was a comedy, Royall Tyler's *The Contrast* (1789), in which the character Brother Jonathan represented the commonsense hero discussed above. The popular theater presented, in addition to comedies, skits, comic songs, and dances, variety entertainments, and other short acts, most of which involved humor. These early theatrical endeavors, in urban theaters and in traveling tent shows, gave rise to the minstrel theater in which the humor of the skits, variety entertainment, and primitive musical comedy was cemented by a running comedy act in which two end men—Tambo and Bones— put on blackface makeup, representing caricatures of licentious behavior attributed to blacks, and engaged in a running debate with the Interlocutor, a formally attired, stuffy caricature of the upper classes. This routine provided an opportunity to laugh *at* blacks, and at alcohol abuse, sexual promiscuity, ignorance, and other negative behavior, but a look at the scripts suggests that it also gave the audience an opportunity to laugh *with* Tambo and Bones, their laziness a protest against the hard life of the working classes, their loose morality a counterculture statement aimed at middle-class mores and the restraints on human nature imposed by them, their topical humor an opportunity to criticize "official" social, political, and cultural opinion from the perspective of a marginal member of society, one who cannot be expected to understand or obey the rules (which the audience might react to ambivalently).

Medicine shows, the circus, traveling variety shows, and other popular entertainments provided a similar opportunity for audiences to laugh at material that is, on the surface, mere comic antics and patter, but that masks a serious, if not entirely conscious, exploration of cultural complexities, changes, and concerns. The 20th century saw vaudeville, the urban variety theater (e.g., Earl Carroll's Vanities, the Ziegfeld Follies), and burlesque continuing in the same traditions, perhaps with more polish and professionalism, and the further development of popular plays, including social comedies such as those of George S. Kaufmann and his various collaborators. Nightclubs and resorts added opportunities for standup comedians, heirs to the mantles of the minstrel, vaudeville, burlesque, and lecture circuit comedians, to provide a topical and social commentary. The so-called Borscht Belt was just one of the training grounds for the comedians who would dominate the vaudeville tour in its last hours, and the mass media of film, radio, television, and recordings in their first hours.

Live performance is still a very significant aspect of humor in the popular culture. The concert tours, colleges, and theaters have been added to the club dates as the goals of successful comedians, and in addition to making it in the mass media, a young comic can aim at a career in the many new comedy clubs which have sprung up all over the country following the success of the Improvisation, the Comedy Store, the Comic Strip, and the other NY-LA meccas. Improvisational theater, circus, comedy magic acts, the legitimate theater (e.g., the comedies of Neil Simon and the continuing presence of musical comedy are all proof of the ability of humor in popular entertainments to coexist with the mass media.)

Mass Media

The mass media, however, provide the most effective source of humor in the popular culture (see Chapter 9 by Brown & Bryant). The early silent comedy films presented simple physical, sight humor that was perfect to entertain the growing urban blue-collar population, and at their peak, in the 1920s, several hundred of them were produced each year. Comic geniuses such as Buster Keaton, Harry Langdon, Harold Lloyd, and, of course, Charlie Chaplin went beyond the intricate, but shallow physical comedy in creating comic personae that exemplified the wise fool and "little man" traditions and married pathos, sensitivity, ambition, and other emotions to the aggressiveness and combativeness of the silent-film comedy genre. They portrayed lower-middle-class antiheroes, vulnerable to the confusion and complexity of modern life, alternatively covetous of and cowered by material possessions and technology, but ultimately surviving, bouncing back with optimism and enthusiasm despite the misfortunes and disasters that inevitably shadowed them. Toward the end of the silent era, a romantic comedy began to prevail, flowering in the early sound films and throughout the subsequent decade as "screwball comedy," a mixture of physical humor, anti-upper-class satire, and a basic romantic comedy plot that presented the argument that love indeed conquers all, transcending social and personal differences, initial hostility, and the conflicts and confusions of relationships to lead to the centrality of marriage and middle-class family life that the society-at-large was beginning to establish as the paramount virtue of the American dream. In the 1960s new life was injected into this paradigmatic theme as individual artists created social satires outside of the standard formulas. Stanley Kubrick, Robert Altman, Woody Allen, Mel Brooks, and many other directors and writers produced individual films that provide a more mature, sophisticated humor for an audience that has been becoming increasingly more educated, more intellectually demanding. While Hollywood has witnessed a revival of the formulaic adventure films and other nonhumor genres, the comedy film has continued to be creative thematically as well as technically.

Radio and television served, initially, as repositories of the traditions of live comedy performance, but they too developed their own distinctive genres (Wertheim, 1979). Fred Allen, Jack Benny, George Burns and Gracie Allen, and others presented ensemble companies of familiar characters in continuing roles with whom the audience could identify comfortably. Milton Berle, Jackie Gleason, and Sid Caesar, among others, carried the ensemble approach to television, merging the comedy characteristics of the popular entertainments— verbal and physical—with some of those common to film humor. But the dominant television formula soon became the situation comedy, and it remains so today. The prototypical sitcom was *I Love Lucy*, a continuing series of adventures in which the central character, played by Lucille Ball, gets into some kind of trouble, either caused by her own scatterbrained ambition or by some minor problem that her misguided activity escalates into potential disaster. The situation comedy's structure is almost never violated. The characters face a problem, take action that exacerbates rather than solves it, and are rescued, ultimately, by a fortuitous intervention or by a realization that the problem or the endeavor that has been troubling them has not been significant except in their own confrontation of it. Lucy is ultimately "rescued" from her self-made mess, forgiven by her temperamental but loyal husband, and restored to her "proper place" as a housewife, providing the overt message that the society wanted to assert during that era—that a woman's place was in the home and that "outside" ambition could only threaten her happiness, but also covertly suggesting that an energetic, enthusiastic woman would never be content in that role. Dozens of other sitcoms emerged carrying a similar structural message— not for women only—that frantic action only makes problems worse. The ideal way to face life is with a calm, restrained, rational fortitude; characters who struggle and squirm are to be laughed at, gently, for their unrealistic ambition, their cosmic conceit. Newer situation comedies, liberated by the topical shows of Norman Lear (e.g., *All in the Family, Maude, The Jeffersons*), may deal with more modern, more realistic problems, and many of them are more sexually oriented than were the early programs, but the formula survives intact, deviated from in exceptional episodes and/or exceptional shows (e.g., M*A*S*H).

Serendipitous Popular Humor

Most of the activity in the study of popular culture is devoted to expressions of the various commercial arts, such as those that we have been considering so far, but it is necessary to expand our definition and our scope to consider more spontaneous, quasi-folk manifestations, such as the various joke fads and cycles that become codified in commercial forms and such ephemera as graffitti, comical bumper stickers, T-shirts, posters, and advertising campaigns. Collectively these "texts" outweigh in quanity and perhaps in importance their more formally recorded cousins. Joke fads and cycles such as the "elephant jokes," the non sequitur "moby grape/moby pickle" jokes, "Tom Swifties," so-called "sick" jokes, "lightbulb jokes," and the various ethnic joke cycles are all folk sources that spread more ‘rapidly in the modern society because they are exploited by book publishers, professional comedians, and other popular culture enterprises. Folklorists and historians have just begun to interpret these public manifestations of humor, and the results are often fascinating (Davies, 1982; Dundes, 1971; Fine, 1981; also see Chapter 8, Volume I, by Fine). The jokes are adaptable to social issues and concerns; for example, the "lightbulb joke" genre can express the alleged characteristics of racial, ethnic, regional, professional, and other subcultures, political and other topical jokes allow people to express their feelings in an acceptable, safe form. The great wave of immigration in the late 19th and early 20th centuries, for example, gave rise to a remarkable number of ethnic jokes, precisely for the reason that America was self-defined as a great melting pot, and yet in their day-to-day lives, people were confronted not by a homogeneous mixture of *homo Americanus*, but by a lumpy and only partially assimilated coterie of Europeans who retained many habits and customs that were decidedly "not American" (Davies, 1982; Goldstein, 1981). How is one to handle such contradictions? Humor, whether of American origin or not, is at one and the same time, a means of acknowledging a problem, fear, or contradiction, and, paradoxically, a means of resolving it.

Humorous bumper stickers, T-shirt imprints, and graffitti allow for further expressions of identity, and in a modern society where alienation and estrangement are always threatening, they permit one to assert one's belief and self-perceptions to like-minded strangers and to an undefined opposition. Often the bumper stickers counter or "answer" one another, as in the case of the pro- and anti-nuclear-power arguments commonly proclaimed in a humorous dialogue on cars in the western states, or in the humorous rebuttals of serious proclamations ("I Found It"—"I Never Lost It"—"Who Needs It"—"Now Let Me Tell You What You Can Do With It"—a theological disputation).

Humorous advertising compaigns are, of course, intended to sell products by amusing the audience and thus calling attention to the brand being advertised, but their success reveals cultural predilection as readily as do the other sources of humor in the popular culture. The beer commercials, for example, that pit former professional athletes in an on-going argument over the primary merits of the product have used many of the traditional motifs—wise fools, "little men," and others—and they provide vignettes of both cultural cliches (the huge, violent "jock" as a Paul Bunyon/Mike Fink comic brawler) and new, subconscious perception (the smaller Japanese baseball player intimidating the larger American athlete into acquiescence). Analyzing the humor of the advertising campaigns alone would provide the student of American humor with enough material to occupy years of labor. But, as we have seen, lack of material for the examination of humor in popular culture is hardly a problem. Popular culture virtually blankets all modern societies, and a large proportion of it is in the humorous mode of expression. This overview merely points to some of the more prominent examples of humor in popular culture.

The theoretical and methodological concerns with which contemporary popular culture scholars wrestle are intimidating for the humor researcher as well—is popular culture a reflection of popular attitudes, or an influence generating the dispositions of the creators and distributors? How can we "decode" visions of reality that are mythic, distorted by emotional needs, commercial dictates, aesthetic considerations, technical capacities, and other interferences that obscure the motives and functions of the enterprises? How do we account for variances, contradictions, and mutually exclusive parallel trends and tendencies when we try to draw broad cultural conclusions from so enormous and varied a body of material? What is universal, both cross-culturally and historically, and what is bound to particularities of time and place, and how are the two related to basic humor theory? Such questions are not easily, or perhaps even ultimately, answerable, but we cannot permit them to interfere with the specific, individual studies that advance both our knowledge of the matter at hand and the state of the art of popular-culture and humor analysis. The importance of both humor and popular culture is obviously too central to any sensible investigation of personality, culture, and society.

REFERENCES

Berger, A. A. *The comic-stripped American*. New York: Walker, 1973.

Bier, J. *The rise and fall of American humor*. New York: Holt, Rinehart & Winston, 1968.

Bigsby, C. W. E. *Approaches to popular culture*. Bowling Green, Ohio: Popular Press, 1977.

Blair, W., & Hill, H. *America's humor: From Poor Richard to Doonesbury*. New York: Oxford University Press, 1978.

Bouissac, P. *Circus and culture: A semiotic approach*. Bloomington, Ind.: Indiana University Press, 1976.

Browne, R. B. *Rituals and ceremonies in popular culture*. Bowling Green, Ohio: Popular Press, 1980.

Chaney, D. *Fictions and ceremonies: Representations of popular experience*. New York: St. Martin's 1979.

Charney, M. *Comedy high and low*. New York: Oxford University Press, 1977.

Davies, C. Ethnic jokes, moral values, and social boundaries. *British Journal of Sociology*, 1982, *33*, 383-403.

Davison, P., Meyersohn, R., & Shils, E. *Literary taste, culture and mass communication* (14 vol.). Teaneck, N.J.: Somerset House, 1978.

Dundes, A. A study of ethnic slurs. *Journal of American Folklore* 1971, *84*, 51-61.

Dunlop, D. Popular culture and methodology. *Journal of Popular Culture*, 1975, *9*, 375-383.

Fine, G. A. Popular culture and social interaction: Production, consumption, and usage. *Journal of Popular Culture*, 1977, *11*, 453-466.

Fine, G. A. Rude words: Insults and narration in preadolescent obscene talk. *Maledicta*, 1981, 5, 51-68.

Gans, H. *Popular culture and high culture: An analysis and evaluation of taste.* New York: Basic Books, 1974.

Gilbert, D. *American vaudeville.* New York: Whittlesey House, 1940.

Gillespie, D. F. Sociology of popular culture: The other side of a definition. *Journal of Popular Culture*, 1972, *6*, 292-300.

Glanz, R. *The Jew in early American wit and graphic humor.* New York: KTAV, 1973.

Goldstein, J. H. American humor. Paper presented at The Free Library of Philadelphia, November, 1981.

Inge, M. T. *Handbook of popular culture* (3 vols.). Westport, Ct.: Greenwood Press, 1978, 1980, 1981.

Kando, T. M. *Leisure and popular culture in transition.* St. Louis: C. V. Mosby, 1980.

Landrum, L. Proteus at bay: Methodology and popular culture. *Journal of Popular Culture*, 1975, *4*, 497-608.

Mintz, L. E. Recent trends in popular culture studies. In R. Walker (Ed.), *American studies.* Westport, Ct.: Greenwood Press, in press.

Rubin, L., Jr. *The Comic Imagination in American Literature.* New Brunswick, N.J.: Rutgers University Press, 1973.

Schutz, C. E. *Political humor.* Canbury, N.J.: Associated University Presses, 1977.

Wertheim, A. F. *Radio comedy.* New York: Oxford University Press, 1979.

White, D. M., & Pendleton, J. *Popular culture: Mirror of American life.* Del Mar, Cal.: Publishers, Inc., 1977.

Zinsser, W. K. *Pop goes America.* New York: Harper & Row, 1966.

Chapter 9

Humor in the Mass Media

DAN BROWN and JENNINGS BRYANT

Humor is ubiquitous in contemporary mass media fare. In the present chapter we examine reasons why humor is such a pervasive phenomenon, strategies for its use, the ways it is employed in different media, the social content of humor, and the effects of its use on enjoyment, persuasion, learning, and antisocial behavior. The present chapter does not purport to explain *why* humor is enjoyed since our focus is somewhat more "applied" than "basic." Moreover, it should be noted that attempts to explain the appeal of humor greatly predate the mass media and span more than two millenia, from Plato (c. 355 B.C., 1871) to the present (e.g., Goldstein & McGhee, 1972; Zillmann & Bryant, 1980).

RATIONALES FOR HUMOR USE

The most obvious reason for employing humor in the American mass media is that humor does what our media messages are supposed to do: attracts a large audience (which, in turn, brings fame and fortune to the message designers, producers, and distributors). As will be discussed in more detail later, during an average week, there will be more than 500 billion viewings of televised comedy; a "hot" comedy movie can earn more than $100 million in a single year; and veritable multitudes of "mass consumers" regularly read newspaper comics or humor magazines, are drawn to friendly banter between local newscasters, and watch with rapture and amusement the latest witty commercial or advertisement. The average American laughs 15 times per day (Feinsilber & Mead, 1980); a great deal of this mirth is elicited "in unison" by messages from our mass media.

Of course, there are other rationales for employing humor in the mass media. Humor is employed in children's educational television to maintain interest in and attention to the educational messages; humor in entertainment programs may serve to divert attentions from the problems of the day, or humor may provide the consumer with relief from frustration or boredom. But all of these rationales seem secondary or subsidiary to the "drawing power" of humor.

The Practitioners

Most writers and producers of mass media humor, and most comedians whose material is presented regularly via the mass media, appear to be too busy creating and performing humor to systematically analyze their strategies of humor use. Or perhaps they feel that humor is such an art form that to subject it to systematic or scientific scrutiny would be anathema. Or maybe they do not want to reveal trade secrets. Occasionally, however, practitioners do examine their art critically. One contemporary example of this is a humorous article by Yanok and Yanok (1977), entitled "What's Funny?," that examines the mechanics of comedy. After discussing some of the tricks of the trade, the authors conclude that the mass media, especially electronic media, have changed the very nature of professional humor:

> E very soul among us is tied to every other by electronic circuitry. A joke used to take weeks to travel coast to coast. Now a funny line on television is heard simultaneously by one of every four people in the country. In twenty-four hours it's an old joke. (p. 37)

Many writers and producers of contemporary mass media humor seem to find that the key element in successful comedy is *reality*. According to Norman Lear, producer of *All in the Family* and its television legacy, "If you want to make people laugh, hit them where they breathe and where they live. It's much easier to get an audience to laugh after they care a lot" (Wilde, 1976, p. 197). Lear believes that his programs succeed in capturing large audiences because the humor exploits the reality of living.

Carl Reiner, another successful producer of television programs and films, sees the best jokes as developing from natural conversation when there is an unexpected turn from the reality of situations. Reiner cites the success of comedians such as Groucho Marx who derived humor from the truth of living, as in telling a woman, "Lady, you're fat," or "You're standing on my foot." Reiner does not, however, rely on a formula of humor, believing that an intuitive approach is needed (Wilde, 1976).

In spite of his considerable success in print media, Art Buchwald has argued that humor is easier when presented audiovisually. He observes that the humor in media forms in which characters are seen and heard permits a closer audience member identification with the characters than is possible in print media, where the lines of type appear more impersonal. Buchwald believes that the first step in writing humorous newspaper pieces is winning the confidence of the reader, a difficult task in a column of limited space. For Buchwald, the use of dialogue about topics familiar to the readers works best, but he finds predicting what readers will find funny almost impossible (Wilde, 1976).

Neil Simon, the playwright, differs from Reiner and Buchwald. He describes his most popular style as bringing together people of opposing tendencies in unreal situations. The resulting conflict produces situations that are funny in spite of the fact they would be intolerable in real life (Wilde, 1976).

The Scholars

While most contemporary humor practitioners tend to view their technique as successful because they make the humorous content as real as possible, many humor scholars apparently have a different view. Mendelsohn (1966, p. 108) wrote that "most students of humor and laughter are in agreement that the pleasures we derive from the comic represent a shedding of the 'grim reality' and a temporary 'healthy' recourse to the playfulness of childhood." Piddington (1963) saw laughter accompanying play as fulfilling an "expressive" function and a "communicative" function. Mendelsohn found both functions applicable to humor in the mass media, with the first function being the expression of pleasure to others in a habitual way (beginning in infancy) and the second function representing communication of pleasure to other people in an effort to promote a nonserious frame of mind. In other words, the communicative function would apply to the message, while the expressive function pertains to the receiver. The humorous activity was seen by Mendelsohn, not as a category of behavior, but as a mode of expression. He cited Freud's (1938) assertion that being "in the mood for laughing" provides a condition favorable for pleasure. Mendelsohn contended that the communicator of humor through the mass media "cues" the audience members (communicative function) to maximize the opportunity for the audience members to experience pleasure by regressing to a temporary state of childish playfulness.

Mendelsohn also noted the power of humor to assist in the overcoming of difficulty, as with anxiety, fear, guilt, or embarrassment. Freud distinguished between the "wit" and the "comic," with the former being unconscious and psychological in nature and the latter being ordinarily the product of the environment or social circumstances. In media, the comic can be produced through a variety of techniques, including imitation, caricature, parody, travesty, exaggeration, and many other devices. Mendelsohn saw the pleasure derived from humor as the result of "humoristic displacement, a process whereby we are able to recognize the funny or ludicrous aspects of situations in which normally we might manifest a strong emotion such as anger, sympathy, pain, or pity" (p. 116). Humor in the mass media, he believed, provides the means of expression, in socially acceptable ways, the pleasures of carefree childhood.

Some of the most systematic scholarly attempts to establish strategies for humor use in mass communication have come from those attempting to teach and inspire future generations of humor practitioners. One excellent pedagogical attempt is a chapter entitled "Comedy" in Willis's *Writing Television and Radio Programs* (1967). After delineating the difficulties of trying to write humor and reviewing classic attempts to explain the motivations for laughter, Willis explicates strategies for using three basic elements of humor: triumph (see Chapter 5 by Zillmann in Volume I on disparagement humor), incongruity (see Chapter 3 by Suls in Volume I on cognitive humor), and surprise (see Suls chapter). It is impossible to effectively summarize the richness of strategy found in Willis's chapter; however, a hint can be seen in the questions students are implored to employ for self-evaluation of material written according to the strategies presented:

[1] Does the comedy material manifest one or more of the elements that constitute the roots of all laughter? (p. 298)
[2] Is the material arranged in a way that will secure the maximum possible effect? (p. 299)
[3] Have you presented the material with the maximum economy? (p. 301)
[4] Do your jokes spring from the situation as if there were an inevitability about them, as if they were happening in spite of themselves, so to speak? (p. 301)
[5] Is your material completely clear? (p. 301)
[6] Can your audience see what you mean instantly? (p. 301)
[7] Is your comedy writing appropriate to the situation? (p. 302)

Whether mass media humor operates through bringing content close to the reality perceived by receivers of messages, through aiding in the inducement of pleasure by reminding audience members of pleasant experiences, or through a variety of other strategies, the belief appears to be common that humor facilitates the causes of mass communication. The presence of humor in entertainment programming, advertising content, news presentations, editorial messages, and educational communications signifies the confidence in humor of communicators using the mass media.

The Appeal of Humor and Patterns of Humor Use

The audience appeal of comedy and other forms of humor has received a relatively sparse amount of basic research, although considerable applied television audience research is available in the form of "ratings."

Norback and Norback (1980) have utilized ratings to record the drawing power of television comedy through the years. In the 1950-1951 season, three of the top ten programs on television were comedies occupying positions one, three, and five in popularity. The 1960s evidenced a trend toward situation comedies with rural settings and characters. Examples include *Andy Griffith*,

Gomer Pyle, Green Acres, Petticoat Junction, and Mayberry RFD. The most successful of these programs, *The Beverly Hillbillies*, produced 9 of the top 50 programs of all time (Norback & Norback, 1980). In the 1970s, the networks began dropping many of these comedies in favor of dramatic fare targeted to younger audiences. In the 1970-1971 season, comedy shows occupied positions two and three in the top ten most popular programs, but the other eight positions were filled by dramatic offerings. By the 1973-1974 season, comedy had begun a resurgence, capturing six of the top ten spots. In 1978-1979, comedy shows filled nine of the top ten positions on television.

Since that year the appeal of comedy has waned. A. C. Neilsen figures for the week ending May 1, 1983 placed five comedy programs in the top ten, but five more occupied places in the second ten most popular shows.

Cantor (1977) found that humor penetrates virtually all television programming, including news, sports, soap operas, and religious programs. Approximately 15–20% of television commercials contain humor (Cantor, 1976; Kelly & Solomon, 1975). Zillmann (1977) reported that in 1975 about 15% of all television prime-time programs were comedies, and these shows accounted for about 17% of the audience. The average half-hour comedy was viewed by about 19 million people, and a week of comedies was seen by 551 million people.

Zillmann (1977) reported the results of a content analysis of prime-time commercial network television directed to the amount of joke-work involved in humorous incidents. "Blunt" humor was defined as being immediately apparent (e.g., pie in the face, direct insult). "Refined" humor dealt in subtleties involving such elements as incongruity, novelty, surprise, ambiguity, polysemy, and so forth. When a week of all prime-time comedy was analyzed, 58% of all funny incidents were classified as blunt humor, and when comedy-variety shows only (excluding situation comedies) were considered, 62% of the humor was of the blunt variety. Zillmann concluded a lack of emphasis in prime-time humor in cognitive capabilities and skills.

With humor so prevalent in television fare, the question arises as to the proportion of humor in the daily lives of people that emanates from the mass media. Graeven and Morris (1975) compared college humor in 1930 and 1972, using data from Kambouropoulou's (1930) study involving 100 students who recorded incidents in a 7-day humor diary. Graeven and Morris asked 42 students to record all incidents involving humor and laughter within one entire day. No large differences were observed between the two time periods. Humor from mass media sources occurred with about the same frequency as telling of events, and these two categories ranked above memorized jokes and below spontaneous interpersonal humor in frequency.

The Audience Research Department of the Independent Broadcasting Authority (IBA) in Great Britain attempted to define and study the reasons why television comedy shows were rated as successful or not by viewers (IBA Audience Research Department, 1976). Among two IBA shows receiving mostly favorable comments from viewers, the frequently cited characteristics were the high quality of the script writing, performance of leading character, original idea, characterization, acting, suitability for family viewing, "realistic" and "natural" tone, the basic situation, the quality of individual plots. Negative comments on the programs receiving mostly favorable treatment included the criticism of glamorizing prison life and criminals, unrealistic situations, slow pace, and unnecessary sexual references. A program receiving predominantly negative comments was cited for poor acting, overacting, and poor script writing. This program received approving comments on its all black cast, its racial treatment, and the suggestion that it might improve race relations.

The mention of humor in television almost certainly evokes images of situation comedies, variety programs, or talk shows, but humor has played a prominent role in educational television as well. Bryant, Hezel, and Zillmann (1979) analyzed how humor was used in *Mister Rogers Neighborhood*, *Captain Kangaroo*, *Sesame Street*, and *The Electric Company*. Program elements were classified as humorous when the implied intention was to be funny, and distinctions were made between visual and auditory humor. Further classification divided humor into categories of tendentious, nonsense, or prosocial humor and determined the relationship of humor to the educational point. The sampled material revealed the following proportions of visual humor: *The Electric Company*, 38%; *Sesame Street*, 33%; *Captain Kangaroo*, 18%; and *Mister Rogers Neighborhood*, less than 3%. Auditory humor was found in these proportions: *The Electric Company*, 29%; *Sesame Street*, 25%; *Captain Kangaroo*, 15%; and *Mister Rogers Neighborhood*, 4%. Humor tended to accompany the educational message in *The Electric Company* and *Sesame Street* but not in the other two programs. Considering all the programs together, the incidence of humor was frequent, with each 29-minute-and-45-second program segment using on the average 51 incidents of visual humor and 39 incidents of auditory humor. Of these incidents, 23 were tendentious and 67 were nontendentious. However, no incidents of tendentious humor occurred on *Mister Rogers Neighborhood*. Most of the tendentious humor (86%) and the nonsense humor (85%) was rated as being somewhat related to the educational point. Humor directly related to the point comprised only 7% of the tendentious humor and 5% of the nonsense humor, and humor that was rated as totally unrelated to the educational point amounted to 7% of the tendentious humor and 8% of the nonsense humor.

Huston, Wright, Wartella, Rice, Watkins, Campbell, and Potts (1981) examined the format features of television programming directed to children, concluding that animated programs tend to contain certain features when the programs are humorous (visual tricks, visual change, and music and noise), while other features (higher rate of visual change and somewhat more rapid tempo) tend to be found in serious animated programs. Live presentations used moderate action, singing, and long zoom shots with the cameras frequently, but very few formal features were found to be specific to either humorous or serious programs. Nonhuman dialogue tended to be found with both humor and animation, while human dialogue (both child and adult) was associated with live, serious productions. Singing was associated with live, humorous programs. Saturday morning programming relied heavily on perceptually salient and visual/auditory attention grabbing features (rapid action, rapid tempo, variability, music, noise), while features providing linguistic information (dialogue) or emphasizing carefully organized formats that were reflective in nature tended to be avoided. Commercial programs designed for children tend to be heavily animated and rely extensively on humor, especially nonverbal humor. Hayes and Birnbaum (1980) reported that children pay greater attention to visual than to auditory parts of television cartoons.

Other than these few studies on television humor, normative data on humor use in the mass media are missing. Conspicuously absent are systematic examinations of the way humor is used in newspapers, magazines, or motion pictures.

The Context and Social Content of Mass Media Humor

In marked contrast to the paucity of investigations into patterns of humor use, numerous investigations of the social content of mass-media humor have been conducted, as have critical reviews of the historical developments of media forms.

Newspaper Cartoons and Comic Strips

Cartoons, manifestations of much humor in modern media, have been drawn for centuries. Johnson (1937) described the discovery of the oldest existing caricature in Egypt dating back to 1360 B.C. Early cartoons often featured exaggerations of personal characteristics. But a trend away from personal caricature occurred during the middle of the 19th century, and modern cartoons are often subtle and intellectually oriented.

Modern newspapers have sometimes prominently featured political cartoons. Front page cartoons appeared in 90% of the issues of the Chicago *Tribune* between 1951 and 1959 (Rothman & Olmstead, 1966).

Political cartoons over a 100-year period were studied by Meyer, Seidler, Curry, and Aveni (1980) to examine the roles of women depicted in major newspapers' July Fourth editions. In early years (1890–1930s), female figures represented abstractions of liberty and independence, but in later years (1950s–1970s) more diversity occurred, with the number of cartoons dealing with women in contemporary situations declining. The researchers found evidence in the cartoons of "resistance to changing old norms and difficulty in coping with emerging ones" (Meyer et al., 1980, p. 28).

From the single cartoon grew the sequence of panels known as the comic strip. Richard Outcalt's *The Yellow Kid* was an immediate success in 1895 and became a featured item of the newspaper, especially in the Sunday color comics. Early comic strips (e.g., *The Katzenjammer Kids*, *Krazy Kat*, and *Buster Brown*) were full of anarchy, violent acts, disruption of social patterns, and resistance to authority. Speigelman, Terwilliger, and Fearing (1947) found affluent comic strip characters possessing noble goals such as aiding fellow humans and working for the good of the community. Disadvantaged characters, however, were seen as having shortsighted goals, especially emphasizing gaining money, and using frequently violent means to obtain goals. Ryan (1936) was even less favorable, reporting the content of comic strips to consist of sadism, cannabalism, bestiality, eroticism, violence, melodrama, tales of crime and criminals, and other negative elements.

Barcus (1961) studied the cartoons of three Boston Sunday newspaper comic strips from 1900 to 1959 and noted a trend toward "the development of continuity, the increase in action and adventure types, as well as the accompanying themes of love and romance, crime and adventure, and attention to interpersonal relations" (p. 179). While Barcus found the comics not necessarily representative of American life, the strips did reflect some of the needs, fears, and values of the culture.

Saenger (1955) content analyzed the nine leading newspapers in New York City with respect to their comic strips in 1950. He classified the strips as domestic, adventure, or comedy and found the characters in comedies more concerned with the seeking of leisure than the pursuit of success. The three categories appeared with similar frequencies in the sample. Several trends in roles were found in the comics. The rank of power in the comic strip family as rated by foreign observers was: (1) child, (2) mother, and (3) father. This relationship was often reflected in humorous or satirical treatment. Single men and married women were rated as the most aggressive characters, and marked "premarital" and "postmarital" personalities were symbolically expressed, with men being weaker and shorter after marriage. While the typical adventure comic strip man was a fighter, the typical males in domestic and comedy strips were bumblers who lacked persistence.

Comic Books

Closely related to comic strips but different in style and readership were the comic books, which first appeared in 1934 as a color magazine from Delacorte Publishers. Original stories and characters were featured in *Detective Comics*, published by National Publications in 1937, and comic books carried on the tradition of the pulp magazines of the 1920s and 1930s. Early comic books "relied on vivid, flashily rendered covers, depicted torture, half clad women, ugly gangsters, guns, etc. to broaden their audience and boost their sales (Cahill, Note 1). Thorndike (1941) content analyzed the words of four complete DC/ National comic books (*Superman*, *Batman*, *Action*, and *Detective Comics*), classifying standard words, words of recent currency, homemade compounds, contradictions, proper names, and respectable or vulgar slang. He found that each book contained about 10,000 words. About 1,000 different words that did not fall into the most common 1,000 words of Thorndike's list appeared in each book, and the four books together contained about 3,000 words not on the list. While the books did contain many slang words, the bulk of the vocabulary consisted of standard English words, and the reading level was estimated to approximate that of the fifth or sixth grade.

Following the end of World War II, comic books turned to heavy emphasis on crime-related content to contend with the sagging sales that followed the war. Comic books featuring crime and horror stories came under the scrutiny of the U. S. Senate Subcommittee to Investigate Juvenile Delinquency during May and June of 1954. In October of that year, the Comics Magazine Association of America adopted a code of regulations that was especially stringent on crime and horror comics. Sales suffered until Stan Lee at Marvel Comics introduced Spiderman and the Fantastic Four in 1962, and a period began in which the comic heroes dealt with the problems of real people.

Magazine Cartoons

Along with comic strips and comic books, cartoons have been popular features of a variety of magazines otherwise emphasizing photographs and/or the printed word. Anderson and Jolly (1977) performed trend analysis on 430 cartoon people in 195 cartoons appearing in the *Saturday Evening Post*, *Saturday Review*, and *Playboy* magazines. From each magazine, 15 cartoons from each of the following years were sampled randomly: 1952, 1957, 1962, 1967, and 1972. Since *Playboy* was not in publication in 1952 and the *Saturday Evening Post* was no longer published in 1972, cartoons from those magazines in those years were not available. The authors reported their findings of five dominant stereotypes: seductive female, sensually assertive male, disconsolate man, incompetent woman, and angry woman. Occurrence of the angry woman interpersonal putdowns were reported as having declined over the last 20 years covered by the study. Anderson and Jolly interpreted their findings as indicative of popular humor as a valid social indicator that provides information beyond the range of demographic statistics and opinion surveys.

Greenberg and Kahn (1970) reported on the treatment of black characters in *Playboy*, "this country's chief humor magazine" (p. 557), in all issues of 1956, 1958, 1960, 1964, 1968, and the first seven months of 1969. The researchers found very few black characters in the cartoons until 1967, and only 4% of the cartoons in the later issues contained black characters. However, the authors wondered whether any other medium could match that figure. The basis for the humor in nearly half of the cartoons depicting contemporary black characters tended toward racially motivated humor, and the proportion was closer to 75% during the last two years studied. Prior years had a small emphasis on racial humor "because blacks were presented in background roles, e.g., servant or waiter, and had no role in the humor situation" (p. 559). Only one third of the black cartoon characters appeared in a sex-related cartoon, and cartoons with black characters were less likely than those with white characters to appear in a middle-class setting. Contemporary black characters "reflected distinctly black patterns in their dress or appearance, e.g., Afros, dashikis, etc." in increasingly larger proportions of the cartoons as time passed: 1956-1966 = 0; 1967 = 7%; 1968 = 32%; and 1969 = 41%.

Cantor and Richardson (Note 2) drew samples of cartoons from *Playboy*, *Cosmopolitan*, *Esquire* and *Ladies Home Journal*. They found, as did the earlier research, cartoons depicting only females to be the most rare. However, the presence of both males and females occurred more frequently in this sample than in earlier ones, making the occurrence of males and females not significantly different from each other. Males disparaged other cartoon characters in humor more often than did females, but the difference was not significant; such was true of males as victims of humor as well. No difference was found in the frequency with which males victimized females in humor and the frequency with which females disparaged males. Considering the four magazines separately, no differences were found between the proportion of male/female to female/male disparagement in magazines targeted to men and those aimed for women. When all cartoons and all magazines were included, males were victims of ridicule significantly more often than females. However, when only cartoons depicting both males and females are considered, the difference was not significant. The same pattern existed in the four magazines considered separately.

Cantor and Venus (Note 3) studied the cartoons from *Look* and *The New Yorker*, popular national magazines, and found male characters appearing in 283 cartoons while females appeared in only 136 cartoons. Males appeared without females in 154 cartoons, while females appeared without males in only seven. The characters were classified according to whether they exhibited stupidity, and males displayed the trait more often than females. However, in cartoons in which both males and females appeared, females more often displayed stupidity. Males were classified more often than females as disagreeable or submissive. Equivalent numbers of cartoons depicted people of each gender as being disagreeable or submissive when people of the opposite gender also appeared in the cartoon. Attractiveness was equally apportioned to males and females for all cartoons, but when people of both genders appeared together, a slightly greater but nonsignificant tendency of females to be unattractive was observed. More males than females were the butt of the cartoon humor overall. But females were insignificantly more often the object of the humor when people of both genders were depicted. Males were found to receive more cartoon ridicule than females, but the difference apparently can be attributed to the more frequent appearance of males in cartoon humor. When people of both genders appeared together, the difference tended to be equalized.

Smith (1979) also studied magazine cartoons, but he focused on the portrayal of elders in eight popular national publications after 1970, analyzing 2,217 cartoons. He found that elders appeared infrequently in the cartoons (4.3%), especially in women's magazines, and recurring negative themes such as sexual dysfunction and ultraconservatism were associated with elderly characters. Positive portrayals of elders were often represented as departures from "normal" behavior. The themes were considered as negative when the elderly character was the object of the joke or when the shortcomings of the character provided the basis for the humor. The author concluded that the elderly, while not generally depicted in cartoons favorably, were depicted less often in cartoons than in jokes.

Malamuth and Spinner (1980) studied the pictures and cartoons appearing in all issues of *Playboy* and *Penthouse* magazines from January 1973 through December 1977. The focus of the study was sexual violence and was hampered by differences in rater judgments that were not expected. The authors called for future research to develop reliable categories for rating sexual violence within cartoons, but they did note the findings on which their raters agreed. *Penthouse* displayed a linear trend of increase in sexual violence over the 5-year period with respect to the absolute number of incidents of such violence in cartoons. However, the increase was not linear if a measure of proportion of cartoons depicting sexual violence was used. The proportion of cartoons containing sexual violence over the period was greater in *Penthouse* than in *Playboy*. The overall proportion was about 10% of all cartoons having sexually violent content.

Jokes

Palmore (1971) content analyzed 265 jokes from a joke anthology and other jokes and found that stereotypes with respect to elderly people in the jokes predominated, emphasizing declining mental and physical abilities, especially for women. Richman (1977) selected jokes at random from three jokebooks and found similar negative images projected with respect to elders but not for children who were the objects of the humor in the jokes. Davies (1977) content analyzed six books purchased from stores along a Toronto street and agreed with the other two researchers about the presence of negative images of elders. He contended that humor may serve as an effective transmitter of false stereotypes about elderly people. Weber and Cameron (1978) challenged the reliability of all of these studies and cautioned against making premature policy statements designed to promote social change until more research could be performed and evaluated.

Sexism

The treatment of the elderly by television has been studied by Harris and Feinberg (1977), who found that the frequency of presentation of the elderly resembled their actual proportion in the population. People over 60 were present in these proportions: 7% of game show participants, 6% of drama and soap opera characters, 9.5% of comedy show characters, and 10% of news and talk show characters and children's program characters. The characters were found to be generally one dimensional, inadequately developed, and usually not included in love relationships. Women were seen in especially low esteem with increasing age.

In a study of the roles and statuses of women on children and family television programs shown in the late afternoon, early evenings, or on Saturday mornings, Long and Simon (1974) found differences in the treatment of women and men. Men were often portrayed as influential or as leaders in professional positions. Men were generally seen as capable, except in comedy programs, where they were portrayed as "stupid and bungling." Women were seen in less diverse roles, occupying less varied statuses, and having less complex personalities than men. The women tended to appear as wives and mothers or in comic roles, an assessment also made by Tedesco (1974). Comedy shows commonly used the "put down" device in provoking audience laughter directed both at and with the female characters. The authors concluded that the general image of women in these programs (produced in 1971-1973) was one of "tradition and sexism."

Ellis (1977) viewed women in situation comedies as exhibiting evidence of change in society while the men were not. She believed this situation to have existed through the years but noted that the "classic way of containing this disturbing social reality" has been to depict the changing social pattern within comedy. To have the changes occur outside comedy would, in Ellis' opinion, threaten the patriarchy operative in society.

The Mary Tyler Moore Show, which premiered in 1970, triggered a trend of comedies featuring women. The lead character, unlike most female characters on television was single and was depicted as a professional woman whose primary interest was not marriage. Most single female television characters were depicted as unmarried by some reason other than divorce, such as in *Here's Lucy* and *Julia*, where the characters were depicted as widows. Later programs such as *Rhoda*, *Fay*, and *One Day at a Time* began to deal extensively with the problems of women living alone.

Streicher (1974) found traditional and sexist patterns for males and females in cartoons appearing on Saturday morning television. She noted the finding by Streicher and Bonney (1974) that young girls mention situation comedies as their favorite programs, while young boys name cartoons as their top choices, and Streicher speculated that girls may not be so pleased with cartoons because so few female characters appear in them.

Stocking, Sapolsky, and Zillmann (1977) sought to determine whether females were more often than males the butt of humor in prime-time television. The authors concluded that in a 1-week sample drawn in November 1975, males were more often victimized in hostile humor than were females, and males also more often delivered the humor. Males were found to be ridiculed as frequently by females as females were ridiculed by males. More than two-thirds of the humor (69%) was hostile, and most of the humorous incidents occurred within the family viewing hour.

Racism

Reid (1979) compared the behavior of black and white television characters in a sample of comedy shows aired in the spring of 1977, including four black-oriented programs, three white-oriented programs, and three mixed programs. Of the 110 characters identified, 40% were black, "the proportion of white females to white males was low (1:2), and the proportion of black female characters to black males was greater (1:1)" (Reid, 1979, p. 467). In a two-way analysis of variance of the factors of race by sex, significant differences by race were found for achievement-sex interaction, sex effects in dominance and nurturance, and race effects in recognition. When the characters were rated on achievement, black females scored lowest, black men highest, and white women second highest. On dominance, males were rated higher than females. On recognition ("self-forwarding attitude and calling attention to one's own achievements"), blacks were rated higher than whites. On nurturance, females were rated higher than males. No significant differences were found based on race or sex for measures of activity, deference, harm avoidance, succorance, aggression, autonomy, or self-recognition. Black versus white male characters were not found to behave differently in any of the categories, but significant differences as measured by t-tests were reported between black and white females on succorance and recognition. In summarizing his findings for the behavior of white characters on black-oriented shows, Reid concluded that "the data as a whole clearly indicate a pattern in which whites on black programs are depicted as generally unpleasant and possessing undesirable characteristics" (p. 470), more aggressive and active, lower in autonomy, nurturance, and succorance.

Hinton, Seggar, Northcoot, and Fontes (1974) noted that in 1965, five consecutive hours of monitoring the three major networks revealed the appearance of only three blacks, two of whom remained on for less than three minutes. By 1967, blacks appeared frequently, reported the authors, and blacks became even more prominent by 1973. Hinton et al. collected a random sample including 133 programs of drama and comedy from the network shows aired for six consecutive weeks in February and March 1973 between the hours of 5:00 p.m. and 11:00 p.m. Data were collected on every ninth white character and all black characters. The sample included 168 whites and 149 blacks, representing a "real ratio" of 10:1 whites to blacks. By network, ABC and CBS portrayed whites and blacks in a 12:1 ratio, while the ratio on NBC was 5:1. A half-hour comedy program (*Sanford and Son*) was the only network program with a primarily black cast. The authors concluded support for charges that a policy of tokenism was operating at the networks, but the charges that the networks were portraying blacks as possessing consistently negative stereotypical traits were not supported. Black characters were found to be portrayed as industrious, competent, and law abiding, although blacks were usually relegated to insignificant roles in the programs.

A report by the U. S. Commission on Civil Rights (1977) noted a trend in realism in television situation comedy spurred by Norman Lear, who treats controversial issues and contemporary social and personal problems realistically in his humorous productions. These comedies were quite different from their counterparts of the 1950s (e.g., *Make Room for Daddy, Leave It to Beaver, Ozzie and Harriet*) where white, middle-class suburban families were depicted in situations where the parents solved all problems flawlessly and no serious problems existed. Lear's programs (e.g., *All in the Family, Maude, Good Times, The Jeffersons*) addressed real life problems (menopause, cancer, aging, death, racism, etc.). Critical response to the programs was widely varied, ranging from rave reviews to indictments, and programs such as "All in the Family" became the objects of frequent analysis (cf. Brigham & Giesbrecht, 1976; Chapko & Lewis, 1975; Meyer, 1976; Slawson, 1972; Stein, 1974; Surlin, 1974; Surlin & Tate, 1976; Tate & Surlin, 1976; Vidmar & Rokeach, 1974; Wilhoit & De Bock, 1976). Televison bigots such as Archie Bunker and Fred Sanford provided opportunities for treatment of racial issues, but many black people charged that television blacks were depicted as dumb and that black-oriented television comedies were written to appeal to whites.

During the 1974 season, the National Black Feminist Organization listed several objections to the portrayal of blacks on television, including a lack of positive images to counter the ridiculous ones of comedy shows. In the 1975-1976 season, several situation comedies emerged in which ethnic characters provided the basis for the humor. Unlike Lear's programs, which explored realistic issues, many of these shows (e.g., *Chico and the Man, Welcome Back, Kotter, On the Rocks*) relied on ethnic stereotypes for comedy. These ethnic shows and others (e.g., *Barney Biller, Joe and Sons, Popi*) largely excluded female characters except in secondary roles.

Advertising

Unlike the proliferation of attention given to the social content of television program humor, especially the humor in situation comedies, humor in advertising has not been so thoroughly studied. Much of the work relevant to humor in advertising has arisen from concern with treatment of women and minorities by advertisers. The National Advertising Review Board (1975) reported on advertising portraying or directed to women, noting that the depiction of stupidity in both males and females is a standard comedic device often used in advertising. Many advertisers have fallen into the trap of attempting to be funny but succeeding only in offending members of the public.

The report found that women are frequently portrayed as stupid or too dumb to handle routine tasks without advice from children, men, or male voices from nowhere. The advertising industry in the sixties and seventies, while under attack from minority groups and women for racist and sexist stereotyping abandoned many stereotyped caricatures, such as Frito Bandito. These images were often replaced by portrayals of the white middle-class.

EFFECTS OF HUMOR USE

This section treats the effects of humor as it pertains to interest, appeal, or entertainment, to persuasion, and to recall or learning. A brief look at the side effects of humor use is also included.

Entertainment

One area in which substantial basic research on mass media humor has been conducted is in entertainment. Zillmann and Cantor (1976) in presenting a disposition theory of humor and mirth, posited that the degree of enjoyment derived from the witnessing of the disparagement of some person/object is a function of the degree of hostility felt toward that person/object. That is, a negative disposition toward other people is a prerequisite to the enjoyment of seeing those people suffer misfortunes, and a strong sentiment is necessary for the elicitation of reactions of great joy. Substantial evidence has been obtained to support their theory (e.g., Zillmann & Cantor, 1972; Cantor & Zillmann, 1973; Chapman, Smith, & Foot, 1977).

Bryant (1977) examined the effect of degree of hostility in written jokes. He concluded that in fair exchanges of hostile behavior between the characters, when the reader holds no strong predisposition toward either character, moderate hostility in both provocation and retaliation defines the optimum condition for mirth. Extremely minimal hostility in the interchanges or intensely hostile exchanges apparently impair appreciation of the humor in the jokes. Zillmann and Bryant (1974) also found that for printed jokes and cartoons, retaliation equivalent to the degree of provocation is necessary for the optimum humor appreciation, whereas over- or under-retaliation by the disparaged protagonist results in impaired humor appreciation.

In addition to disposition toward humor protagonists and considerations of propriety and equity, affective state and level of arousal of the reader relate to the enjoyment of printed humor. Cantor, Bryant, and Zillmann (1974) exposed college students to a collection of cartoons, jokes, and written excerpts that the students were asked to rate on various measures of humor and appeal. The written excerpts were used to effect a factorial variation in hedonic tone (positive or negative) and excitatory potential (low or high). When the students were exposed to highly arousing communications, subsequently seen cartoons and jokes received higher ratings of funniness than were received after exposure to the lesser arousing stimuli. These findings held for both positive and negative hedonic valence.

An alternative means of manipulating level of arousal in receivers of humorous messages is by controlling for sexual content in the messages. Burns and Tyler (1976) displayed 60 cartoons selected from *Playboy* magazine, 20 having sexual content and 40 having nonsexual content, to college students, who were asked to rate the degree of humor in the cartoons. The cartoons were stacked into two slide projectors, from which the subjects were allowed to randomly select slides for viewing. The cartoons were prejudged for humor and arranged so that each projector was equated for humor. The subjects were divided by gender and scores on the revised Byrne, Barry and Nelson Repression-Sensitization Scale and the Marlowe-Crowne Social Desirability Scale. These divisions produced people classified as sensitizers and repressors. Subjects scoring in the upper half of the Marlowe-Crowne distribution were designated as defensive repressors, and subjects whose scores fell in the lower half of the distribution were classed as nondefensive repressors. Ten subjects were randomly assigned to each of the six groups. Female repressors tended to rate cartoons without sexual humor as funnier than cartoons with sexual humor, while the female sensitizers favored the cartoons containing sexual humor more than did the female repressors. Male repressors and sensitizers were not found to be significantly different, nor were the defensive/nondefensive subgroups within either repressors or sensitizers. The authors concluded that partial support was found for the hypothesis that avoidance of involvement with the sexual content of the cartoons would occur in repressors, who were expected to rate the sexual cartoons as less funny than the nonsexual humor. These results were observed with females but not males. The authors speculated that perhaps the males were more sensitized to the cartoons because of their presumed greater familiarity with *Playboy* magazine.

In a study in which the subjects were all males, Davis and Farina (1970) reported that no statistically significant effect was found for sexual arousal on humor appreciation. The results of their experiment showed that sexual arousal increased the rated funniness of sexual relative to nonsexual cartoons and enhanced the impact of communication between a person showing the cartoon and a person seeing the cartoon for the first time. The displayer of the cartoon was a very attractive female who varied her style of attire as a part of the conditions.

Whereas some investigators have been interested in the characteristic arousal and affective responses of different types of consumers of media humor, other research has emphasized the stimulus aspects of the humor. Shultz (1972), on the premise that incongruity and resolution are structural aspects of a joke that a subject must understand in order to fully appreciate intended humor, displayed cartoons to children in grades two, three, six, and seven. The cartoons were of three versions—original, incongruity removed, and resolution removed—and the children were asked to rate the funniness of 10 cartoons on a scale from 1 to

5. After rating each cartoon, the children were again shown the cartoons one at a time and asked to explain the joke-work of the cartoon and why the cartoon was supposed to be funny. Finally, the children were asked to pick the favorite cartoon successively until the cartoons were ranked from 1 to 10. While the experimenter was showing the cartoons to the children, the mirth reactions of the children were recorded on a 5-point scale. Shultz reported that the results indicated a tendency for the children to identify the incongruity and then resolve it for each cartoon. When the children were unable to discover the incongruity intended by the cartoonist (criterial incongruity), incongruities were devised and resolutions attempted as a general rule. For each type of incongruity, both incongruity and resolution were found to be important for humor appreciation. Younger children tended to enjoy the cartoons more than did the older children through all phases of the experiment. "Both age groups seemed to operate with the same cognitive structures; they differed only in the amount of stored information which could be used to identify the criterial incongruity and the criterial resolution" (Shultz, 1972, p. 476).

In another investigation that varied the characteristics of the humorous message, Zillmann, Bryant, and Cantor (1974) manipulated political cartoons during the 1972 presidential election to assess the effect on humor appreciation of various degrees of brutality of assault between protagonists. College students rated cartoons depicting one of the two major candidates whose identity was also manipulated. Following the experiment, the students indicated their disposition toward the candidate by completing a questionnaire. Under conditions of minimum brutality, victimization of disliked candidates was appreciated more than was victimization of favored candidates, but no differences were found in the condition of intermediate brutality. With extreme brutality in the cartoon, victimization of disliked candidates was less appreciated than that of favored candidates, but the results were not statistically significant. In explaining the findings, the authors exposed the rationale that the perception of an aggressive agent in a cartoon is influenced by the tactics used by that agent, critically affecting the interpretation of the cartoon by viewers.

Two studies have utilized interviews with children to attempt to find age differences in the enjoyment of television humor. Streicher and Bonney (1974) interviewed children of ages 6 to 12 about the ways in which they watched television, thought about it, and talked about it among themselves. They found that boys tended to prefer cartoons over all other types of programs. Although girls favored situation comedies as program types, the evidence that comical programs were clear favorites predominated. As the children grew older, they tended to change their preferences toward other types of programming (e.g., mystery-suspense-drama). When the children talked about disliked programs, generic types (e.g., love movies, war movies, westerns) tended to be named rather than specific programs (e.g., *Captain Kangaroo, Romper Room*), which the children often considered "babyish," The children tended to express dislike for commercials, usually because the ads interrupted regular programming, but the children appeared to also obtain amusement from commercials.

Bryant, Meyer, and Comisky (Note 4) interviewed 120 children of ages 5 to

10 to discover the children's favorite funny television segments. These segments were examined by a panel of judges using numerous criteria that either have been demonstrated to be or would appear on intuitive grounds to be relevant components of the kind of television that adults and older children find entertaining (Bryant, Meyer, & Comisky, Note 4). While age differences were found for the dimensions of surprise, abstraction, fantasy, and visual nature of the segment, no such differences by age emerged with respect to degree of logical elements, creativity, cognitive complexity, or intellectual sophistication of the segments. It was suggested that some of the criteria used to evaluate children's appreciation of humor in television must be different from those used to predict or evaluate adult humor appreciation.

In a study employing a different measure of appeal, Wakshlag, Day, and Zillmann (1981) found that the inclusion of humor in educational television programming facilitated selective exposure to the educational messages in first and second grade boys and girls. In other words, when children are free to choose whether to watch programs, they will chose humorous over non-humorous fare. Moreover, rapid pacing of the humorous material is superior in attracting and holding the viewers than slower pacing. These findings were also replicated with high school seniors (Schleicher, Bryant, & Zillmann, Note 5). Furthermore, Zillmann, Williams, Bryant, Boynton, and Wolf (1980) reported that fast pacing of humor in a children's educational television program increased visual attentiveness and enjoyment of the educational messages.

Children often are quite attentive to humorous programming designed for adults. *All in the Family*, a television situation comedy program, was the top ranked of all television programs from October 1971 through April 1976 (Norback & Norback, 1980). Meyer (1976), noting that the program appeared to be popular with children even though it was oriented to adults, reported nonuniform effects of viewing *All in the Family* on 6- to 10-year-old children. He found race and economic status of the child to be the most powerful response discriminators of dimensions of character preferences, understanding of the contents of the show, and moral/ethical judgments of program-related behavior. Gender of the child discriminated well for character preference, and learning ability of the child did so for moral/ethical judgments. The children were often unable to understand the situations, and the moral/ethical lessons of the program did not appear to have as great an impact on the children as did the physical appearance of the characters, role stereotypes, comic behavior, and so forth.

Chapko and Lewis (1975) reported that *All in the Family* has appeal for both high and low ethnocentric people, and that members of the two groups were likely to interpret the content consistently with their value positions. These findings contradicted those of Vidmar and Rokeach (1974) who found a clear association between frequency of viewing the program and prejudice for American viewers, although the same results were not found in Canadians. Slawson (1972) believed the program to be detrimental to society. He felt that successful treatment of bigotry by means of satire would require that the bigot be subjected to ridicule, derision, and irony. Surlin (1974) wrote that viewer interest was enhanced by the content of the program at the expense of "polarizing a portion of the viewing public psychologically least capable of coping with the overwhelming social problems of our society" (p. 41). Surlin and Tate (1976) examined the humorous content of the show, specifically that which was expressed by Archie Bunker. They reported cultural differences in the appreciation of the humor, with Americans enjoying it more than did Canadians. Tate and Surlin (1976) reported that people in a culture into which *All in the Family* had been imported (Canada) did not perceive the show to be as humorous or realistic as did Americans. Wilhoit and DeBock (1976) reported that viewers of the program in Holland found Archie Bunker to be funny and understood the character (partly as a result of expert subtitling). The authors reported a "clear tendency for persons scoring higher on parental authoritarianism or lifestyle intolerance scales to avoid watching" the show (p. 83). Such people were found to be more likely to report that watching the program made them uncertain about their own ideas.

Brigham and Giesbrecht (1976) found that neither the extent to which viewers enjoyed *All in the Family* nor the frequency with which they watched the program was related strongly to the racial attitudes of either blacks or whites. Although racial attitudes were found to be important in the prediction of the reactions of whites to the show and its characters, such was not the case with blacks. Liking for and identification with program characters was closely related to racial attitudes of whites in the study. More racially prejudiced whites tended to express agreement with Archie Bunker and liking for him, while such likelihood was less among less prejudiced whites. Smaller, but still significant, reactions in the opposite direction occurred for Mike Stivic, Archie's son-in-law. Highly prejudiced whites tended to express agreement with Archie's ideas about blacks, but liking the program was not significantly related to agreement with or liking of Archie. Among blacks, however, reactions were not strongly related to racial attitude.

In summary, the effects of the use of humor on various measures of entertainment are dependent on factors of the humor itself (e.g., propriety, equity, cognitive complexity) and characteristics of the receivers of humorous messages (e.g., disposition toward protagonists, affective stage, level of arousal, cognitive ability). The "goodness of fit" between the humor and the receiver also is important in the determination of the appreciation of humor. The power of humor to induce enjoyment is so great that experimenters have used entertainment in the form of television cartoons to reinforce children's behavior (Stumphauzer & Bishop, 1969), but the mechanisms of humor in promoting the appreciation of entertainment are still inadequately understood.

Persuasion

Many of the findings regarding the enjoyment of humorous programming may be extended in principle to the use of humor in advertising and other types of ulterior or persuasive communication. Gruner (1976) traced the examination of humor in persuasive messages, citing several studies involving the use of humor in persuasive speeches. The first study mentioned by Gruner involving mass media (Gruner & Lampton, 1972) included eight items (previously test-marketed for humor) in a sermon that was tape-recorded before a live audience. A nonhumorous version was created by editing out the humorous items and the responding laughter, and the two speeches were played to randomly grouped college students. Tests for agreement with the thesis of the sermon indicated that humor had no effect on the persuasiveness of the message.

Gruner (1976) discussed political cartoons with respect to the relationship between humor and satire. He described the work of Annis (1939) as being the earliest known study of satirical materials as rhetoric, but Gruner found the one paragraph report that newspaper editorials were more persuasive than editorial cartoons on the same topics as "too brief to allow for useful evaluation" (Gruner, 1976, p. 293). Gruner reported that the early study by Asher and Sargent (1941) did not actually involve editorial cartoons but caricatures, which were reported as having a short term effect on persuasion.

Gruner (1976) also reviewed a series of his own studies assessing the effect of satire in newspaper columns, concluding that satire may be useful in producing attitude change but only if the readers perceive the persuasive intent of the piece, a perception that frequently does not occur. In his dissertation, Gruner (1965) prepared a satirical speech on censorship, which was presented to a live audience and tape-recorded for use as a stimulus for an experiment. Gruner (1976) reported that college students who listened to the speech (via audio tape) apparently missed the serious point and interpreted the speech as designed to be funny. The funnier they found the speech, the less intelligent they found the speaker.

Bryant, Brown, and Klein (Note 6) examined the use of humor in event promotion. They found that for business events, humorous promotion did not facilitate attendence; whereas for social events, humorous promotion significantly enhanced attendance and nonverbally expressed enjoyment of the event. For reported anticipation of enjoyment of the social event, a similar pattern of responses resulted, although the findings were not statistically significant.

Brinkman (1968), examining the persuasive effect of editorial cartoons related to nonhumorous editorials, found support for the propositions that: (1) cartoons with printed editorials produce greater opinion change than cartoons alone; (2) an editorial alone results in greater opinion change than an editorial cartoon alone; (3) an editorial opposing the premise of a cartoon results in reversion, while an editorial supporting the argument of a cartoon results in a conversion; (4) in order of effectiveness in producing opinion change, the most effective combination is editorial and cartoon presented together, cartoon presented first and then the editorial, and finally the editorial presented first and then the cartoon; and (5) presenting the same arguments in both cartoon and editorial is more effective in establishing closure than is presenting alternative arguments in the editorial and cartoon. In general, Brinkman found that editorials and cartoons do bring about opinion change, and certain strategies are particularly effective.

Carl (1968) found that the message received by people from editorial cartoonists was often quite different from the message intended by the cartoonists. Carl's survey found 15% of the people in agreement with the cartoonist, 15% in slight or partial agreement, and over 70% in complete disagreement about the intended messages of cartoons. The discrepancy between the message intended and the message received is likely to be related to Sorel's (1981) contention that in political cartooning, the joke tends to be more important than the message.

Berlo and Kumata (1956), according to Gruner (1976), used a radio drama satirizing United States congressional investigating committees generally and Senator Joseph McCarthy in particular. With attitudes tested before and after college students listened to the drama, hearing the satire resulted in decreased regard for congressional committees, although attitudes toward McCarthy improved by an insignificant amount.

A decrease in comprehensibility of the selling point of media messages has often been cited as the reason why advertisers have frequently avoided humor in advertising content. Sternthal and Craig (1973), in a frequently cited study, concluded that evidence of an effective advantage of humorous advertising over serious advertising is lacking, but they suggested these generalizations: Humorous messages (1) attract attention; (2) may lead to decreased comprehension; (3) may serve to distract audience members, reducing counter argumentation; (4) do not usually increase persuasion; (5) tend to enhance source credibility: (6) should be related to the target audience; (7) may promote a positive mood and increase liking for the source; and (8) may increase message effectiveness when used in reinforcing attitudes already accepted by the audience.

Seely (Note 7) wrote that much of the humor in advertising escapes members of the target audience, but that humor has, at times, been very successful in advertising, having the best chance of success with segmented rather than mass audiences by appealing to desires for distinction and superiority of the audience members.

Markiewicz (1974) examined the effects of humor on attitude change. "Generally: humor integral to or adjacent to a persuasive message does not influence persuasion significantly; humor's effects of comprehension and source evaluations are inconsistent; and retention does not appear to be altered by humor usage" (p. 407).

In her dissertation, Markiewicz (1972) conducted seven experiments pertaining to the use of humor in learning or persuasion, only one of which resulted in a positive relationship. The addition of a humorous cartoon to a letter requesting the return of a post card apparently facilitated the return of the cards. Perreault (1972) did not find that humorous printed advertisements outperformed nonhumorous ones in promoting audience recall, but Gruner (1976) reported that advertising campaigns utilizing humor extensively had been followed by "drastic sales increases" for a variety of products. Gruner noted the different conditions operating in the cases of experimental attempts to enhance persuasion by use of humor and the effort to sell a product using humorous advertising, particularly with respect to exposure to the messages, initial attitudes toward the object of the persuasive messages, and the length of time between exposure and the measured effect.

Reid, Vanden Bergh, and Krugman (Note 8) studied nonsensical and sexual humor used in liquor advertisements in 1976 and 1977 issues of *Time*, *Newsweek*, and *Sports Illustrated*. Among male readers who remembers seeing or reading some part of the advertisements, no differences were found. However, for male readers who remembered reading more than half of the copy in the advertisements, greater recall of the humorous ad content was measured. The authors concluded that employing nonsensical humor can improve the likelihood that males readers will read more of the advertisement than with the use of sexual humor, cautioning that the instrument used measures only the amount of information read, not attitude change.

Cantor (Note 9) exposed children of ages 3 to 9 to a half hour of television programming in which advertisements were manipulated. A humorous versus a serious public service announcement advocating better nutrition was followed by an advertisement for sweet desserts or a toy. The week before the experiment, the choices of the children between a fruit and a sweet were recorded, and similar records were kept the week after the manipulations. The children chose fewest sweets and most fruits when the serious version of the nutrition ad was followed by the toy advertisement. Cantor concluded that, at least in the absence of a counter-advertisement, the serious advertisement was more effective in persuading the children than the humorous ones. These findings are consistent with those for the use of humorous radio commercials (Cantor & Venus, 1980).

Although the effects of humor on persuasion have generally been found to be either negative or minimal, several questions remain to be resolved concerning the use of humor in persuasive messages. Humorous content apparently fosters attention to messages, but at issue is whether it serves to draw that attention away from the serious point and toward the humor itself. The existence of numerous successful humor-oriented advertising campaigns in which humor is believed to attract people begs systematic analysis. Kowet (1982) claims that the secret to the rise of Miller Lite beer is an ad campaign based on humorous television commercials. Lite has the enviable position of selling more of its product than all its competitors combined among low-calorie beers and ranks third among all beers. The commercials for Miller are the most popular ones in television, and the "hook is their self-mocking humor" (p. 21). These commercials and the sales performance of the product are, according to Kowet, no coincidence. If humor is effective in generating persuasive messages as measured in sales of advertised products, experimental research should be able to demonstrate such results; however, research to date has not done so.

Learning

The goal of persuading receivers is closely related to the effort to promote learning, and humor has often been employed to facilitate information acquisition. While some earlier studies (e.g., Lumsdaine & Gladstone, 1958; McIntyre, 1954) found humor a detriment to the objectives of instructional films, later evidence has suggested the opposite conclusion. Davies and Apter (1980) and Chapman and Compton (1978) found that humorous slide presentations produced higher learning than did nonhumorous ones for children of ages 5, 6, 7, and 11. Zillmann et al. (1980) reported similar results for 5- and 6-year olds viewing specially-created educational television programs with versus without humorous excerpts. Bryant, Zillmann, Wolf, and Reardon (Note 10) found similar results with 7- and 8-year-old children, but indications were noted that the facilitating impact of humor diminishes with increasing age (cf. Hezel, Bryant, Harris, & Zillmann, Note 11). Sapolsky (Note 12) found that varying the funniness of the humor did not improve learning and that only mildly funny humor produces desirable results. Although a funny source makes the watching of educational television more enjoyable, the funniness of the source does not apparently produce strong educational effects (Sapolsky & Walker, Note 13; Wakshlag, 1981). Working from the question of whether humor that facilitates learning functions by grabbing the attention of the viewers, Bryant and Zillmann (Note 14) compared the use of humor with the use of audio-visual "fireworks" in television as attention-getters. No differences by type of attention-grabber were found with audiences of 5-through 8-year-old children. For a more complete summary of the findings of the research on effects of humor in children's educational television, see Bryant, Zillmann, and Brown (1982). Research on the effects of educational television programs that frequently employ humor and various other entertainment features has been summarized by Bryant, Alexander, and Brown (1982).

Bryant, Zillmann, Brown, and Parks (Note 15) tested the effectiveness of ridicule as an educational and social corrective when used in children's educational television programs, and reported that 4-year-old children re-sponded best when commands were given rather than ridicule, but 6-year-old children were more responsive to ridicule.

Bryant, Brown, Silberberg, and Elliott (1981) found that humorous illustra-tions in college textbooks had no effect on information acquisition and motivation. Positive effects, however, were noted on appeal, and negative effects were found for humor on persuasibility.

The effects of humor on information acquisition and learning, as with persuasion, have often been considered negative. However, positive effects of humor have been found with young children, even though with increasing age the humor impact apparently diminishes. The chief advantage of using humor to promote educational goals is apparently in gaining or maintaining the attention of the message receiver.

Side Effects

The use of humorous forms in media have frequently produced side effects that go beyond the intentions of message producers. We will make no attempt to be exhaustive in reviewing this literature. Rather, a sampling of studies that presents a few of the several research traditions will be mentioned.

When comic strips came under the scrutiny of Senator Estes Kefauver and his Senate subcommittee in the 1950s, research on the effects of comics became important. Witty (1941) found that the reading of comics had beneficial side effects: Such reading improved children's learning of reading skills when the comics were part of an otherwise adequate reading program. He reported that when children who read comics extensively were compared with children who seldom read them, little difference was observed in the patterns of noncomic reading of the two groups with respect to amount of or nature of reading.

Another side effect of humor use—this one potentially detrimental—involves the relationship between television viewing and the learning of sex-role stereotypes. Davidson, Yasuna, and Tower (1979) exposed girls of ages 5 and 6 to one of three cartoon television programs taken from Saturday morning fare. The authors reported that the girls who viewed a low-stereotyped program received significantly lower sex-role stereotype scores than did the girls in the high-stereotyped and neutral program conditions. The high-stereotype and neutral program-viewing groups did not differ from each other, and the authors concluded that the neutral version may not have been neutral after all.

Certainly the most extensive study of the potentially dysfunctional side effects of entertaining programs has been associated with the investigation of media violence. Examining the impact of cartoon violence, Haynes (1978) found that fifth and sixth grade children recognized violent content in comic cartoon programs as being antisocial. Numerous findings from other studies suggest that cartoon violence is an effective facilitator of antisocial behavior.

Side effects of humor have been studied in widely varying contexts. As with humor and entertainment, persuasion, and learning, the role of humor with respect to side effects apparently lies chiefly in facilitating exposure to or in attracting attention to media messages.

SUMMARY

The power of humor in the mass media as entertainer, persuader, and educator apparently lies chiefly in the ability of humor to attract audiences. This chapter has documented research findings revealing this capacity for appeal to the masses via both entertainment and education-oriented media, especially television. Moreover, cartoons in the media were popular long before television and have appeared widely in the form of caricatures, political cartoons, comic strips, and comic books. Formal content analyses, however, are missing to chronicle the certainly frequent use of humor in advertising and motion pictures.

Not everyone is pleased about the humorous treatment of serious issues in the mass media. Women, elderly people, blacks, and other minority group members have been active in voicing objections to humorous portrayals emphasizing the shortcomings of various groups or presenting false stereotypes, which are often criticized as promoting bigotry, racism, sexism, or other negative attitudes. Hostile humor and violent comedic behavior have also been criticized as being staples in the humor diet in mass media messages.

Although the social content and context of humor in the mass media have frequently been studied, investigations of the roles and effects of humor per se have not been frequent. A few studies have examined the effect of humor on persuasion and learning, generally finding humor ineffective in promoting either, except with young children. Most positive effects of humor tend to relate to humor as an attention-getter. Even though speculation about the mechanisms of humor is thousands of years old, neither researchers nor mass media practitioners are able to agree completely on how and why people find certain messages funny. But progress has been made.

REFERENCE NOTES

1. Cahill, J. *The American comic book: An integration of its evolution and its effects as a mass medium.* Unpublished manuscript, 1977.
2. Cantor, J., & Richardson, C. *Content analysis of the humor in* Playboy, Cosmopolitan, Esquire, *and* Ladies Home Journal. Unpublished manuscript, 1976.
3. Cantor, J., & Venus, P. *Content analysis of the humor in* The New Yorker *and* Look. Unpublished manuscript, 1975.
4. Bryant, J., Meyer, T., & Comisky, P. *A developmental analysis of children's favorite humorous television segments.* Paper presented at the meeting of the International Communication Association, Berlin, June 1977.
5. Schleicher, M. P., Bryant, J., & Zillmann, D. *Voluntary selective exposure to educational television programs as a function of differently paced humorous inserts.* Manuscript in preparation, 1980.
6. Bryant, J., Brown, D., & Klein, D. M. *The judicious use of humor in event promotion: A series of field studies.* Paper presented at the meeting of the Advertising Division of the Association for Education in Journalism, Athens, Ohio, July 1982.
7. Seely, J. *Humor in advertising: The language pun.* Paper presented at the meeting of the Rocky Mountain Modern Language Association, Denver, October 1980.

8. Reid, L. N., Vanden Bergh, B. G., & Krugman, D. M. *Male readership differences in liquor magazine ads employing nonsensical and sexual humor.* Paper presented at the meeting of the Association for Education in Journalism, Boston, August 1980.
9. Cantor, J. *Modifying children's eating habits through television ads: Effects of humorous appeals in a field setting.* Paper presented at the meeting of the International Communication Association, Acapulco, Mexico, May 1980.
10. Bryant, J., Zillmann, D., Wolf, M. A., & Reardon, K. *Learning from educational television as a function of differently paced humor: Further evidence.* Manuscript in preparation, 1981.
11. Hezel, R. T., Bryant, J., Harris, L., & Zillmann, D. *The relationship between humor and educational information: Lectures and learning.* Manuscript in preparation, 1981.
12. Sapolsky, B. S. *The degree of funniness of humor accompanying informative messages and its effect upon children's rote learning.* Manuscript in preparation, 1981.
13. Sapolsky, B. S., & Walker, B. A. *The effect of mood and source on children's attention, enjoyment, and learning from educational television.* Paper presented at the Second International Conference on Humor, Los Angles, August 1980.
14. Bryant, J., & Zillmann, D. *Humor and audiovisual fireworks in educational television: Effects on learning.* Unpublished manuscript, 1981.
15. Bryant, J., Zillmann, D., Brown, D., & Parks, S. *The effect of ridiculing a model on children's imitation of televised instruction.* Paper presented at the meeting of the Speech Communication Association, Anaheim, 1981.

REFERENCES

Anderson, R. E., & Jolly, E. Stereotyped traits and sex roles in humorous drawings. *Communication Research,* October 1977, *4*(4), 453-484.
Annis, A. D. The relative effectiveness of cartoons and editorials as propaganda media. *Psychological Bulletin,* 1939, *36,* 628.
Asher, R., & Sargent, S. Shifts in attitude caused by cartoon caricatures. *Journal of General Psychology,* 1941, *24,* 451-455.
Barcus, F. E. A content analysis of trends in Sunday comics: 1900-1958. *Journalism Quarterly,* Spring 1961, *38,* 171-180.
Berlo, D. K., & Kumata, H. The investigator: The impact of a satirical radio drama. *Journalism Quarterly,* 1956, *33,* 287-298.
Brigham, J. C., & Giesbrecht, L. W. "All in the Family": Racial attitudes. *Journal of Communication,* Autumn 1976, *26*(4), 69-74.
Brinkman, D. Do editorial cartoons and editorials change opinions? *Journalism Quarterly,* Winter 1968, *45*(4), 724-726.
Bryant, J. Degree of hostility in squelches as a factor in humor appreciation. In A. J. Chapman & H. C. Foot (Eds.), *It's a funny thing, humour.* Oxford: Pergamon Press, 1977.
Bryant, J., Alexander, A., & Brown, D. Learning from educational television programmes. In M. J. A. Howe (Ed.), *Learning from television.* London: Academic Press, Ltd., 1983.

Bryant, J., Brown, D., Silberberg, A., & Elliott, S. Effects of humorous illustrations in college textbooks. *Human Communication Research*, 1981, *8*(1), 43-57.

Bryant, J., Hezel, R., & Zillmann, D. Humor in children's educational television. *Communication Education*, January 1979, *28*(1), 49-59.

Bryant, J., Zillmann, D., & Brown, D. Entertainment features in children's educational television: Effects on attention and information acquisition. In J. Bryant & D. R. Anderson (Eds.), *Children's understanding of television: Research on attention and comprehension*. New York: Academic Press, 1983.

Burns, W., & Tyler, J. Appreciation of risque cartoon humor in male and female repressors and sensitizers. *Journal of Clinical Psychology*, April 1976, *32*(2), 315-321.

Cantor, J. Humor on television: A content analysis. *Journal of Broadcasting*, Fall 1976, *20*, 501-510.

Cantor, J. R. Tendentious humour in the mass media. In A. J. Chapman & H. C. Foot (Eds.), *It's a funny thing, humour*. Oxford: Pergamon Press, 1977.

Cantor, J. R., Bryant, J., & Zillmann, D. Enhancement of humor appreciation by transferred excitation. *Journal of Personality and Social Psychology*, 1974, *30*(6), 812-821.

Cantor, J., & Venus, P. The effect of humor on recall of a radio advertisement. *Journal of Broadcasting*, Winter 1980, *24*(1), 13-22.

Cantor, J. R., & Zillmann, D. Resentment toward victimized protagonists and severity of misfortunes they suffer as factors in humor appreciation. *Journal of Experimental Research in Personality*, 1973, *6*, 321-329.

Carl, L. M. Editorial cartoons fail to reach many readers. *Journalism Quarterly*, 1968, *45*, 533-535.

Chapko, M. K., & Lewis, M. H. Authoritarianism and "All in the Family". *Journal of Psychology*, 1975, *90*, 245-248.

Chapman, A. J., & Crompton, P. Humorous presentations of material and presentations of humorous material: A review of the humor and memory literature and two experimental studies. In M. M. Gruneberg, P. E. Morris, & R. N. Sykes (Eds.), *Practical aspects of memory*. London: Academic Press, 1978.

Chapman, A. J., Smith, J. R., & Foot, H. C. Language, humour and intergroup relations. In H. Giles (Ed.), *Language: Ethnicity and intergroup relations*. New York: Academic Press, 1977.

Davidson, E. S., Yasuna, A., & Tower, A. The effects of television cartoons on sex-role stereotyping in young girls. *Child Development*, June 1979, *50*(2), 597-600.

Davies, A. P., & Apter, M. J. Humor and its effect on learning in children. In P. E. McGhee & A. J. Chapman (Eds.), *Children's humor*. New York: Wiley, 1980.

Davies, L. J. Attitudes toward old age and aging as shown by humor. *Gerontologist*, 1977, *17*, 220-226.

Davis, J. M., & Farina, A. Humor appreciation as social communication. *Journal of Personality and Social Psychology*, 1970, *15*(2), 175-178.

Ellis, K. Queen for one day at a time. *College English*, 1977, *38*(8), 775-781.

Feinsilber, M., & Mead, W. B. *American averages*. Garden City, N.Y.: Dolphin Books, 1980.

Freud, S. Wit and its relation to the unconscious. In A. A. Brill (Ed.), *The Basic Writings of Sigmund Freud*. New York: Modern Library, 1938.

Goldstein, J. H., & McGhee, P. E. (Eds.), *The psychology of humor*. New York: Academic Press, 1972.

Graeven, D. B., & Morris, S. J. College humor in 1930 and 1972: An investigation using the humor diary. *Sociology and Social Research*, 1975, *59*(4), 406-410.

Greenberg, B., & Kahn, S. Blacks in "Playboy" cartoons. *Journalism Quarterly*, 1970, *47*, 557-560.

Gruner, C. R. An experimental study of satire as persuasion. *Speech Monographs*, 1965, *32*, 149-153.

Gruner, C. R. Wit and humour in mass communication. In A. J. Chapman & H. C. Foot (Eds.), *Humour and laughter: Theory, research, and applications*. London: John Wiley & Sons, 1976.

Gruner, C. R., & Lampton, W. E. Effects of including humorous material in a persuasive sermon. *Southern Speech Communication Journal*, 1972, *38*, 188-196.

Harris, A. J., & Feinberg, J. F. Television and aging: Is what you see what you get. *Gerontologist*, 1977, *17*(5), 464-468.

Hayes, D. S., & Birnbaum, D. W. Preschoolers' retention of televised events: Is a picture worth a thousand words. *Developmental Psychology*, 1980, *16*(5), 410-416.

Haynes, R. B. Children's perceptions of "comic" and "authentic" cartoon violence. *Journal of Broadcasting*, 1978, *22*(1), 63-70.

Hinton, J. L., Seggar, J. F., Northcott, H. C., & Fontes, B. Tokenism and improving imagery of blacks in TV drama and comedy: 1973. *Journal of Broadcasting*, 1974, *18*(4), 423-432.

Huston, A. C., Wright, J. C., Wartella, E., Rice, M. L., Watkins, B. A., Campbell, T., & Potts, R. Communicating more than content: Formal features of children's television programs. *Journal of Communication*, 1981, *31*(3), 32-48.

Independent Broadcasting Authority, Audience Research Department. *Situation comedies: A study of viewers' comments on six programmes*. London: Author, 1976.

Johnson, I. S. Cartoons. *Public Opinion Quarterly*, 1937, *1*, 21-44.

Kambouropoulo, P. Individual differences in the sense of humor and their relation to temperamental differences. *Archives of Psychology*, 1930, *19*(121), 5-77.

Kelly, J. P., & Solomon, P. J. Humor in television advertising. *Journal of Advertising*, 1975, *4*, 31-35.

Kowet, D. And then Big Ben broke Deacon Jones' foot. *TV Guide*, 1982, 20-22.

Long, M., & Simon, R. J. The roles and statuses of women on children and family TV programs. *Journalism Quarterly*, 1974, *51*, 107-110.

Lumsdaine, A. A., & Gladstone, A. I. Overt practice and audio-visual embellishments. In M. A. May & A. A. Lumsdaine (Eds.), *Learning from films*. New Haven, Conn.: Yale University Press, 1958.

McIntyre, C. J. *Training film evaluation: FB 254-cold weather uniforms*. (Technical Report SDC 269-7-51.) Port Washington, N.Y.: U. S. Naval Special Devices Center, 1954.

Malamuth, N. M., & Spinner, B. A longitudinal content analysis of sexual violence in the best selling erotic magazines. *Journal of Sex Research*, 1980, *16*(3), 226-237.

Markiewicz, D. *The effects of humor on persuasion*. Unpublished doctoral dissertation, Ohio State University, 1972.

Markiewicz, D. Effects of humor on persuasion. *Sociometry*, 1974, *34*, 407-422.

Mendelsohn, H. *Mass entertainment*. New Haven, Conn.: College & University Press, 1966.

Meyer, T. P. The impact of "All in the Family" on children. *Journal of Broadcasting*, 1976, *20*(1), 25-33.

Meyer, K., Seidler, J., Curry, T., & Aveni, A. Women in July fourth cartoons: A 100-year look. *Journal of Communication*, 1980, *30*(1), 21-30.

Miller, G. R., & Bacon, P. Open- and closed-mindedness and recognition of visual humor. *Journal of Communication*, 1971, *21*(2), 150-159.

National Advertising Review Board. *Advertising and women: A report on advertising portraying or directed to women*. Washington, D.C.: Author, 1975.

Norback, C. T., & Norback, P. G. (Eds.), *TV Guide Almanac*. New York: Ballantine Books, 1980.

Palmore, E. Attitudes toward aging as shown by humor. *Gerontologist*, 1971, *11*, 181-186.

Perreault, R. M. *A study of the effects of humor in advertising as can be measured by product recall tests*. Unpublished masters thesis, University of Georgia, 1972.

Piddington, R. *The psychology of laughter*. New York: Gamut Press, 1963.

Plato. Philebus. In B. Jowett (Ed. & Trans.), *The dialogues of Plato*. London & New York: Oxford University Press (Clarendon), 1871.

Reid, P. T. Racial stereotyping on television: A comparison of the behavior of both black and white television characters. *Journal of Applied Psychology*, 1979, *64*(5), 465-471.

Richman, J. The foolishness and wisdom of age: Attitudes toward the elderly as reflected in jokes. *Gerontologist*, 1977, *17*, 210-217.

Rothman, R. A., & Olmsted, D. W. "Chicago Tribune" cartoons during and after the McCormick era. *Journalism Quarterly*, 1966, *43*, 67-72.

Ryan, J. K. Comic strips and morals. *Forum*, 1936, *95*, 11-13.

Saenger, G. Male and female relations in the American comic strip. *Public Opinion Quarterly*, 1955, *19*(3), 195-205.

Shultz, T. R. The role of incongruity and resolution in children's appreciation of cartoon humor. *Journal of Experimental Child Psychology*, 1972, *13*, 456-477.

Slawson, J. How funny can bigotry be? *Educational Broadcasting Review*, 1972, *6*(2), 79-82.

Smith, M. D. The portrayal of elders in magazine cartoons. *Gerontologist*, 1979, *19*(4), 408-412.

Sorel, E. The limits on drawing power. *Washington Journalism Review*, 1981, *3*(8), 30-31.

Spiegelman, M., Terwilliger, C., & Fearing, F. Goals and means to goals as seen in comics characters. *Journal of Social Psychology*, 1947, 46-52.

Stein, H. F. "All in the Family" as a mirror of contemporary American culture. *Family Process*, 1974, *13*(3), 279-315.

Sternthal, B., & Craig, C. S. Humor in advertising. *Journal of Marketing*, 1973, *37*, 12-18.

Stocking, S. H., Sapolsky, B. S., & Zillmann, D. Sex discrimination in prime time humor. *Journal of Broadcasting*, 1977, *21*(4), 447-457.

Streicher, H. W. The girls in the cartoons. *Journal of Communication*, 1974, *24*(2), 125-129.

Streicher, L. H., & Bonney, N. L. Children talk about television. *Journal of Communication*, 1974, *24*(3), 54-61.

Stumphauzer, J. S., & Bishop, B. R. Saturday morning television cartoons: A simple apparatus for the reinforcement of behavior in children. *Developmental Psychology*, 1969, *1*(6), 763-764.

Surlin, S. H. Bigotry on air and in life: The Archie Bunker case. *Public Telecommunications Review*, 1974, *2*(2), 34-41.

Surlin, S. H., & Tate, D. C. "All in the Family": Is Archie funny. *Journal of Communication*, 1976, *26*(4), 61-68.

Tate, E. D., & Surlin, S. H. Agreement with opinionated TV characters across cultures. *Journalism Quarterly*, 1976, *53*(2), 199-203, 210.

Tedesco, N. S. Patterns in prime time. *Journal of Communication*, 1974, *24*(2), 119-124.

Thorndike, R. Words and the comics. *Journal of Experimental Education*, 1941, *10*, 80-81.

U.S. Commission on Civil Rights. *Window dressing on the set: Women and minorities in television*. Washington, D.C.: U.S. Government Printing Office, 1977.

Vidmar, N., & Rokeach, M. Archie Bunker's bigotry: A study in selective perception and exposure. *Journal of Communication*, 1974, *24*(1), 36-47.

Wakshlag, J. J. Effect of humorous appearance of teacher on effectiveness of television programs as a function of differently paced humorous inserts. *Journal of Educational Psychology*, 1981, *73*(1), 27-32.

Wakshlag, J., Day, K. D., & Zillmann, D. Selective exposure to educational television programs as a function of differently paced humorous inserts. *Journal of Educational Psychology*, 1981, *73*(1), 27-32.

Weber, T., & Cameron, P. Humor and aging—a reply. *Gerontologist*, 1978, *18*, 73-76.

Wilde, L. *How the great comedy writers create laughter*. Chicago: Nelson-Hall, 1976.

Wilhoit, G. C., & De Bock, H. "All in the family" in Holland. *Journal of Communication*, 1976, *26*(4), 75-86.

Willis, E. *Writing television and radio programs*. New York: Holt, Rinehart and Winston, Inc., 1967.

Witty, P. Children's interest in reading the comics. *Journal of Experimental Education*, 1941, *10*, 100-104.

Yanok, G., & Yanok, S. H. What's funny? *Mainliner*, 1977, 35-37.

Zillmann, D. Humour and communication: Introduction to symposium. In A. J. Chapman & H. C. Foot (Eds.), *It's a funny thing, humour*. Oxford: Pergamon Press, 1977.

Zillmann, D., & Bryant, J. Retaliatory equity as a factor in humor appreciation. *Journal of Experimental Social Psychology*, 1974, *10*, 480-488.

Zillmann, D., & Bryant, J. Misattribution theory of tendentious humor. *Journal of Experimental Social Psychology*, 1980, *16*, 146-160.

Zillmann, D., Bryant, J., & Cantor, J. R. Brutality of assault in political cartoons affecting humor appreciation. *Journal of Research in Personality*, 1974, *7*, 334-356.

Zillmann, D., & Cantor, J. R. Directionality of transitory dominance as a communication variable affecting humor appreciation. *Journal of Personality and Social Psychology*, 1972, *24*, 191-198.

Zillmann, D., & Cantor, J. R. A disposition theory of humor and mirth. In A. J. Chapman & H. C. Foot (Eds.), *Humor and laughter: Theory, research and applications*. London: Wiley, 1976.

Zillmann, D., Williams, B. R., Bryant, J., Boynton, K. R., & Wolf, M. A. Acquisition of information from educational television programs as a function of differently paced humorous inserts. *Journal of Educational Psychology*, 1980, *72*(2), 170-180.

Chapter 10

Uses and Effects of Humor in Educational Ventures

DOLF ZILLMANN and JENNINGS BRYANT

Traditionally, education has been thought of as a most serious and sober undertaking. In recent years, however, it has become permeated with humor and other elements of entertainment. Notwithstanding contentions of great reluctance in the involvement of merriment (e.g., Browning, 1977), education has not just tolerated, but has eagerly embraced the merger with entertainment. Humor, in particular, is apparently thought to aid the educational mission in a grand fashion. As a result, levity that seemed appropriate for kindergarten can now be found in the college classroom and in introductory science texts. Instructors at all levels seem to work from the premise that teaching in an entertaining fashion can only help the cause of education (e.g., Adams, 1974; Bradford, 1964; Earls, 1972). Humor consequently abounds in educational efforts from grade to graduate school (Bryant, Comisky, & Zillmann, 1979) and from the first reader to the university textbook (Bryant, Gula, & Zillmann, 1980). But nowhere is the marriage of education and entertainment more obtrusively evident than in educational television, especially in educational programs for children (Bryant, Hezel, & Zillmann, 1979).

ATTRACTING AUDIENCES

Although some programs (e.g., *Mister Rogers' Neighborhood*) get by with little humor, most popular programs (e.g., *Captain Kangaroo, Sesame Street, The Electric Company*) rely heavily on many forms of humor—along with much other visual and audiovisual material adapted from pinball machines and similar devices of the carnival variety. These entertainment-embellished programs proved highly successful in attracting large audiences to the screen, and it has often been surmised that their success would not have been possible without the lavish involvement of elements of entertainment, especially humorous stimuli (cf. Lesser, 1974). It has been suggested, in fact, that educational television, because of its elusive audience, was virtually forced into a union with entertainment. Unlike the captive audience of the classroom, the broadcast audience is free to choose among several simultaneously available offerings. Any member of the television audience can at any moment turn away from an educational message in favor of comedy, drama, games, or sports. And unlike the readers of a textbook who tend to be motivated by interest and/or obligation, the television audience—or at least the majority of this audience—appears to be relatively unmotivated for exposure to information that provides little immediate gratification and that has little instant utility. The noncaptive broadcast audience is truly free to choose, and it presumably uses this freedom to maximize gratification deriving from exposure. Because of this, it must be expected that viewers, especially children, tune into programs that provide a high degree of immediate gratification, and that educational programs that fail to provide such gratification will fail in the competition with noneducational entertainment fare.

Clearly, the attraction of a sizeable audience has to be a primary consideration in educational broadcasting. (After all, what good can come from the finest educational program if it fails to reach its target audience?) One might thus expect that much research has probed variables that could help draw larger audiences. One certainly would expect that the effects of humor and other forms of entertainment have been explored. Oddly enough, until recently there has not been a single study that addressed this issue directly. (The little research there was has been conducted post facto on the success of certain programs; it did not use control conditions and, hence, does not permit an evaluation of the effectiveness of particular variables involved.) The investigation that has started to correct this situation (Wakshlag, Day, & Zillmann, 1981) is an experiment that explored the effects of the involvement of humorous episodes in an educational program on selective exposure under competitive viewing conditions.

In this investigation, educational programs were manipulated to create versions without humor and versions with humor in a slow, intermediate, and fast pace. The amount of humor was kept constant in all humor versions by combining episodes into blocks (12 individual episodes in the fast-pace versions; 6 blocks of 2 episodes in the intermediate-pace versions; 3 blocks of 4 episodes in the slow-pace versions). The variation could thus be described as "cluttering" versus "clustering" of humor in an educational message. These manipulated messages competed against two others that were simultaneously available for display on the television monitor. Ostensibly in a waiting period, first- and second-grade school children could watch any of these programs for as long as they pleased: or they could, just like at home, turn off the set. Unknown to the children, their program selections were automatically recorded. This experimental procedure had proved useful as a simulation of noncaptive audience conditions in the study of preferences for different types of entertainment programs (cf. Zillmann, Hezel, & Medoff, 1980).

It was found, first of all, that the presence of humor in educational programs greatly facilitated selective exposure. Both boys and girls spent much more time watching the programs when they were embellished with humorous tidbits than when they were presented in unadorned form. The study, then, leaves no doubt that children whose television viewing is not supervised by parents or guardians (i.e., children who are not coerced into watching certain programs and who are free to watch as they please) will favor humorous over nonhumorous educational television. Or put another way: the findings show that nonentertaining educational television is likely to compete very poorly with other programs, especially with entertaining ones, whenever the respondent is free to choose from several available offerings.

Second, and more important to the message designer, the study revealed significant differences in selective exposure as the result of the particular distribution of humorous episodes in an educational message. As can be seen from Figure 10-1, the fast pacing of humorous stimuli—presumably because in the initial sampling of available programs such stimuli were more frequently

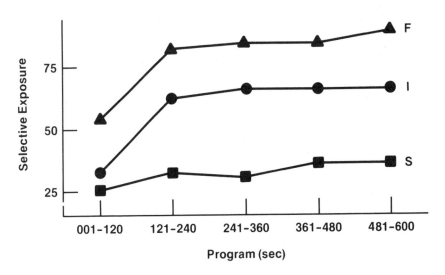

Figure 10-1. Selective exposure to educational programs as a function of differently paced humorous inserts. The programs, one at a time, competed with two others that were simultaneously available for display on a television monitor. The fast-paced interspersion of humor (F, triangles) proved more effective in attracting and sustaining an audience than the interspersion of the same humorous materials at an intermediate pace (I, circles); the latter, in turn, proved more effective than the interspersion of humor at a slow pace (S, square). (Adapted from Wakshlag, Day & Zillmann, 1981.)

encountered and because the more frequent encounter prevented further sampling of competing programs—attracted the viewers more rapidly and held them more effectively to the program. Successively slower pacing of humorous stimuli proved successively less effective in both regards. Clearly, if attracting an audience were the sole objective of educational television, humorous stimuli should be frequently interspersed in educational messages, ideally without disrupting the flow of this message. The continuity of the educational message is, of course, imperative; and to assure this continuity, the limits to placing humorous stimuli need to be recognized. However, for preschoolers demands on attention span have to be kept to a minimum anyway, and the frequent employment of humorous stimuli is unlikely to be disruptive. Similarly, many educational messages to children in the lower grades (e.g., messages designed to teach spelling) are composed of short, self-contained units and can readily tolerate the frequent insertion of humorous stimuli. Generally speaking, then, it appears that, as long as essential message continuities are not disrupted, the employment of humorous tidbits in a rapid pace—the so-called cluttering—is superior to any slower-pace "time outs for humor"—the so-called clustering— in attracting and sustaining a broadcast audience.

The audience-drawing capacity of rapidly paced humor has also been demonstrated for adolescents. In an investigation that used high school seniors as subjects (Schleicher & Bryant, Note 1) it was found that the fast pacing of humorous stimuli in educational programs attracted more students for longer periods of time to the screen than did the interspersion of the same stimuli at a slower pace.

Although selective exposure to printed materials has not been examined experimentally, it should be expected that the promise of gratification manifest in the obtrusive presence of humorous materials in educational magazines and books will similarly foster increased exposure. This phenomenon appears far less important than selective exposure to educational television programs, however, as printed educational offerings rarely compete against one another under comparable circumstances. Educational magazines and books are ordinarily chosen by teachers for the students, not by the students themselves. But to the extent that teachers are partial to humor or deem humor a useful educational aid (e.g., Browning, 1977), the selective bias should be displayed by these teachers.

Returning to educational television where humor now can be considered a proven gratifier capable of fostering increased selective exposure, it must be acknowledged at this point that the involvement of humorous stimuli is by no means the only audience attractant, nor necessarily the most powerful one. It has been shown recently (Wakshlag, Reitz, & Zillmann, 1982), for instance, that appealing rhythmic background music in educational programs can greatly aid in attracting children to the screen. The effect of such music on selective exposure seems comparable to that of the interspersion of humorous stimuli. Meaningful statements about the relative power of music versus humor cannot be made, however, as hitherto the effects of only a few types of music and forms of humorous stimulation have been explored.

EFFECTS ON LEARNING

Attracting and sustaining a broadcast audience, although critically important, is of course only the first step in the process of educating by means of television. The necessary second step is to get the educational message across—that is, to make sure that the information to be acquired is indeed being acquired by the viewers. It is this second step that has produced most of the controversy over the use of entertainment features in contemporary educational television. Specifically, the Singers (Singer & Singer, 1979; Singer, 1980) have taken issue with the fast pace of entertainment-embellished educational television programs for children, arguing that such rapid-fire expositions prevent vital rehearsal processes and ultimately stunt the development of cognitive skills that are essential to learning. Notwithstanding such projections of long-term consequences that are most difficult to ascertain (cf. Zillmann, 1982), concerns that elements of entertainment in education can only distract from the educational message and thus impar the acquisition of information have been voiced for some time. Schramm (1973), for example, speculated that the respondents' enjoyment of humor, in particular, might extend into subsequently presented educational segments. The assumed cognitive preoccupation with humor would then interfere with the reception of educational information; or should the information be received, it would hamper the rehearsal and storage of this information. Early research on the effects of humor in instructional films, mainly conducted with captive and presumably rather attentive military audiences (e.g., Lumsdaine & Gladstone, 1958; McIntyre, 1954), indeed tended to support the conclusion that the involvement of humor is more a hindrance than a help in accomplishing educational objectives (cf. Gruner, 1978; Schramm, 1972). Schramm (1973) further speculated that viewers might perceive educational segments in sharp contrast to any enjoyable humorous stimuli associated with them and thus be more dissatisfied with the educational segments and possibly pay less attention to these segments than to the same educational segments without humor. Recently, McGhee (1980) added the suggestion that humor in educational television might create a playful frame of mind that could interfere with the acquisition of novel information mainly because it would make any rehearsing, which could be construed as effort and labor, seem undesirable or unnecessary.

Theoretical considerations, then, led mainly to the projection of negative effects of the involvement of humor on information acquisition from educational messages (cf. McGhee, 1980). Even writers who promoted fast-paced, entertaining educational programs for children seemed to concede that, on the whole, humor might be distracting; however, they tended to insist that humor that is well integrated in the educational message (i.e., that directly relates to it semantically) might have beneficial effects (e.g., Lesser, 1972, 1974). [The only aspect of humor use associated with unqualified positive projections concerned quizzes and exams and apprehensions connected with them. Based on Freudian reasoning (1905/1958), humor has been expected to alleviate tensions and anxieties; consequently, it should relax students who are uptight

about exams and improve their performance. The evidence on this point (e.g.,
Horn, 1972; Mechanic, 1962; Smith, Ascough, Ettinger, & Nelson, 1971;
Terry & Woods, 1975; Weinberg, 1973) is quite inconsistent, however (cf.
Chapman & Crompton, 1978; McGhee, 1980).]

Positive Effects of Humor

Evidence suggesting that, counter to the distraction concerns, the involvement
of humor in educational television might actually facilitate information
acquisition comes from investigations by Hauck & Thomas (1972), Kaplan &
Pascoe (1977), Davies & Apter (1980), and Chapman & Compton (1978).

Hauck and Thomas observed that elementary school children recalled
humorous associations better than common nonhumorous ones, but only under
conditions of incidental learning. Humor was of no consequence when learning
was intentional and presumably associated with high levels of attention. The
distinction between incidental and intentional learning, together with its
implications for attention and information rehearsal, is an important one
because it offers an explanation for the earlier failures to obtain facilitatory
effects of humor use on learning (cf. Schramm, 1972). As already pointed out,
the early investigations tended to involve attentive, motivated audiences. Under
the conditions of intentional learning that were created, information acquisition
from nonhumorous messages was apparently sufficient, and potentially more
attractive, enjoyable presentations of the same facts thus could not achieve
notably superior effects.

Kaplan and Pascoe manipulated videotaped lectures for college under-
graduates. They created a control condition without humor and three humorous
versions. The humor employed was either related to the concepts to be taught,
unrelated to them, or partly related and partly unrelated to them. Subjects'
information acquisition was assessed immediately after exposure and, for a
second time, six weeks after exposure. There were no appreciable effects on
concept learning overall, either immediately after exposure or in the delayed
retest. However, when the items to be learned were separated into those
associated with the humor manipulation and into others, specific effects of
humor use did emerge.

In the immediate test, the involvement of the various forms of humor was
without effect on information acquisition of manipulated items. This finding
seems in line with the argument that under conditions of intentional learning
humorous embellishments have zero impact. The lecture employed by Kaplan
and Pascoe actually was an integral part of a course the subjects were taking.
The students thus must have been highly motivated to acquire the information
presented. Information acquisition of unmanipulated items, in contrast, was
affected by the presence of humor. Specifically, the involvement of concept-
related humor led to a reduction in the acquisition of information concerning the
unembellished concepts in the lecture. This finding appears to support

Schramm's (1973) contention that any gain in learning due to attentional enticements by humor comes at the expense of less attention, and hence, less learning of other portions of educational messages.

In the retest, the pattern of effects inexplicably reversed. Humor was of little moment in the learning of unmanipulated items. It enhanced information acquisition of the manipulated items, however. The involvement of concept-related humor fostered superior learning of the concepts to which the humor related. This finding may be interpreted as showing that relevant humor, especially when rehearsed (as in a test), can greatly aid information acquisition and, perhaps more importantly, information retention.

The investigations by Davies and Apter and by Chapman and Crompton pertain to educational television for child audiences. Slide presentations that can be regarded as acceptable simulations of standard educational television fare were employed in both studies. The effects of humor involvement were assessed by comparing a humorous version with a nonhumorous control. The two studies produced consistent findings. In immediate postexposure tests, information acquisition from the humorous version of a program proved superior to that from its nonhumorous counterpart.

In the investigation conducted by Chapman and Crompton there was a very close correspondence between humor and the information to be acquired. Children (5 and 6 year olds) who had been exposed to zoo animals that were drawn either in a "funny" or "serious" fashion had to retrieve as many species as possible upon a letter cue. For example, the initial presentation of a camel was connected with the statement, "c is for camel;" and in the test for retention, "c" was the cue for retrieval. Because of this linkage between humor and the item of recall, it can be argued that in this investigation it was the humorous item itself (not a potentially nonhumorous, educational item) that was better recalled. However, in the investigation by Davies and Apter in which somewhat older children (8 to 11 year olds) served as subjects, the humorous stimuli were only minimally relevant to the topics being taught, and it appears that the humorous format alone effected superior retention of the educational items presented.

Effects of Different Distributions of Humor

An experiment conducted by Zillmann, Williams, Bryant, Boynton, and Wolf (1980) explored the effects of humor on information acquisition from educational television more directly than other investigations. Educational television programs were specially designed and produced on topics that were novel to the children (kindergarten and first-grade students). In order to test for information acquisition, tests were constructed to determine the extent to which subjects recall items and comprehend significant relationships. Various experimental programs were then created by inserting humorous stimuli that are characteristic of children's fare. Humorous episodes were edited into the educational message proper, and these episodes were distributed differently to create a condition of fast pace (individual episodes) and a condition of slow pace (two episodes blocked together, without changing either the sequence of presentation or the amount of material. (Since the humorous materials were added to the message proper, the humorous versions of the program were necessarily longer. Also, since the two distributions of humorous stimuli can be construed as different sets of message disruptions that may uniquely affect information acquisition, controls for both time and particular distribution of humorous inserts were necessary. However, these additional controls produced effects that did not appreciably differ from the effect produced by the message proper, and it consequently suffices here to compare the humor versions against the message proper alone.)

The study thus explored not only the effect of the involvement of humor, but the effects of the pacing of humorous episodes throughout an educational television program as well. The variation in pace should be of particular interest to the message designer, because it is a variable that lends itself to arbitrary manipulation. In this connection, it should be pointed out that in the discussed investigation the humorous episodes employed bore no particular semantic relationship with the educational message. Pace manipulations using such "unrelated" humor are obviously virtually unlimited. Implications for message design notwithstanding, however, the use of such humor to achieve positive ends may seem futile because, as will be recalled, only the involvement of humor that relates directly to the educational message has been viewed as having a chance to facilitate the learning of educational materials.

But is any beneficial effect of humor on the acquisition of information from educational television really limited to "related" humor? Does "unrelated" humor necessarily function as a distractor? It seems that in the past much of the reasoning on humor in educational television was based on the premise that audiences are highly attentive to educational programs. Indeed, if this premise is adopted it is difficult to see how humor can enhance information acquisition because, regardless of particular message characteristics, information acquisition should always be at a high level. This premise can readily be challenged, however. In general, television audiences are all but fully attentive; and children, in particular, may watch a cut-and-dried educational program with little interest and be semiattentive at best. Just as the most motivated college student may find it difficult to be fully alert through a lengthy lecture, so may the child watching educational television, even if essentially interested in the contents, become nonalert, if not drowsy at times. And as the experienced lecturer might be able to break the monotony and regain the attention of the audience by saying something funny or doing something amusing, so might children's attention to the screen be revived by an occasional humorous episode.

If, then, one accepts the premise that attention cannot be at maximum levels for long periods of time and that educational messages are often met with less than maximum interest—a condition conducive to the rapid fading of alertness—it becomes possible to project positive effects on information acquisition as the result of the involvement of humor, especially of humor that is rapidly paced. In line with this reasoning, Zillmann et al. proposed, in fact, that the interspersion of humorous stimuli in an educational program, whether or not the humor is semantically related to the educational materials covered, is likely to serve an alerting function. The respondent who vigilantly reacts to a humorous episode will remain vigilant and alert for some time thereafter (cf. Berlyne, 1960, 1970; Buchwald & Humphrey, 1973; Lynn, 1966; Zillmann, 1982); and during this period, they may more closely attend to the educational portions of a program and process incoming information more actively. As a result, the presence of humor should facilitate learning, especially when vigilance is revived often through the fast-paced placement of humorous stimuli.

The findings of the investigation by Zillmann et al. are entirely consistent with such a projection. As can be seen from Figure 10-2, the interspersion of

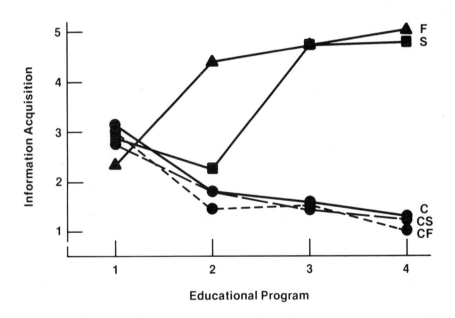

Educational Program

Figure 10-2. Acquisition of information from educational programs as a function of the involvement of differently paced humorous inserts. The fast-paced interspersion of humor (F, triangles) proved most effective. The effect of interspersing humor at a slow pace (S, squares) developed more slowly. However, both versions containing humor proved to be more effective than any of the three nonhumorous control versions (circles). Of the controls, the solid line identifies the educational message proper (C), the short-segment broken line identifies the version that controls for the fast-paced insertion pattern (CF), and the long-segment broken line identifies the version that controls for the slow-paced insertion pattern (CS). (Adapted from Zillmann, Williams, Bryant, Boynton, & Wolf, 1980.)

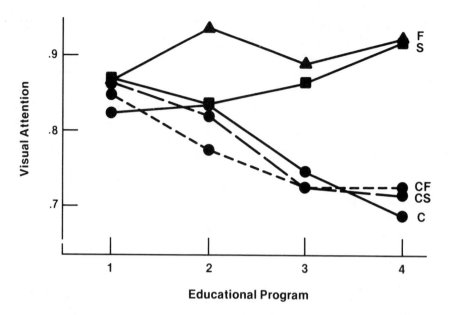

Figure 10-3. Visual attention to educational programs as a function of the involvement of differently paced humorous inserts. All effects parallel those on information acquisition. The nomenclature of Figure 2 applies. (Adapted from Zillmann, Williams, Bryant, Boynton, & Wolf, 1980.)

"unrelated" humorous stimuli in an educational program resulted in information acquisition from that program that was superior to that from the educational message proper. The fast-pacing of humorous episodes proved to be particularly effective. It produced the facilitating effect on learning more rapidly and, mostly because of this early effect, tended to produce a stronger overall facilitation. The vigilance interpretation is further supported by the findings on visual attention presented in Figure 10-3. Humor-induced vigilance apparently carried over into the subsequently presented portions of the educational message. There can be no question, then, that "unrelated" humor, especially when paced rapidly, can enhance children's acquisition of information from educational television programs.

Bryant, Zillmann, Wolf, and Reardon (Note 2) carried out essentially the same investigation with somewhat older children (7 and 8 year olds). The findings were consistent with those of the earlier study, but there was some indication that the learning-facilitating effect of humor becomes weaker as the child's age increases.

Table 10-1. Information Acquisition from Educational Television Programs as a Function of Interspersed Humor and Audiovisual Gimmicks

	Attentional potential			
	Low		High	
	Hedonic quality			
Stimulus	Low	High	Low	High
Humor	2.35	2.58	3.20	4.10
Gimmicks	2.32	2.50	3.80	4.65

Note. A no-humor, no-gimmicks control condition yielded a mean score of 2.15. From Bryant & Zillmann, 1982.

Vigilance as a Mediator

An experiment designed to test the vigilance explanation of the observed facilitatory effect of humor on learning more directly has been conducted by Bryant and Zillmann (Note 3) with children (5 and 6 year olds) as subjects. These investigators argued that, if humor has its effect—in large measure— through the stimulation of vigilance, nonhumorous stimuli, as long as they have a similar effect on vigilance, should similarly facilitate learning. Consequently, nonhumorous stimuli that are commonly used as attention-getters (the audio-visual gimmicks of "fireworks" on children's television; i.e., fast-moving colorful objects, exploding stars, and the like) were sampled, and their attention-getting potential and hedonic value (neutral vs. pleasant) were determined in a pretest. Humorous stimuli were similarly pretested and matched up on these criteria with the nonhumorous materials. In the main experiment, it was found that the interspersion of stimuli with a high potential to attract attention, whether humorous or not and whether pleasant or not, facilitated the acquisition of information from an educational program. No appreciable differences were found in the effect of humorous and nonhumorous stimuli. There was a tendency, however, for pleasant stimuli to be more effective than hedonically neutral ones of a similar attention-getting capacity.

The same investigation was carried out with 7 and 8 year olds. The effects of humorous and nonhumorous stimuli were comparable once again. However, in this investigation the effect of hedonic valence was stronger than that observed for the younger children. The more pleasant stimuli yielded substantially greater information acquisition than the less pleasant ones. The effect of the variation in attention-getting potential was in the same direction as before, but was somewhat weaker than in the prior investigation. It thus appears that as the child grows older, attention and learning become less mechanical and are increasingly influenced by hedonic stimulus properties.

Surely, these two investigations lend strong support to the vigilance explanation. Their practical implications are less clear, however. The studies show that audiovisual fireworks may do as good a job as humorous stimuli in recapturing the attention of an audience whose alertness is fading. This should not be taken to mean that both types of stimuli function equally well in the facilitation of learning from educational television. It should be remembered that in the investigations by Bryant and Zillmann the children could not turn to another program. Had they not been a captive audience, they may well have turned away from the fireworks presentations. Content-free audiovisual gimmicks or displays with little meaning, especially when used very frequently, are unlikely to attract and sustain selective exposure as effectively as humorous materials; and their beneficial effects on learning may well be limited to captive audiences—or to messages that feature these gimmicks and displays infrequently enough to be tolerated by a noncaptive audience.

Effects of Variations in Funniness

While research on the effects of the distribution of humorous stimuli in educational television programs for children has produced clear-cut results, many aspects of the use and the effects of humor in such programs have remained obscure.

Variations in the funniness of humor, for example, failed to produce strong effects (Sapolsky, Note 4). There are indications, however, that only mildly funny humor has a facilitatory effect on information acquisition. The involvement of highly enjoyable humor had no appreciable effect on learning. It is conceivable, then, that humor that triggers intense mirth reactions—because, as Schramm (1972, 1973) had suggested, it preoccupies the respondent—might interfere with information acquisition to the point where it is inferior to that from the educational message without humor.

Research on the funniness of the source of educational information (i.e., the speaker or presenter) also failed to exhibit strong effects on learning (Sapolsky & Walker, Note 5; Wakshlag, Note 6). All a funny source seems to accomplish is to make the experience of watching educational materials somewhat more enjoyable. On the other hand, a study conducted by Cantor and Reilly (Note 7) showed that a teacher's use of a jocular language style enhanced information acquisition. At the same time, however, the joking teacher was less favorably evaluated by the children (sixth-, seventh-, and eighth-grade students).

Related versus Unrelated Humor

Cantor and Reilly's investigation also included a variation in the use of "related" humor. Compared to a no-humor control, the use of such humor (i.e., humor that is relevant to the concepts taught by the educational message) had no appreciable effect overall. Tracing the effect of the various humorous stimuli that were employed suggested that the use of irony, in particular, may have been confusing and have caused misinterpretations that impaired information acquisition. For example, the educational message used was about the culture of a fictitious South American tribe, and it involved—among many other things—information about the size and weight of the people. The fact that they were extremely short and light was nonhumorously expressed as follows: "They are very small people by our standards. The average male is four foot two and weighs approximately 80 pounds. The women average three foot eleven and weigh 70 pounds." In the relevant-humor version the latter sentences were modified to read: "The average male is a towering four foot two and weighs approximately 80 pounds. The women average three foot eleven and tip the scale at 70 pounds." The humorous statements thus are contradictory to the information to be acquired. The child—or the adult, for that matter—who is not fully attentive and properly dismisses the incongruous part of the information concerning height and weight may suffer from the humorous interference with information rehearsal and storage and be left confused. In fact, he or she might focus attention on the humorous part and come away with the impression of great height and weight.

Since irony and similar message-distorting techniques are heavily used in children's educational television (Bryant, Hezel, & Zillmann, 1979), this observation by Cantor and Reilly may prove highly significant. One immediate consequence is that it now appears that the classification of humor as "related" is a confusing oversimplification. Finer distinctions within this class are necessary. In fact, making these finer distinctions holds promise of clarifying and reconciling the conflicting findings on the effects of "related" humor in children's educational television.

The issue of humor that is related versus humor that is unrelated to educational messages is significant in yet another way: It seems to define a turning point in the effects of the involvement of humor in educational television programs for children versus for adult audiences. For one thing, humor is usually not well integrated, semantically, with educational materials in programs for children. Visual and auditory humorous cues are, by and large, as often lacking correspondence with topics taught as they are directly related (Bryant, Hezel, & Zillmann, 1979). In lectures delivered by college professors, in contrast, the use of humor that helps to make educational points dominates other uses, the involvement of "unrelated" humor being comparatively rare (Bryant, Comisky, & Zillmann, 1979). The authors of textbooks similarly integrate humor rather well (Bryant, Gula, & Zillmann, 1980). These uses seem to reflect a good intuitive grasp of the effects of humor in educational endeavors—that, at least, is what recent research suggests. As has been shown, totally "unrelated" humor in educational messages can greatly facilitate information acquisition in children. With age, this beneficial effect seems to weaken. The involvement of "related" humor, on the other hand, poses a risk for children in that, while some forms of relatedness may achieve highly beneficial effects, many other forms such as irony, cynicism, and sarcasm—because they distort the related educational point—may foster misconceptions and thus impair information acquisition. It can be assumed that adult audiences, because of superior information processing skills, are far less likely to misinterpret reality-distorting forms of humor, and "related" humor can thus be expected to be devoid of the discussed ill effects. Additionally, one might expect that adult audiences respond unfavorably to the involvement of obviously forced-in "unrelated" humor. Humor that is well integrated and used to make points of interest can readily be accepted, but humor that has no apparent connection to the educational message, obviously interspersed to liven things up, may be met with impatience, if not with annoyance.

Recent research has produced findings that seem highly consistent with such theorizing. A correlational study of the use of humor by college teachers in the classroom and of its implications for students' perception of their teachers (Bryant, Crane, Comisky, & Zillmann, 1980), for instance, revealed that the frequent employment of humor, whether semantically well integrated with lecture materials or not, is associated with enhanced appeal of male professors, but only the use of humor related to the topics covered was viewed as significantly facilitating their teaching effectiveness. Essentially the same relationships emerged in a similar investigation of the use of related and unrelated humor in college textbooks and the students' perception of these books (Klein, Bryant, & Zillmann, 1982). Regardless of the degree of relatedness between humor and topics covered, the books' appeal (as measured in the enjoyment of reading it) increased with the frequency of humor. However, the more unrelated or poorly related the humor was, the less the students thought to have learned from the text. Related humor proved to be the only kind of humor that did not detract from the books' perceived effectiveness. The frequent use of such humor, moreover, made books appear more interesting and promoted the desire to read them. On the other hand, usage of both related and unrelated humor seemed to be linked with a decline in the authors' credibility as scientists.

Experimental investigations yielded comparable results. Bryant, Brown, Silberberg, and Elliott (1981) manipulated written materials for college students by interspersing humorous drawings into the text. Cartoons were either moderately or extensively used to break the monotony of a nonhumorous educational message. In addition to testing for information acquisition, the appeal and the persuasibility of the educational materials were assessed. Consistent with the suggestions from the correlational data, the appeal of the materials gained from the involvement of humor, whereas persuasibility (which presumably reflects competence and authoritativeness) was negatively affected. The employment of cartoons had no appreciable effect on information acquisition, however.

An investigation by Hezel, Bryant, and Harris (Note 8) addressed the relatedness issue directly. Four versions of a television lecture for college students were created. The lecture either contained no humor, humor that was

Table 10-2. Information Acquisition from an Educational Television Program as a Function of Usage of Relevant and Irrelevant Humor

Humor			
None	Unrelated	Related	Relevant
13.47[b]	10.69[a]	11.19[a]	13.59[b]

Note. Means having different superscripts differ at $p < .05$ by Newman-Keuls' test. From Hezel, Bryant, & Harris, 1982.

unrelated to the topics covered, humor that was related (though not relevant to the topic), or humor that was relevant (in that it helped to make a critical point). Gender of the lecturer was varied in addition, as numerous gender differences in the perception of teachers—as a function of humor use—had been observed in other investigations (e.g., Bryant, Crane, Comisky, & Zillmann, 1980; Klein, Bryant, & Zillmann, 1982; Tamborini & Zillmann, 1981). Immediately after exposure, both male and female subjects were tested for information acquisition. Subjects furthermore evaluated the instructors on a battery of scales.

Hezel et al. found, first of all, that the use of unrelated and somewhat related humor, regardless of the lecturer's and respondent's gender, was detrimental to learning. As can be seen from Table 10-2, information acquisition in these conditions fell below the level of the no-humor control.

The involvement of well integrated, relevant humor did not have this negative effect, but—again irrespective of gender considerations—did not lead to any enhancement of learning either. The latter finding confirms the earlier observations by Kaplan and Pascoe (1977). It will be remembered that these investigators also failed to obtain superior information acquisition immediately after exposure to the educational message containing relevant humor.

The findings concerning the perception and evaluation of the humor-using lecturer are presented in Table 10-3. They apply to both male and female instructors and to male and female students equally. As can be seen, the lecturers appeared to be funnier when using humor; but especially so, when using relevant humor. Being witty, interestingly, seems to be construed as a characteristic of greater quality than being funny. The lecturer employing unrelated humor was perceived as funny, but not as witty (compared to the control; i.e., to the condition devoid of humor). The lecturer employing well integrated, relevant humor, in contrast, was deemed both funny and witty. Being witty (rather than being funny) appears to be a highly valued trait of teachers. Students seem to take a fancy to witty professors, not to funny ones. The data show that only witty professors—witty because of the use of integrated, related, and relevant humor—were judged to be interesting. Moreover, only they were judged to be entertaining and enjoyable. Even more importantly, only the highly witty professor was deemed motivating. The instructors' appeal, then, appears to be greatly enhanced by the use of humor that aids in making educational points or, at least, pertains directly to the

Table 10-3. Perception of a Television Lecturer as a Function of Usage of Relevant and Irrelevant Humor

| | Humor | | | |
Aspect	*None*	*Unrelated*	*Related*	*Relevant*
Funny	-6.09^a	0.73^b	1.59^{bc}	3.72^c
Witty	-1.50^a	-1.42^a	2.72^b	4.64^b
Interesting	0.61^a	0.88^a	4.42^b	4.92^b
Enjoyable	-0.83^a	-0.64^a	3.30^b	5.31^b
Entertaining	-1.08^a	-0.73^a	3.38^b	4.97^b
Appealing	-1.58^a	0.72^b	2.58^b	2.45^b
Motivating	0.55^a	-0.52^a	1.63^a	3.77^b
Clarity	2.91^b	0.34^a	4.06^b	4.69^b
Intelligent	5.77^b	3.17^a	5.83^b	5.13^b
Informed	5.38^b	2.78^a	3.98^{ab}	4.36^{ab}

Note. Means having no letter in their superscripts in common differ at $p < .05$ by Newman-Keuls' test. From Hezel, Bryant, & Harris, 1982.

educational message. This is in sharp contrast to the employment of humor without apparent justification—other than to break the monotony. Teachers using such unrelated humor may well be perceived as being funny and possibly gain appeal in the sense of being liked. They seem unable, however, to involve and motivate their audiences. The findings concerning competence further stress the risks associated with the use of unrelated humor in educational messages for college students. Unrelated humor was viewed as detracting from the clarity of the educational presentation. Its use, as can be seen from the table, had a devastating effect on the perception of the teachers' intelligence, and it prompted appraisals of inferior informedness. In summary, then, the use of unrelated humor was not only a detriment to teacher-student rapport but proved to be most harmful to assessments of the teachers' competence. These deleterious effects on teacher perception may be assumed to mediate a loss in mature students' attentiveness and ultimately result in reduced information acquisition from educational messages in which unrelated humor abounds.

SUMMARY

It should be clear from the preceding discussion that any unqualified generalizations, whether they project good or bad consequences of humor use for teaching and learning, are untenable. Humorous stimuli differ in many regards. In the educational setting, the varied forms of humor may uniquely impact teacher-student rapport, attention to educational materials, and learning. Moreover, dependent upon developmental circumstances, respondents may differ greatly in their acceptance of humor in education. Situational factors have to be reckoned with in addition.   All this does not mean, however, that generalizations are impossible. The discussed research allows several conclusions, in fact, and they are offered below as tentative generalizations to be further evaluated by future research.

1. The involvement of gratifying humor in educational messages that compete with other messages for attention fosters superior selective exposure.
2. For child audiences, comparatively dense distributions of brief humorous episodes have stronger effects on selective exposure than the less frequent interspersion of larger humorous episodes.
3. For child audiences, the interspersion of humor that is unrelated to the educational message fosters superior attention and information acquisition.
4. For these audiences, the frequent interspersion of small units of unrelated humor is more effective than the less frequent use of larger units.
5. As the children's age increases, the positive effect of the use of unrelated humor on attention and information acquisition seems to grow weaker.

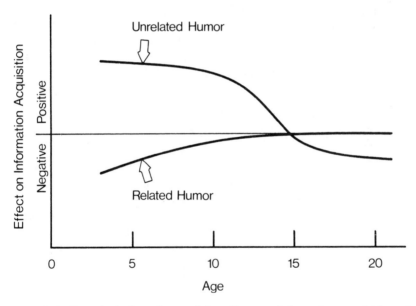

Figure 10-4. Hypothetical gradients of the effects on information acquisition of the involvement of humor that is unrelated or related to the educational message. The horizontal line signifies the effect of an educational message without humor. Unrelated humor fosters vigilance, attention, and superior learning in children. This effect is lost with the development of attentional discipline and motivation. Finally, the initial effect reverses for adults, as the use of irrelevant humor undermines teacher-student rapport. The negative effect of the use of integrated relevant humor diminishes and vanishes with the child's advancement to improved information processing skills, this advancement making confusions in the intepretation of reality-distorting humor increasingly unlikely.

6. For child audiences, the use of humor that is well integrated with the educational message, especially reality-distorting forms such as irony, may be confusing and impair information acquisition.
7. For child audiences, the funniness of humorous stimuli involved in educational materials appears to be of little moment.
8. For these audiences, the funniness of the source of educational information appears to be of no consequence for information acquisition.
9. For adult audiences in an educational setting such as the classroom, the involvement of humor that is unrelated or irrelevant to the educational message has detrimental effects on information acquisition.
10. For these audiences, the involvement of relevant humor that is well integrated in the educational message is without immediate consequences for learning, but may lead to superior retention of educational information.

Statements 3 through 6, 9, and 10 are summarized in Figure 10-4.

11. For adult audiences, the involvement of unrelated and irrelevant humor in educational messages presented in educational settings (classroom, textbook) is detrimental to teacher-student rapport.
12. For these audiences and under these circumstances, the involvement of relevant, well integrated humor seems without appreciable consequence for teacher appeal and the perception of competence, but is likely to make the learning experience more enjoyable.

ACKNOWLEDGMENTS

The authors' research discussed in this chapter is part of a program of research into the uses and effects of elements of entertainment in educational television that was supported by Grant APR77-13902 from the National Science Foundation. In that program, Drs. Joanne R. Cantor, Kenneth D. Day, Richard T. Hezel, Barry S. Sapolsky, Jacob J. Wakshlag, and Brien R. Williams, whose research is cited, collaborated with the authors. The various contributions of these investigators are gratefully acknowledged.

REFERENCE NOTES

1. Schleicher, M. P., & Bryant, J. *Voluntary selective exposure to educational television programs as a function of differently paced humorous inserts.* Manuscript in preparation, 1982.
2. Bryant, J., Zillmann, D., Wolf, M. A., & Reardon, K. R. *Learning from educational television as a function of differently paced humor: Further evidence.* Manuscript in preparation, 1982.

3. Bryant, J., & Zillmann, D. *Humor and audiovisual fireworks in educational television: Effects on learning.* Manuscript in preparation, 1982.
4. Sapolsky, B. S. *The degree of funniness of humor accompanying informative messages and its effect upon children's rote learning.* Manuscript in preparation, 1982.
5. Sapolsky, B. S., & Walker, B. A. *The effect of mood and source on children's attention, enjoyment, and learning from educational television.* Paper presented at the Second International Conference on Humor, Los Angeles, August 1979.
6. Wakshlag, J. J. *Effect of humorous appearance of teacher on effectiveness of televised educational programs.* Manuscript in preparation, 1982.
7. Cantor, J., & Reilly, S. *Jocular language style and relevant humor in educational messages.* Paper presented at the Second International Conference on Humor, Los Angeles, August 1979.
8. Hezel, R. T., Bryant, J., & Harris, L. *The relationship between humor and educational information: Lectures and learning.* Manuscript in preparation, 1982.

REFERENCES

Adams, W. J. The use of sexual humor in teaching human sexuality at the university level. *The Family Coordinator*, 1974, *23*, 365-368.

Berlyne, D. E. *Conflict, arousal, and curiosity.* New York: McGraw-Hill, 1960.

Berlyne, D. E. Attention as a problem in behavior theory. In D. I. Mostofsky (Ed.), *Attention: Contemporary theory and analysis.* New York: Appleton-Century-Crofts, 1970.

Bradford, A. L. The place of humor in teaching. *Peabody Journal of Education*, September 1964, 67-70.

Browning, R. Why not humor? *APA Monitor*, February 1977, 32.

Bryant, J., Brown, D., Silberberg, A. R., & Elliott, S. M. Effects of humorous illustrations in college textbooks. *Human Communication Research*, 1981, *8*, 43-57.

Bryant, J., Comisky, P., & Zillmann, D. Teachers' humor in the college classroom. *Communication Education*, 1979, *28*, 110-118.

Bryant, J., Crane, J. S., Comisky, P. W., & Zillmann, D. Relationship between college teachers' use of humor in the classroom and students' evaluations of their teachers. *Journal of Educational Psychology*, 1980, *72*, 511-519.

Bryant, J., Gula, J., & Zillmann, D. Humor in communication textbooks. *Communication Education*, 1980, *29*, 125-134.

Bryant, J., Hezel, R., & Zillmann, D. Humor in children's educational television. *Communication Education*, 1979, *28*, 49-59.

Buchwald, J. S., & Humphrey, G. L. An analysis of habituation in the specific sensory systems. In E. Stellar & J. M. Sprague (Eds.), *Progress in physiological psychology.* New York: Academic Press, 1973.

Chapman, A. J., & Crompton, P. Humorous presentations of material and presentations of humorous material: A review of the humor and memory literature and two experimental studies. In M. M. Gruneberg, P. E. Morris, & R. N. Sykes (Eds.), *Practical aspects of memory*, London: Academic Press, 1978.

Davies, A. P., & Apter, M. J. Humor and its effect on learning in children. In P. E. McGhee & A. J. Chapman (Eds.), *Children's humor.* New York: Wiley, 1980.

Earls, P. L. Humorizing learning. *Elementary Education*, 1972, *49*, 107-108.

Freud, S. *Der Witz und seine Beziehung zum Unbewussten*. Frankfurt: Fischer Bücherei, 1958. (Originally published, 1905.)

Gruner, C. R. *Understanding laughter: the workings of wit and humor*. Chicago: Nelson-Hall, 1978.

Hauck, W. E., & Thomas, J. W. The relationship of humor to intelligence, creativity, and intentional and incidental learning. *Journal of Experimental Education*, 1972, *40*, 52-55.

Horn, G. Laughter . . . a saving grace. *Today's Education*, December 1972, pp. 37-38.

Kaplan, R. M., & Pascoe, G. C. Humorous lectures and humorous examples: Some effects upon comprehension and retention. *Journal of Educational Psychology*, 1977, *69*, 61-65.

Klein, D. M., Bryant, J., & Zillmann, D. Relationship between humor in introductory textbooks and students' evaluations of the texts' appeal and effectiveness. *Psychological Reports*, 1982, *50*, 235-241.

Lesser, G. Assumptions behind the production and writing methods in "Sesame Street." In W. Schramm (Ed.), *Quality in instructional television*. Honolulu: University Press of Hawaii, 1972.

Lesser, G. *Children and television: Lessons from Sesame Street*. New York: Random House, 1974.

Lumsdaine, A. A., & Gladstone, A. I. Overt practice and audiovisual embellishments. In M. A. May & A. A. Lumsdaine (Eds.), *Learning from films*. New Haven, Conn.: Yale University Press, 1958.

Lynn, R. *Attention, arousal and the orientation reaction*. Oxford: Pergamon Press, 1966.

McGhee, P. E. Toward the integration of entertainment and educational functions of television: The role of humor. In P. H. Tannenbaum (Ed.), *The entertainment functions of television*. Hillsdale, N.J.: Erlbaum, 1980.

McIntyre, C. J. *Training film evaluation: FB 254—Cold weather uniforms*. (Technical Report SDC 269-7-51.) Port Washington, N.Y.: U.S. Naval Special Devices Center, 1954.

Mechanic, D. *Students under stress: A study of the social psychology of adaptation*. New York: Free Press of Glencoe, 1962.

Schramm, W. What the research says. In W. Schramm (Ed.), *Quality in instructional television*. Honolulu: University Press of Hawaii, 1972.

Schramm, W. *Men, messages, and media: A look at human communication*. New York: Harper & Row, 1973.

Singer, J. L. The power and limitations of television: A cognitive-affective analysis. In P. H. Tannenbaum (Ed.), *The entertainment functions of television*. Hillsdale, N.J.: Erlbaum, 1980.

Singer, J. L., & Singer, D. G. Come back, Mister Rogers, come back. *Psychology Today*, March 1979, pp. 56; 59-60.

Smith, R. E., Ascough, J. C., Ettinger, R. F., & Nelson, D. A. Humor, anxiety, and task performance. *Journal of Personality and Social Psychology*, 1971, *19*, 243-246.

Tamborini, R., & Zillmann, D. College students' perception of lecturers using humor. *Perceptual and Motor Skills*, 1981, *52*, 427-432.

Terry, R. L., & Woods, M. E. Effects of humor on the test performance of elementary school children. *Psychology in the Schools*, 1975, *12*, 182-185.

Wakshlag, J. J., Day, K. D., & Zillmann, D. Selective exposure to educational television programs as a function of differently paced humorous inserts. *Journal of Educational Psychology*, 1981, *73*, 27-32.

Wakshlag, J. J., Reitz, R., & Zillmann, D. Selective exposure to and acquisition of information from educational television programs as a function of appeal and tempo of background music. *Journal of Educational Psychology*, 1982, *74*, 666-677.

Weinberg, M. D. *The interactional effect of humor and anxiety on academic performance.* Unpublished doctoral dissertation, Yeshiva University, 1973.

Zillmann, D. Television viewing and arousal. In D. Pearl, L. Bouthilet, & J. Lazar (Eds.), *Television and behavior: Ten years of scientific progress and implications for the eighties* (Vol. 2). *Technical reviews.* U.S. Public Health Service Publication No. (ADM) 82-1196. Washington, D.C.: U.S. Government Printing Office, 1982.

Zillmann, D., Hezel, R. T., & Medoff, N. J. The effect of affective states on selective exposure to televised entertainment fare. *Journal of Applied Social Psychology*, 1980, *10*, 323-339.

Zillmann, D., Williams, B. R., Bryant, J., Boynton, K. R., & Wolf, M. A. Acquisition of information from educational television programs as a function of differently paced humorous inserts. *Journal of Educational Psychology*, 1980, *72*, 170-180.

Author Index

Roman type refers to page numbers in Volume I, *italic type* refers to page numbers in Volume II.

Subject Index

Roman type refers to page numbers in Volume I, *italic type* refers to page numbers in Volume II.